Good Films, Cheap Wine, Few Friends:
A Memoir

by Juan Luis Buñuel

Edited, and with an introduction, by Linda C. Ehrlich

Design by Jared Bendis

Good Films, Cheap Wine, Few Friends: A Memoir
by Juan Luis Buñuel
First Edition

ISBN 978-0-9858786-4-1
Library of Congress Control Number 2014936939

Published by Shika Press Ltd.

Shika Press Ltd.

Shaker Heights, Ohio, USA

ACKNOWLEDGEMENTS

We would like to thank: María Carmen Cabrera. Jared Bendis (Creative New Media Officer for Kelvin Smith Library, CWRU), the office of the Dean of the College of Arts and Sciences, and the Freedman Center, CWRU, Elena Fernández, Charlotte Sanpere-Godard, Christine Cano, John Givens, Richard Cooper, Esq., Corey Wright, Phyllis Goldenberg, Amy Heller and Dennis Doros of Milestone Film and Video, Linda Dittmar, and Ian Gibson.

∞ ∞ ∞

As editor, I dedicate my efforts on this memoir to the memory of my dear Spanish colleague Antonio Candau (1962-2013) who once wrote to me that editing Juan Luis Buñuel's memoir would be "a true challenge. *Aparte de interesante seguro que es muy divertido....*"

TABLE OF CONTENTS
A roadmap though my life

Note: There will be comments and indications, *"truffées,"* throughout this work which will help with problems of daily living. Such as...how to make good rice.

Introduction 1

Dedication 23

Early Years 25
    PARIS - *SNOW WHITE* (1934 to 1938)... 27
    MADRID, LEAVE FRANCE, 1939 33
    CROSSING THE UNITED STATES 35
    NEW YORK, 1939 to 1944.. 41
    SCHOOL IN NEW YORK, BUTTERFLY IN CLASS................. 49
    VACATIONS.. 53
    RETURN TO CALIFORNIA, 1945 57
    LIFE IN LOS ANGELES... 59
    COMIC BOOKS... 69
    END OF WWII, MOVE TO MEXICO CITY (D.F.) 75
    DIFFERENT HOMES, D.F... 79
    CALLE EXTREMADURA & PANTEÓN DOLORES................... 85
    SCOUTS & SNIPE HUNT 87
    AMERICAN FOOTBALL... 93
    VISA FOR U.S., 1953 97
    CABARETS IN MEXICO... 99
    RANCHO DEL CHARRO 103
    CERRADA FÉLIX CUEVAS... 105
    OBERLIN COLLEGE, OHIO.. 109
    TRIP TO FLORIDA (1956) 117
    TRIP TO TEXAS 123
    ACCIDENTS 127

Filming.. 129
    DON QUIXOTE + ORSON WELLES 131
    ACAPULCO AND END OF *QUIXOTE*.................................. 137
    LITTLE GIANTS 145

VOYAGE TO EUROPE 149
48 RUE MAZARINE 153
MONACO BAR AND TRIP WITH CHARLES 155
ZARAGOZA AND FAMILY, CALANDA 161
THE CONTRESCARPE 185
THE YOUNG ONE (La joven), GABRIEL FIGUEROA 191
INTERLUDES 207
Recipe for a Dry Martini 215
VIRIDIANA 219
GARRET-RUE MAZARINE 225
LES HALLES 227
SMUGGLE OUT FLN AGENT 229
CAMBODIA (1961) 233
SONATAS 237
TLALOC 239
ANTS 241
NICHOLAS RAY, SAMUEL BECKETT 245
VIVA MARÍA 249
SHOOTING AND GUNS 255
ST. MARK'S PLACE 259
MALRAUX IN MEXICO 267
MAY 1968 PARIS – MEXICO 269
PANAMA 277
BLACK PANTHERS 281
WILLARD, CALDER AND MIRÓ 283
LEONOR 289
BILBAO FILM FESTIVAL 293
YUGOSLAVIA 295
WOMAN WITH RED BOOTS, 1974 297
MASTROIANNI - BERGMAN 299
SYNOPSES OF FEATURE FILMS 305
HOUSE IBIZA (1977) 307
DEATH OF MY FATHER 311
THOUGHTS OF LORCA 313
GUANAJUATO 317

Later Years & Family Histories 323

CAN'T SLEEP.. 325

DREAMS 327

CHILE 331

UNFORGETTABLE MEALS 333

LA COUPOLE... 337

TRIP TO NORMANDY: LETTER TO JERRY LINDNER....................... 339

BUÑUEL FAMILY HISTORY AND STORIES: 345

LEMPEREUR-SÉNÉCHAL-RUCAR (mother's side)...................... 355

DEATH OF MY MOTHER (1994) 361

STORIES MY FATHER TOLD ME 363

MUSIC 371

SAN JOSÉ PURUA, MEXICO.. 373

1996 - 2010 379

THINGS I LIKE & DISLIKE... 387

People I Have Met.. 391

A Few More Thoughts... 425

NAMES & *HOLA* 427

DEATH 429

ON THE WRONG TRACK 431

SPANISH CIVIL WAR (An Introduction)................................. 433

Juan Luis' article about ALEXANDER CALDER............................ 437

COLLECTIONS 447

INTRODUCTION

by Dr. Linda C. Ehrlich

Juan Luis Buñuel with his art work in the background

The memoir of Juan Luis Buñuel (b. 1934 in Paris) offers a first-hand look at the life of a vibrant man who has lived through momentous times. The eldest son of filmmaker Luis Buñuel, Juan Luis is a *flâneur* in a life that spans France, the U.S., Mexico, Spain, and several other intriguing locations. A filmmaker, sculptor, and raconteur in his own right, Buñuel grew up surrounded by important figures of the twentieth century. These include Alexander Calder, Man Ray, Joan Miró, Nicholas Ray, Samuel Beckett, Ingmar Bergman, André Malraux and Eldridge Cleaver, among many others. As his writings reveal, the Buñuelian lucid, dark humor and outrage over society's pretensions and inequities have certainly passed from father to son.

1

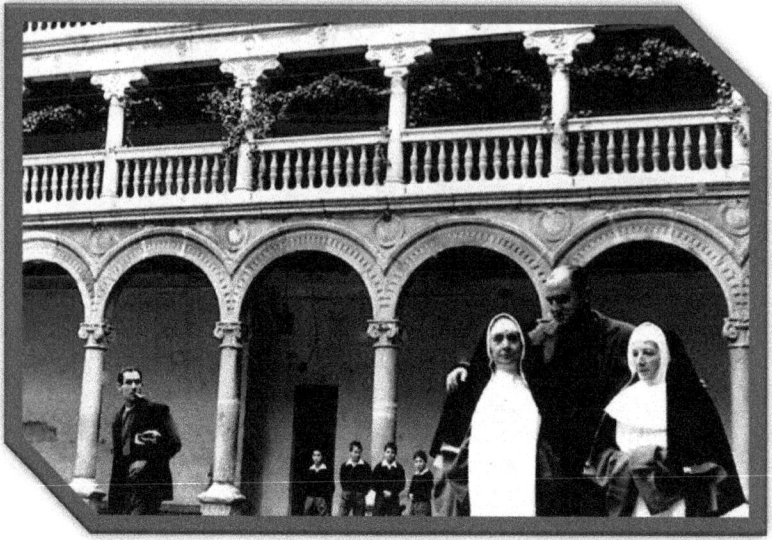

Juan Luis and two "nuns," filming of *Viridiana*

In this memoir (originally written for his three children), Juan Luis Buñuel offers us a writing style that is imaginative and often surprising. He combines fascinating anecdotes with an acute sense of time and place. The memoir is full of ironies, gaps, and an overarching acceptance of time passing. They are never dull; rather, they present a very human voice, full of irreverence and enthusiasms. The memoir gives us an intimate portrait of Buñuel family life in exile and descriptions of the extended family, all told by Juan Luis with great affection and an eye for the telling detail.

You will find Juan Luis an amicable and insightful companion. His engaging stories range from how he dealt with "monkey spectators" while working on a documentary in Cambodia to his childhood recollection of how the great sculptor Alexander Calder would make small wire toys for him that he would play with and then toss in the garbage! We learn how Buñuel explored the Mexican visual art scene, how he taught

Brigitte Bardot how to shoot a pistol, and how he assisted with the filming, and the subsequent scandalous screening, of his father's *Viridiana* at the 1961 Cannes Film Festival (where it won the Palme d'Or and then was immediately denounced by the Vatican).

Juan Luis' memoir has something for everyone—for film fans, lovers of Spanish and Mexican culture, students of twentieth-century history, and everyone who relishes a good story. They provide another window into a family that has understandably guarded its privacy even as its activities have influenced history. Juan Luis' memoir can be placed on the bookshelf beside his father's 1982 autobiography *My Last Sigh*, and those of his mother Jeanne Rucar de Buñuel entitled *Memorias de una mujer sin piano* (*Memories of a Woman Without a Piano*).[1]

As a writer, Juan Luis Buñuel is not in a hurry, nor does he feel a compulsion to remember everything. So you can also meander and pause during this roughly chronological journey. There are leisurely digressions of lists of collections, dreams and recipes, and practical notes of advice to his children from a watchful father. On these pages you will even find directions on how to create the famous Buñuel dry martini (and a correction to the recipe revealed in *My Last Sigh*), and how to savor life...and paella, *cocido madrileño, huevos rancheros, chorizo, mole poblano*, sea urchins, octopus *a la gallega*....

---

[1]This autobiography was published first in French as *Mon dernier soupir* with the collaboration of Jean Claude-Carrière (1983), and in Spanish translation by Ana María de la Fuente, as *Mi último suspiro: memorias*, published by Plaza y Janés. Translated into English by Abigail Israel, and published by Knopf (1984).

Jeanne Rucar de Buñuel's memoir was written in Spanish with Marisol Marín del Campo (Madrid, Alianza, 1991).

The memoir includes first-hand accounts of many important historical events, including the 1968 student uprisings in Paris, the Black Panther movement in the U.S., the ups and downs of Orson Welles' work in Mexico on his (never-finished) Don Quixote film, and the smuggling of the undeveloped reels of his father's controversial film *Viridiana* from Spain to France under the cloaks of toreadors.

Beneath his joie de vivre and sense of mischief lies Juan Luis' serious concern for the forces that bind life unnecessarily, and for the chasm beneath our surface decorum. As he wrote in a note to me:

> I was born near the middle of the 20th century...and I lived through the Spanish Civil War, World War II, the French war in Algeria, and another dozen wars fought throughout the world since then. I was lucky. I did not fight in any of them. In fact, in France during the Algerian War, I was considered a deserter. I refused to fight against my fellow man.

An Overview: Juan Luis Buñuel's Career

This memoir will take you to various countries and continents. You will sometimes see Juan Luis credited as Jean Louis Buñuel, John Buñuel, J.L. Buñuel, etc.. After attending elementary and secondary schools in New York City, Hollywood, and Mexico City, Juan Luis received a B.A. in English Literature from Oberlin College (Ohio) in 1957.

He went on to make film and television documentaries in a host of countries: Mexico, Argentina, Venezuela, England, Paris, Chile, and Cambodia, to name a few. One of Juan Luis' key documentaries turns the lens onto his father's hometown of Calanda in the province of Teruel with its insistent drum festival (*Calanda*, 1967) during Semana Santa. *Calanda* (filmed by Jacques Renoir, of the famous painter and filmmaker family) won the first prize at the Tours International Film Festival for the Documentary, and was invited for screenings at the London Film Festival and the New York Film Festival at Lincoln Center.

Juan Luis revisited the city in 2006 to film *Calanda: 40 Years Later (Calanda: 40 años después)*, with his son Diego and Christian Garnier as cameramen. *Calanda: 40 Years Later*, produced with the assistance of the Centro Buñuel de Calanda (CBC) and Aragon TV, has received screenings at the Berlin Film Festival and in Amsterdam.

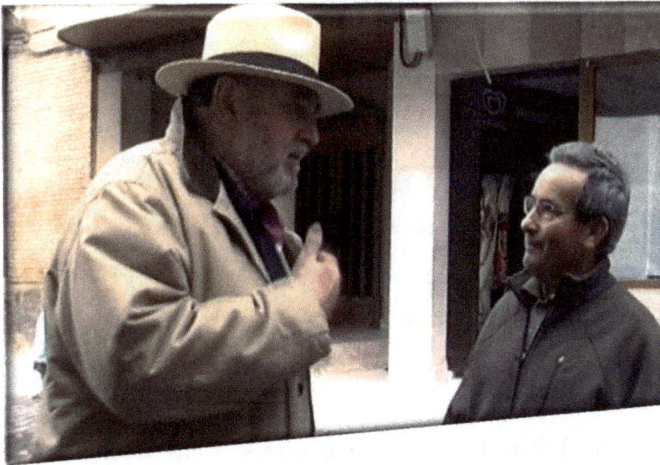

Juan Luis and the cultural attaché of Calanda, 2007

The new film is punctuated with interviews of local residents: a shepherd, the mayor, drum makers, a young Spanish woman who has adopted a daughter from China, men from Morocco, Uruguayan bar owners, among others.[2] Rafael, Juan Luis' younger brother, is invited for the *rompida* (break of the hour at noon) to start off the drumming.

As Juan Luis noted in one email to me (24 Feb. 2007): " In *Calanda: 40 Años Después*, I combine both films and show the town in the Middle Ages (40 years ago) and today, in its modern form, as a European village with several factories, foreign workers, etc." This documentary contrasts the monster-like mechanization of the factories and their polluting billows of smoke with the work of craftsmen, who still make the drums largely by hand.

For the UNESCO Heritage series, Juan Luis made three documentaries: *Gaudí: To Dream in Barcelona* (1989, about architect Antonio Gaudí, narrated by actor John Hurt); *Guanajuato, una leyenda* (1990, which focuses on the ancient city of

---

[2] For additional information on *The Last Script* and *Calanda: 40 Years Later*, see my review in the online journal *Senses of Cinema* (51: 2009).

Guanajuato in central Mexico); and *The Years of Change* (1994, filmed in Chile about the educational system there after the Pinochet dictatorship).

These UNESCO documentaries take us soaring to the heights of creativity (*Gaudí*) and deep into the depths of the earth's dark caverns (*The Years of Change*) and their unfortunate miners. *Gaudí: To Dream in Barcelona* approaches the city as a "vast dream state...a territory of infinite possibilities" as it highlights the sinuosity of the architecture. Juan Luis imaginatively cross-cuts between details of the architecture and the natural forms that inspired them, including shots of huge tortoises and hippos cavorting in the water, and the eyes of a komodo dragon. The camera waltzes lyrically along the mosaic tiles of the benches of Parc Güell as kids "take possession" of the space.

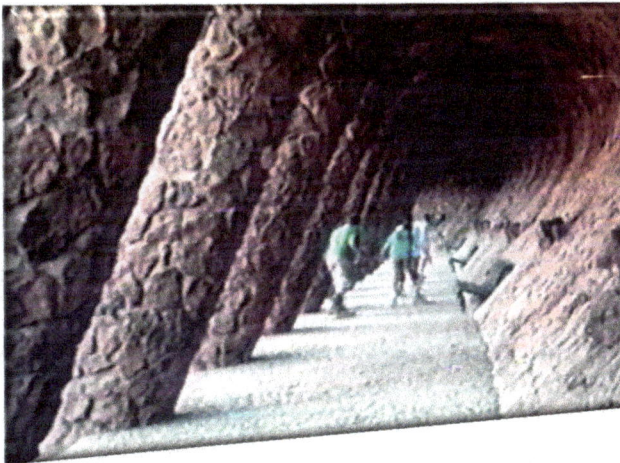

Gaudí: To Dream in Barcelona

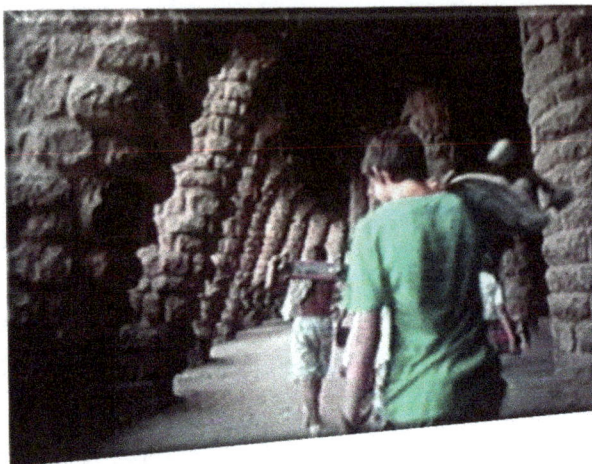

In the footage he shot of the May 1968 protests in Paris, Juan Luis, a fledgling filmmaker, captures the sense of unrest and exhilaration in the crowds of students and workers symbolically "waving goodbye" to French President Charles de Gaulle. In the row of young filmmakers locking arms and marching, we can spot a young Alain Resnais, a bearded Louis Malle, and even a glimpse of the elusive Chris Marker!

During my visit to Paris in December 2013 to work with Juan Luis, I was fortunate to be able to view another of his short documentaries, *The Great Camembert Race* (not to be confused with the Paris-Camembert bicycle race). Buñuel recorded this truly surreal event with the same care one might expect of a film about a famous marathon or horse race. We see a Danish engraver living in Paris inspect each contribution of cheese for insects, and a woman (wearing empty camembert boxes as earrings) oil a special surface on a slant. Children vociferously cheer "their" camemberts as the half-chunks of cheese slide down. Alas, the cheeses seem to have a mind of their own. The documentary ends with lovingly captured portraits of some of the key players, as the day ends with glasses of table wine and (of course) bread and cheese.

8

Juan Luis has also written and directed three feature-length films: *Au rendez-vous de la mort joyeuse* (*At the Meeting with Joyous Death*, 1973, shot in France, with Gérard Depardieu); *The Woman with Red Boots* (*La femme aux bottes rouges*, 1974, shot in Spain, with Catherine Deneuve and Fernando Rey); and *Leonor* (1975, shot in Spain, with Swedish actress Liv Ullmann, French actor Michel Piccoli, and Italian actress Ornella Muti). His first film, *At the Meeting with Joyous Death*, brought him several prestigious awards: the Georges Sadoul Award in Paris, the Silver Hugo at the Chicago International Film Festival, and the Clavel de Oro (first prize) at the Sitges Film Festival (Spain). *The Woman with Red Boots* features Deneuve as a strikingly beautiful, but rather detached, artist with a special skill for strategy on a transparent three-level chess set.

Juan Luis' feature films for French television continue his role as artistic *flâneur*. To list just a few: *Mort de Franco* (filmed for Gaumont, 1976); *Ressac* (1979, filmed in Normandy with André Dussolier); *Les brus* (1981); *Aveugle, que veux-tu?* (1984); and *Adriana* (1991). His mini-series for television were filmed around the world: Patagonia, Argentina (*Tropique du crabe*, 1986); Venezuela (*Barrage sur l'orénoque* (1996); Mexico (*Rebellion of the Hanged / La rebellión de los colgados*, 1986); and France (two episodes of *Fantômas*, with Helmut Burger, 1980), and *L'homme de la nuit*, 1983). The latter production (also filmed in Alsace, with George Wilson, Bulle Ogier, Pierre Clementi, and with Tía Conchita Buñuel's youngest son Pedro Cristián as an extra) won the prize for Best Series of the Year from the French Critics Award. *Tropique du crabe*, based on a true event, tells of residents on an island with few supplies, the tyranny of one man over many women and children, and the eventual murder of the man by the Captain's wife. Juan Luis ponders the question of why the women did not rise up and rebel earlier.

Juan Luis' one-hour specials include *Maelzel's Chess Player* (*Joueur d'échecs de Maelzel*, with Jean-Claude Drouot, 1981, based on an Edgar Allan Poe story, shot in Mexico); *You'll Never See Me Again* (shot in Bristol, England, 1986); *The Devil's Lair* (1980, Spain); and *Un homme ordinaire* (1982) and *Le Libertin* (France).

He even has a few actor credits. He appeared as an actor in the 1990 film *Henry and June* (directed by Philip Kaufman), with Mickey Rooney (in an uncompleted film by one of his colleagues), and in several other films, including an (uncredited) role as a torturing monk in *Viva María!* with the Spanish actor Francisco [Paco] Regueiro (another Republican in exile) as the deceitful Father Superior. (For another Regueiro role, see Juan Luis' description in this memoir of his work with Orson Welles.) Juan Luis also appeared in television documentaries such as *Orson Welles in the Land of Don Quixote* (2000), *Buñuel in Hollywood, A propósito de Buñuel* (*Speaking of Buñuel*, from the same year), and in the earlier *Les paradoxes de Buñuel* (1997, which he co-wrote).

In 2007 he served as narrator-character, with Jean-Claude Carrière, of the documentary *The Last Script: Remembering Luis Buñuel* (*El ultimo guión: Buñuel en la memoria*). This documentary circumambulates the places most prominent in the family's history: Calanda, Zaragoza, Toledo, Madrid, Paris, the U.S. (New York City and Hollywood), and Mexico. *The Last Script: Remembering Luis Buñuel* is designed as a loosely chronological visual "scrapbook" marking the 25th anniversary of the death of Luis Buñuel. It is also a relaxed chat between the two narrators, who were both intimately connected with the life of the Aragonese director. Returning to the Studio des Ursulines in Paris, where *Un chien andalou* was first screened, the two men declare that the place is *"lleno de fantasmas y recuerdos"* (full of ghosts and memories).[3]

The Last Script (2008): Juan Luis and Jean-Claude Carrière

This documentary offers us glimpses of directors who touched Buñuel's life, including Jean Epstein, Fritz Lang, Nicholas Ray, Charlie Chaplin, Alfred Hitchcock, and Jean Cocteau.

Along with his solo achievements, Juan Luis Buñuel served as assistant director to Orson Welles (the unfinished *Don Quixote*), Louis Malle (*Viva María*, 1965, and *Le Voleur / The Thief of Paris*, 1967), Juan Antonio Bardem (*Sonatas*, 1959), Henri Verneuil (*Guns for San Sebastián / La bataille de San Sebastián*, 1968), among

---

[3] This documentary, directed by Gaizka Urresti and Javier Espada of the Centro Buñuel de Calanda, is available as an extra feature on the Criterion DVD of *The Exterminating Angel (El Ángel exterminador)*. The theatrical version is 118 minutes long, but there are also 45-minute and 85-minute versions.

others. He also assisted his father on the following films: *Fever Mounts at El Pao* (1959), *The Young One* (1960), *Viridiana* (1961), *Diary of a Chambermaid* (1964), and *That Obscure Object of Desire* (1977).

As one would expect, he has often been called to participate on film juries, including serving as president of the jury in Dijon, Nantes, and Peñiscola, and as a member of the jury in Avoriaz, Biarritz, Madrid, Porto, Brussels, Sitges, and Bilbao. From time to time he participates in various exhibitions, symposia, and homages to the legacy of his father's work.

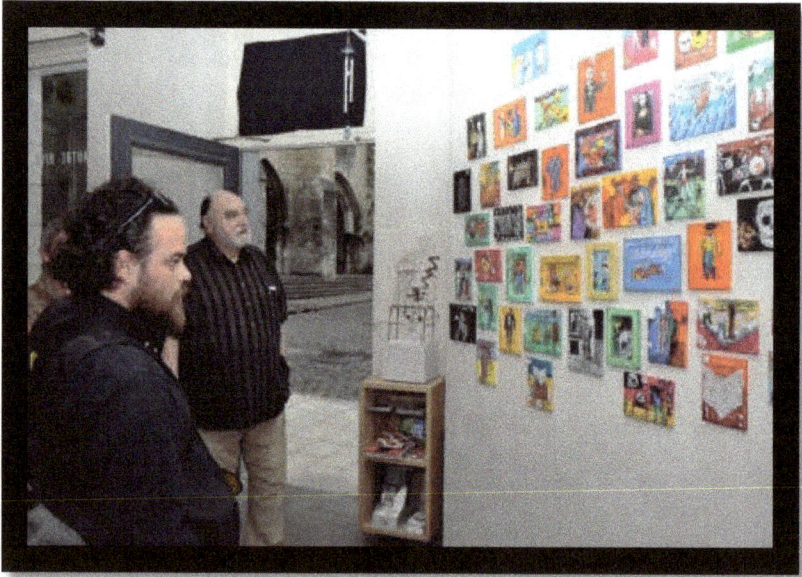

Juan Luis with a wall of his paintings, Bourges, France

As a sculptor and painter, Juan Luis has held one-man exhibitions in Mexico City (Misrachi Gallery, the Salon de Independientes, Galería Diana), New York City (Willard Gallery), San Francisco (Wenger Gallery), Paris (Salon de la jeune sculpture,

Palais Royale), Barcelona (Galeria Pecannins), Palma de Mallorca, Cadaqués (Galería Carlos Lozano), Bourges (Galeria Autre Rives), and Madrid.

He has also participated in collective shows in Paris and Mexico City. His early art lessons with Mexican painter Rufino Tamayo (recounted in the memoir) and his childhood times with American sculptor Alexander Calder had a lasting effect. Juan Luis' imaginative brass and copper wire figures give the illusion of people, objects, and animals moving through three-dimensional space.

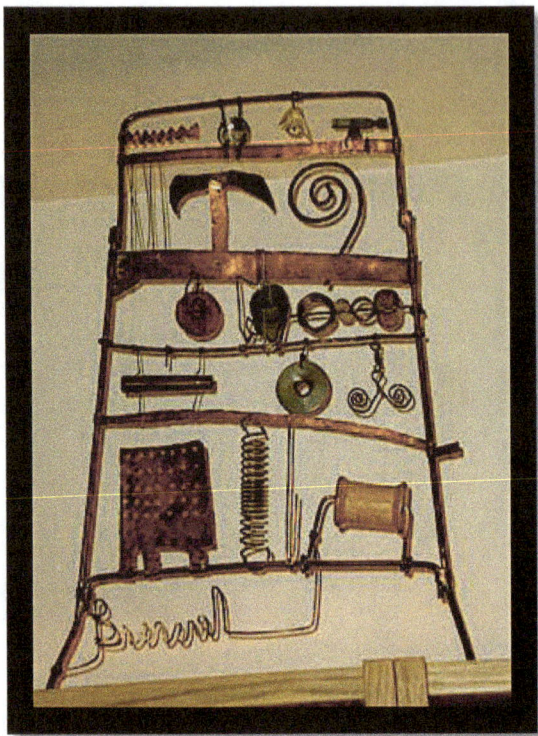

"Letter to Smith" sculpture (wood, wire, and found objects)

In his sculptures and paintings, he is not confined to the everyday but also includes such images as skulls, mummies, and skeletons strumming guitars. Found objects are transformed into whimsical, often dreamlike, compositions with such titles as "Nocturnal insects," "*Poulet sans espoir*" (chicken / police officer without hope), "*Lagunilla*" (small lake / lacuna), and *La nonne* (the nun). This latter work is an elaborate wire sculpture resembling a great, but unwieldy, ocean vessel with sails, and punctuated with circles that seem to soar off into space.

A Few notes on Luis Buñuel (Juan Luis' Father)

Luis Buñuel in the late 1920s

One of the world's foremost filmmakers, Luis Buñuel (1900-1983) was a wild and disciplined poet of the cinema. With the help of cinematographers like Gabriel Figueroa, José Aguayo, and Edmond Richard, Luis Buñuel exposed the hypocrisies of the Church, the horrors of Fascism, and the inadequacies of a bourgeois complacency.

When Spain kicked Buñuel out for the honesty of his filmmaking, he began what film scholar Marsha Kinder described as "many successive periods of exile."[4]

Because of the Spanish Civil War and World War II, he lived in Paris, New York City (where he worked at the Museum of Modern Art from 1940-43), Los Angeles, and Mexico.

Novelist Henry Miller reported that people called Luis Buñuel "a traitor, anarchist, pervert, defamer, iconoclast. But lunatic they do not call him."[5] As Luis Buñuel himself said in an influential talk entitled "Cinema as an Instrument of Poetry":

> In the hands of a free spirit, the cinema is a magnificent and dangerous weapon.[6]

Luis Buñuel would not be hemmed in by any interpretation of him. Juan Luis has a keen sense of his father's films. In one correspondence to me, he stressed:

> It makes me really sad to see how solemn-looking and overcomplicated people get about him...He laughed while he was shooting. All the time. There were jokes, ironies...puns on the characters, the actors, the audience

---

[4] Marsha Kinder, *Blood Cinema: The Reconstruction of National Identity in Spain* (Berkeley: University of California Press, 1993): 286.

[5] Note Francisco Aranda, *Luis Buñuel: A Critical Biography*. Translated and edited by David Robinson (N.Y.: Da Capo Press, 1976): 73.

[6] Cited in the collection of writings by Luis Buñuel entitled *An Unspeakable Betrayal: Selected Writings of Luis Buñuel* (Berkeley, University of California Press, 2000): 138.

and, of course, on himself. And as a faithful if low-profile Surrealist all his life, he never shot or edited a single 'symbolic' shot. I think there are no metaphors in Buñuel. If he thought a shot looked suspect, he'd cut it out.

Luis Buñuel and actor Fernando Rey

With Juan Luis Buñuel's memoir, we again have the pleasure of experiencing the Buñuelian tradition of filmmaking based on a Spanish sense of *esperpento* (ironic dark comedy), extending also into other visual arts.

Structure of the Memoir

All of the writings in the actual memoir are by Juan Luis alone. As editor, I have helped shape the book, with the assistance of master designer Jared Bendis. We interspersed photographs, frame grabs, and illustrations of art. (The original memoir had no illustrations or annotations.) The images take us immediately to the places described so vividly in words. During my short visit to Paris (all other technology failing), we took photos of old sepia-toned photos as Juan Luis graciously took out old albums for my perusal. Subsequently, I "grabbed" rare images from documentaries and scanned others to illustrate key points in the memoir.

Juan Luis' intriguing interludes of dreams, practical advice, and digressions are set off from the chronological tale to give readers visual cues. (As his father once stated: "When my films are a little short, I add a dream.")[7] Readers will note that some sections of the memoir are more ample than others, and that some memories are "nested" in larger events that are described or implied.[8] The varied entries in this memoir offers insight into the way of life of a creative man.

It was difficult to decide what material to include as editor's notes and what was sufficient without additional explanation. I decided to err on the side of completeness, and I compiled information from a host of sources to complement the original writings. However, I did not annotate the final " People I Have Met"section. It has an engaging directness just as it is.

The stories meander across several continents, time periods, and languages—a pleasure, but also a challenge, for an editor. For the English-language reader, French and Spanish words are retained with an English translation. Mr. Buñuel is trilingual (English, Spanish, French), so he was able to read my edited draft and add comments and suggestions.

---

[7] Personal correspondence with Juan Luis, 5 Dec. 2006.

[8] For further reading, see Ulric Neisser, "Nested structure in autobiographical memory," in David C. Rubin, ed. *Autobiographical Memory* (Cambridge: Cambridge University Press, 1986).

There are repetitions in the memoir, but in some cases I left them in. As in life, repetition is often welcome. I also decided to keep the basic order of entries of the original memoir, even though this means there are occasional flashbacks and flash-forwards.

The pleasure for me was to share for a while in the Buñuelian universe.[9] A draft of this memoir was in my study closet for several years until I felt the urge to find a way to publish it. For the past nine months, this has been a delightful, challenging project.

Concluding Notes

A memoir is a revisiting and a reinterpreting. Through this memoir we not only catch the outline of a man's life but we also gain new insights into twentieth-century art and history. A memoir is neither a biography nor an autobiography. Omissions and emphases are partially due to the nature of memory and partially due to editorial choice. While this memoir was written over many years for Juan Luis' children, it is not necessarily about his personal family. Rather, it is about his experiences, with an emphasis on artistic experiences and travel. In this sense, it is personal but still preserves a sense of privacy. In *Patterns of Experience in Autobiography*, Susanna Egan notes that memoirs

---

[9] **Editor's Note:** I hosted Juan Luis for a guest talk at Case Western Reserve University in 2004. He spoke on "Freedom—How Not to Make Commercial Films and Survive." We have continued an intermittent email correspondence ever since. When I was in Japan at the time of the earthquake/tsunami/nuclear disaster, Juan Luis was one of the first to send me news (from France) that revealed the true nature of the environmental threat.

(autobiographies) tend to assume certain dominant narrative patterns: childhood as a "paradisal sanctuary," the journey as a recurring metaphor, and "confession" as a mode often used by autobiographers who write later in life.[10] Some of this applies to Juan Luis' memoir, but not all.

To be an embodiment of important memories is both a pleasure and a responsibility. To move forward beyond those memories, to one's own artistic creations, is also crucial. Juan Luis Buñuel understands this dynamic and carries it with grace. As Mieke Bal wrote in her Introduction to *Acts of Memory*:

> Narrative memories, even of unimportant events, differ from routine or habitual memories in that they are affectively colored, surrounded by an emotional aura that, precisely, makes them memorable.[11]

A bon vivant, Juan Luis is as happy singing the praises of a restaurant set up in a humble clapboard shack on a Spanish roadside as he is drinking martinis with French President François Mitterand. In fact, he's probably happier. In one correspondence with me, Juan Luis asserted, "I have faith in the caustic sense of

---

[10] Susanna Egan, *Patterns of Experience in Autobiography* (Chapel Hill, University of North Carolina Press, 1984): 3-4.

[11] Mieke Bal, Jonathan Crewe and Leo Spitzer, *Acts of Memory: Cultural Recall in the Present* (Dartmouth: University Press of New England, 1999): viii. The other two kinds of memory she outlines are background memories and traumatic recall.

humor of the human being."[12] I was reminded of this when I later wrote to him of something humorous I had overhead:

> I was walking to the Cleveland Museum of Art. Behind me was a family with a little girl who was complaining that all she saw in the museum were 'pictures of old ladies and naked people.'

> To which Juan Luis replied dryly, 'Oh, a cultured and intellectual family.'

Juan Luis Buñuel is a wonderful raconteur. His memoir reminds us that what rises to the surface in a life are the stories. Wander through these pages to savor richly lived moments—accompanied by cheap wine, good films, and a few good friends.

Linda C. Ehrlich

May 2014

---

[12] Personal correspondence 27 Oct. 2006.

DEDICATION BY JUAN LUIS BUÑUEL

To Juliette, Diego and Pablo: This, read with MON DERNIER SOUPIR and MÉMOIRE D'UNE FEMME SANS PIANO and seen with all the photo albums, will give you a small idea of how it went.

Juliette as a chef, cooking paella

Diego and Pablo

EARLY YEARS

PARIS - *SNOW WHITE* (1934 to 1938)

Born prematurely (3 weeks) on November 9, 1934. My mother had to stay in bed for the last two months of her pregnancy. Paris. 4eme Arrondissement. Absolutely no memories of the event.

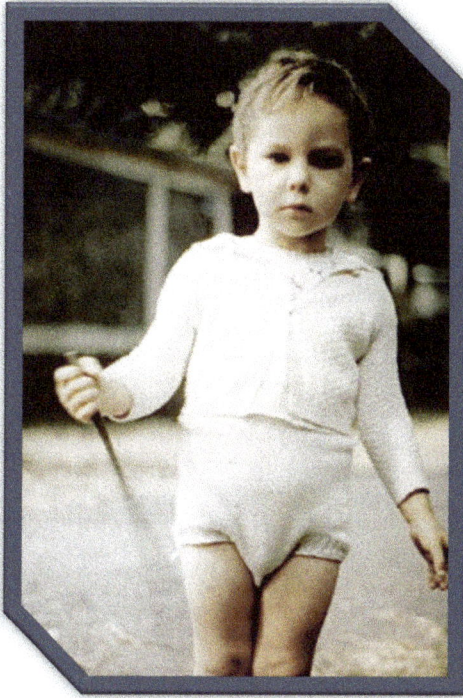

Baby photo, Paris, 1936

Ages One to Three and a half:

First memories: Winter. Paris. Walking up a long snow-covered avenue, holding my mother's hand. Late afternoon. The sun was setting. We seemed to be alone on this street. The snow was clean, with the exception of someone's footsteps who had passed before, leaving their marks ...the steps went ahead of us to disappear over a slight rise in the road. It was almost nightfall. I was wearing rubber boots and tried to put my feet into the footsteps in the snow but since an adult had done them, it was quite difficult for me. Strange feeling, almost as if in a dream.

We were living in a block of brick apartment houses which formed a hollow square ...Square Albin Cachot. In the middle of this complex, a *"marchand de quatre saisons"* (vendors selling seasonal produce on carts) would come every day to sell fruits and vegetables. The pushcart was managed by a large fat lady with rosy cheeks. One day, as we were coming home, my mother told me that the neighbors had informed her that this woman had two hearts.She was leaving her body to science. I was greatly impressed by this news. Though what "leaving your body to science" meant, I was not quite sure. Later I realized they wanted her hearts. If she really had two hearts.

Grandmother's house:

Vague impressions of my grandmother's house...dark furniture, dark piano, huge cupboards, the corners are carved bearded masks. One had to be careful not to scrape one's shins against their grimacing faces.

Once I urinated behind the piano. My excuse: I couldn't find the toilet.

My grandmother kept a canary in her kitchen. I always wanted to hold "Fifi" in my hands. To please me, she took the small yellow bird out of its cage and let me hold him. "Be careful that he doesn't fly away," she instructed. I obeyed and held him very tightly. The bird died, suffocated by my small hands. We buried him in a flowerpot on the balcony.

In this same kitchen, once a week, she would boil her laundry on a large coal-burning stove, wash it by hand and then hang everything all over the room during winter. The apartment would become hot and humid. She did not have central heating but one *"salamandre"* (Ben Franklin stove) in the living room in which coal was also burned.

Hens hatch their eggs by sitting on them. My Aunt Georgette had solemnly informed me of this fact. The eggs must be kept warm. One afternoon, a very fat lady, dressed in many layers of clothing, came to my grandmother's apartment for tea. Knowing that they would sit at the dining room table to gossip and sip their beverage, I fetched an egg from the kitchen and slipped it under the fat lady as she sat down...to see the baby chicken hatch. Everyone but the fat lady laughed.

Les sports d'hiver (Winter sports):

Immense snow-covered slope. Small skis. Very difficult to keep my balance on the skis. I fall into the snow. Huge Saint Bernard comes up, hovering over me, sniffing. I was very frightened.

Zoo Parc de Vincennes:

Walking slowly with my grandfather. We stop in front of a cage which housed wild boars. They tower above me. Years later I visit the wild boars. Now they are much smaller than me. Confusion.

At home:

I had done something wrong and my father had sent me to bed without supper. I was lying in the dark feeling miserable when the door creaked open. My mother came in with some chocolates. Suddenly, the silhouette of my father loomed in the doorway. He took the chocolates away and forced my mother to leave the room. I heard them arguing on the other side of the door.

Another day. I had done something wrong and my mother had bought a cat o' nine tails (a whip with nine lashes or "tails") to threaten me. She shook it in my face and said she would use it if I wasn't going to be obedient. My father appeared, took the whip away from her and threw it into the fireplace. It must have been winter because there was a fire in the hearth. The whip burned.

Cat o' nine tails can be purchased in Paris at the Marchands de Couleurs (hardware stores). These whips are used by housewives who take their bitches-in-heat for a walk in the streets. They lash the interested male dogs away. It's strange that my mother would threaten me with such an instrument. I always considered myself a very obedient child, never causing any problems. I guess I did.

Paris:

One day, in La Librairie Espagnole (Spanish Bookstore) on Rue Gay Lussac where my Tante Geogette worked, an incident occurred which scarred me for life. My aunt was wearing a large sharp brooch. When I walked into the store, she grabbed me, lifting me up for a kiss. As my bare thigh (I was wearing short pants) passed over her ample bosom, the silver jewel slashed through my skin. I bled all over her white blouse. I still have the scar.

Fear of the Eiffel Tower. A terrible fear of heights, of having to go to the top of the Eiffel Tower. Just driving by and seeing it in the distance would make me hide my face in my mother's shoulder.

The first film I saw was Walt Disney's *Snow White*. I was terrorized by the evil Witch. But also fascinated. I nagged my mother, forcing her to take me again to the same theater. Then, almost hysterical with fear, I warned everybody, in a high-pitched voice, when the Cruel Old Hag would appear.

MEUDON

During the Spanish Civil War we moved to Meudon. My father worked at the Republican Spanish Embassy and thought it would be safer to have his family living outside of Paris. He carried a gun with him at all times. I remember sitting on his knees, holding another gun he owned, an air pistol. It was quite heavy. He would help me hold the weapon. From the balcony window we would shoot at leaves in the trees. Once he shot my Aunt Georgette in the ass. She had been sitting below us on a bench in the street, gossiping with some neighbors. Since she wore a heavy rubber girdle, the airgun pellet did not penetrate the flesh, or the girdle...but it did leave a beautiful blue mark on her skin.

About my father's other pistol, a 9 mm. He usually left it in a dresser drawer...loaded. One day he found me playing with this gun, pointing it at him and mother and going, "Poum! Poum!" Slowly, and talking very gently, he worked his way around me and got the gun away without anyone getting shot. After that he was more careful where he kept his guns.

I had a little wagon, which I lent to a playmate. He left it in the street and a truck ran over it.

One night, my mother sang me an old French drinking song, about harvesting grapes, pressing them, making the wine, drinking it ...and then urinating. It embarrassed me tremendously.

In the mornings my mother and I would sit at the dining room table facing each other. She would have *café au lait* and I, a bowl of warm milk *avec une tartine beurrée* (with a buttered piece of French bread). Then she would read *Babar* to me. I would follow the words, from across the table. I thus learned to read *Babar* upside down.

In *L'âge d'or* my father had a scene in which a puppy was to be kicked to death. The actor refused to do it. My father also did not want to do it. He always liked animals. A string was rigged on the dog's collar. In the scene, Gaston Modot (the actor) pretends to kick the dog. This rigging allowed the dog to be pulled out of harm's way. My mother salvaged the puppy and gave it to my grandmother in Paris. They named him Dalou (I suppose after *Un chien andalou)* and when I was born, he became my watchdog. The only person he would growl at would be my grandfather, but only when the old man had had a little too much wine at the café. He could hear my grandfather missing the keyhole as he tried to fit the key into the entrance door lock. Dalou would immediately start growling. Thus my grandfather's lack of sobriety was announced to the family.

Dalou finished his days in the family country home in northern France. He would go into the barnyard and gingerly step around the chicken and turkey droppings. He was very elegant. They called him "Le Parisien."

MADRID, LEAVE FRANCE, 1939

In Madrid, my mother had hired a Nana (maid) to take care of me during the day. But this woman hated the upper class. She was a revolutionary and her family had always suffered from poverty. My mother caught her, as she was carrying me, banging my head against the side of the door as she passed through. I found an explanation to a phenomenon which had been bothering me for many years. At night, the very vision of my face in a mirror scares me. It still does. I don't like to look at my image at night. My mother caught this same maid forcing me to look at myself while I was crying. She pushed my visage right up to the mirror and insisted on how terrifying it looked. I was three years old at the time.

Leaving Paris:

Taking a cab through the streets of Paris. Gare St.Lazare. Last vision of Paris. Rainy day. Tante Georgette giving me a small fuzzy lion. Voice of a newspaper vendor calling out in a deep guttural cry, "*Paris Soir, Ce Soir...Paris Soir, Ce Soir!*"(Those newspapers have since disappeared.)

The boat train...steam, confusion.

On board the transatlantic steamer:

Huge boat looming over us at the docks. Long corridors on the inside of the ship. Finally our cabin.

Wonderful playroom with wooden horses and many toys. I only enjoyed this room for several hours...because, as we crossed the channel, I rapidly became seasick. This lasted throughout most of the trip.

First vision of Jell-O on board: Since the ship swayed back and forth, the brightly colored Jell-O shook and shivered. The Thing from Outer Space. My mother, alarmed, told me not to touch it. "Jean Louis, *touche pas!*" A kindly American man said that it was quite good, that everyone in America ate it. It was my first contact with United States gastronomy.

No memory of the arrival in New York.

CROSSING THE UNITED STATES

We crossed the United States in a car. I sat on my mother's lap all the way. Why she did not put me in the backseat, I'll never know.

Some place in the West, Arizona or New Mexico, a brush fire was burning on both sides of the road. My father rolled up the windows and we barreled our way through.

Driving one early morning on a long and lonely highway in the Arizona desert, a hitchhiker was sitting by the road. He had his head down between his knees. This gave him an aspect of having no head. I was very impressed. He was probably asleep. But I am still convinced that he was headless.

First encounter with an unknown plant: Arizona

Dressed in shorts and sandals, I wandered behind the gas station while my father was getting the car refueled. I saw a strange hairy plant which looked like a small barrel. It looked soft so I kicked it. Bad luck. It was a cactus.

Very hot. In a roadside café, a woman gave some iced water to her small white dog. It lapped it up quickly and fainted dead away.

We finally arrived in Los Angeles.

California:

We lived in a small house on a tree-lined street...Sycamore Street. Back yard, front yard. I had a cowboy hat, a gun and a wooden knife. That's all I remember of that first house. My father had very little money and no job so we moved to...

Juan Luis as a cowboy

Beverly Hills:

We lived with some friends who were also without money but someone had lent them a large house without furniture. They would supply food for one week, then it was our turn. Mattresses on the floor, a table with four chairs. An immense Doberman Pincher guarded the house. He was extremely ferocious. Nobody could get close to him. One day I walked up and started playing with him. He licked me and frolicked like a pup. My frightened parents found me crawling all over him. I was three and a half years old.

First spanking:

It had been raining very hard. Dressed in a new rubber raincoat and boots, I went out in the yard to play. The streets were flooded and very attractive rivers of water were flowing down the gutters. I splashed around happily, even crossed the street...which immediately brought out my father who, out of fear of what could have happened to me...a car or a truck running over the splashing child...gave me my first spanking. Even now I hesitate to cross a street during a rainstorm.

We once went to film director Eric Von Stroheim's house for lunch. For some reason, I was bashful and did not want to meet all these unknown people (I did not know, of course, who Stroheim was). I refused to get out of the car, wrapped myself around the steering wheel and started to cry and yell. My father tried to pull me off the steering column, cursing. I do not remember how it ended.

There were no jobs to be found. One morning, a letter arrived. It was from Paris, from Tante Georgette. In it were five dollars. That night both families feasted: beans, hamburgers and a bottle of wine.

1938 - Fourth birthday:

I received a small iron policeman and motorcycle. The officer could be detached from the machine. No cake. Too costly.

On that morning I awoke crying. My mother asked me what was the matter. "I don't want Pepe (Gaston Rucar — my mother's father) to die!" She calmed me.

A few days later, a telegram arrived that my grandfather had died on the day of my birthday.

∞ ∞ ∞

I remember playing with the iron motorcycle cop around a large (it seemed huge) white fountain in the driveway.

I started to learn English. When playing with American children they suddenly would say a word I did not understand. I would run up the block to my father (who was out of work) and ask him what it meant. "Dog!" "Run!" "Bicycle!" etc. etc. The American kids would laugh when I said, "Yes!" in French. "*Oui, oui!*"

We would take excursions into the Mojave Desert miles from Los Angeles. There my father opened up to me his beloved and mysterious world of insects and spiders found under stones and on cacti. With a bit of luck, a few snakes and lizards would be creeping about.

I had a game of Chinese Pick-Up Sticks. You hold them tightly in one hand, and then let them go. They fall in a clump, and you try to pick one at a time without moving the others. Once

I was playing in the bathroom and let a few fall into the toilet. Then I flushed the toilet and ran to tell my father. He was hysterical. He immediately called a plumber who came, yawned, pushed a long wire down the toilet, found nothing, charged my father five dollars and left.

So many things happen the first few years of our lives, yet we remember so little. How sad that all these events do not remain, even as dreams or visions, to slip back into whenever desired. All those years wasted by forgetfulness. Memories should be like pieces of bread upon which we can nibble. Give us this day our daily thought.

NEW YORK, 1939 to 1944

New York:

When we arrived in New York my father did not have a job. At first we lived in a "kitchenette apartment." The bed would lift up and disappear into a wall closet. The kitchen was hidden in a small cupboard. One month we did not have the fifty dollars needed for the rent. My father was about to get a job with the Museum of Modern Art, but for the moment we needed those 50 dollars. Dalí was living in a luxurious hotel near by and my father asked for a loan to pay the rent. He would pay him back in a month. Dalí answered, to his best friend with whom he had written *Un Chien Andalou*, a letter stating that you didn't lend money to friends and that he was glad that Franco had won the war. And that was the end of that friendship. Later, when my father was working at MOMA, Dalí published his autobiography where he denounced my farther as an atheist and a Communist. Politically, at that time, this was not the thing to be. My father was asked to resign from MOMA. Max Ernst said that one day, walking down 5th Avenue with my father, they ran into Dalí. Max said that my father knocked Dalí down to the ground.

Finally, Alexander Calder let us stay in his apartment on the upper East Side of New York City. It was situated in Germantown.

Alexander Calder

Many friends came over for meals in that apartment...Spanish Republican refugees...also Calder, Miró, Duchamp (years later I heard my father mutter that Duchamp was highly overrated)...the talk centered around the Spanish Civil War and World War II.

At times during supper, the air-raid sirens would wail out. All lights in the city had to be turned off. The adults would rush to the windows to watch New York City extinguish itself. I would wait a few moments, until they were concentrated on the spectacle. Then I would steal the inevitable plate of French fried potatoes my mother had made and hide under the table to eat them at my leisure. The adults were so excited by the air-raid warnings that they never noticed my gastronomic raids...or maybe they did and never mentioned my crimes.

Sunday morning I would listen to the operas on the New York classical radio station. My father would describe the different stories: *Lohengrin, Tristan and Isolde, Romeo and Juliette*. Wagner was his favorite.

There was a good bakery down the street and my mother would ask me to go get the bread. I was scared because I wore short pants (like most European kids of my age) and the toughs (12 year olds) would laugh at me for wearing them. I was really scared to go out.

When my mother went off to the hospital, pregnant, I said, "I hope you bring back a monkey." She brought back a baby. My brother, Rafael, was born in New York City during a typically hot moist summer: 1 July 1940.

Editor's Note: Rafael was named after Rafael Sánchez Ventura [1897-1980], a member of the Residencia de Estudiantes and assistant director of *Las Hurdes: tierra sin pan*.

There are several photos in the album of that period. My father, bare-chested, his hair moist with sweat, is holding my brother in what could be an unclean diaper. Behind him is my mother, also unkempt and sweating. In the background, I lurk with a broken toy and sick with whooping cough. It is a grim picture...until I found a set of these photos, each one a little different. My father had done a little "*mise en scène*," probably to impress his family in Zaragoza...it is true that he did not have a job at this time and that it was bloody hot in New York in August.

A baby crocodile was given to me. The best place to keep this reptile was in the bathtub. To feed it, I would tap the beast on the snout. He would open his mouth to bite me and I would shove hamburger meat down its throat. One day the cleaning lady, who obviously did not like the little creature, turned the hot water on in the bathtub. Boiled crocodile.

My toys at that time were a set of roughly cut and colored wooden animals: a lion, an elephant, a tiger, a giraffe...and the hero, a deer. I played constantly with them in, as I remember it, a dark living room. I would even draw them on paper and send them on magnificent adventures. The living room during the summer was always dark. The shades had been drawn to keep out the broiling New York sun. Television did not exist.

Several times we went to Sandy Calder's home in Roxbury, Connecticut for the weekend. My mother and father would make a paella outside on a wood fire and the adults drank great quantities of California wine which was contained in huge gallon bottles. Louisa Calder would bring out her accordion and everyone would dance. If ever there were any discussions, it would be about the Spanish Civil War and the ongoing World War II. My playmates were Sandra and Mary Calder.

Sandy's studio was a magical place full of wires, mobiles, colors, pliers, hammers...He used to make me little animals, which I immediately threw into the nearest wastebasket. In this way I could ask him to make me another animal. What interested me was watching him make the figurines. He never seemed to mind.

Since I could not pronounce Juan Luís correctly, when asked my name I would mutter Van Vis...(Juan Luís), so Sandy Calder named me Vanvis...which became my nickname for many years.

One day, in a small pond near his house, I caught a small water snake. My father had shown me how to catch these beautiful reptiles: right behind the head, holding him tightly so that it cannot turn around and bite you. There is one danger in catching a snake. Using it as a defense mechanism, he'll turn his body and defecate on you...a foul smelly liquid. Usually you drop him.

Anyway, I had my snake by the throat and was proudly going to show it off to the adults in the house. At that moment, the only person in the house was Sandy Calder, and he was in the bathroom, naked and shaving. I walked in and said, "Sandy, look!" With a roar, he grabbed the snake from my hand, rushed out into the garden and finished off the creature with a shovel. My vision of the event, through my tear-stained eyes, was of a naked giant, half of his face swathed in shaving soap, slaughtering my pet. It took me two days to get over this tragedy.

∞ ∞ ∞

In the large living room Sandy kept a human skeleton in a wooden trunk by the chimney. It had impressed me the way he would pull it out and make it walk and rattle. Then, with a roar he would put it back in the wooden trunk. One day, I had been bad, had disobeyed, and my mother, much to my terror, had locked me in the room with the trunk for a few minutes. After that I was very good.

Note: If you cut a finger or your hand, to stop the bleeding, hold the extremity above your head. Usually it will stop or slow down the bleeding.

One Christmas, at Marion Willard's[13] house in Long Island, my father had bought me a small electric train. I was deliriously happy with my new toy. In the meantime, Christmas cheer had spread throughout the house, and especially at the bar. My father, Calder, Joan Miró and José Luis Sert[14] (also a Spanish Catalan refugee) had pulled mightily at the different bottles that lined the wall. Then they came "en masse" towards me, threw me out of the room and started to play with my train, laughing and reliving their love of the restaurants on European trains. I was furious but they were bigger than me.

---

[13] Marion Willard Johnson, a dealer in contemporary art and founder and director of the Willard Gallery for more than 30 years. She sponsored Northwest Coast painters Mark Tobey and Morris Graves, among others.

[14] Josê Luis Sert (1902-1983), Spanish-born architect, designed the Spanish Pavilion at the Paris World's Fair (1937) along with Miró, Calder, and Picasso. He became a U.S. citizen in 1951 and the Dean of the Graduate School of Design at Harvard University in 1953.

Dream

This is a recurring dream. I am lying in my bed. When I was little, we always had apartments with long corridors. I hear my parents talking, comfortably, quietly in the living room at the end of the corridor, the long dark corridor. I call out, "Can I come with you?" They say I can so I leave my bed and, in my pajamas (I don't know why I am wearing pajamas. I've never owned a pair in my life) and barefooted, race down the interminable hallway towards them. But suddenly, to my great terror, I seem to be moving through quicksand, my movements become more and more difficult. I call out to them but they do not seem to hear me and continue to talk quietly. My movements are now quite labored. Then to my horror, small red devils come after me. I am terrorized. I wake up.

SCHOOL IN NEW YORK, BUTTERFLY IN CLASS

I first went to Dalton School, a progressive school. When it rained, the teacher broke out comic books. My art and/or drawing teacher was a poor Mexican painter, Rufino Tamayo who, years later, helped me with my first sculpture exposition in Mexico City.

Then I went to Public School Number 6...P.S. 6. Most of the kids in school were Jewish. Across the street was a Catholic school. We used to have fights with them. During winter we would put rocks in the snowballs. For a while I thought I was Jewish.

I became friends with the son of Frederick March,[15] a great American film actor. At first we thought that the son was a girl because he had long hair. By the standards of today it wasn't that long. One day we followed him into the boys' toilet to check. He was a boy.

Once he invited me to his house for a Halloween Party. Frederick March ran the party for his son. He taught us new games. Then, while we were eating, he said, "The first one to finish gets this skeleton!" It was a huge multicolored cardboard skeleton. I won...but forgot to pick up my skeleton as I left.

I finally figured out why he wanted us to eat fast...to get the party over a little sooner.

∞ ∞ ∞

---

[15] Frederick March (1897-1975) won an Oscar for Best Actor for *Dr. Jekyll and Mr. Hyde* (1931) and for *The Best Years of Our Lives* (1946).

Since it was during World War II, every act was highly patriotic. Everyday, a different child in my class was asked to hold the American flag and the rest of the pupils would recite the Pledge of Allegiance to the United States. When it was my turn to hold the flag I refused. My excuse: I was French. But the real reason was that I was too bashful to stand in front of the class.

One day the teacher gave us a psychological test: "What is the difference between a fly and a butterfly?" When she read my answer, she quickly called in my father. "The correct answer to the question is: the butterfly is beautiful and the fly is ugly. Your son said: the butterfly eats flowers, the fly eats shit! He is maladjusted and sick!" My father laughed and said that I was right and that I had stated an observation that had been made quite correctly. None of this Walt Disney shit about some animals being more beautiful or better than others. He left the teacher chewing on her Freud.

During this period, I did not stop drawing: crayons, wooden pencils, colored pencils, everything was valid. All the drawings were either science fiction battles, or wars between Germans and Americans or Japanese and Americans. At times the Free French participated. The War was part of our daily lives and the adults would listen to the news every night on the radio.

Finally my father got a job at the Museum of Modern Art. I remember, when going to his office, walking by Picasso's *Guernica* and Le Douanier Rousseau's *Sleeping Gypsy*. This last painting always fascinated me...the gypsy, so calm, sleeping, while a ferocious lion looked over her.

My brother must have been one year old. It was Sunday morning and, as usual, my father and I were listening to the morning concert. My mother called me from the kitchen. My brother was going to try his first egg. Did I want to see the expression on his face? I jumped up and galloped towards the kitchen. Such was my haste that I tripped over the rug and slammed my lower lip onto the sharp corner of the living room table. The lip was perforated and I bled like a stuck pig. My father took me to the emergency ward of the nearest hospital. It took three stitches and some chloroform to fix me up. The Famous First Egg.

My mother would take my brother and me to Central Park religiously every morning, summer and winter. We would go to a little lake or pond just above the Metropolitan Museum of Art. There was a small hut by the water that, during winter, sold hot café au lait. We would stop there to warm our hands on the steaming cups and to sip the sweet coffee and milk. It tasted very good.

There was a snow-covered hill with a huge tree at the summit. All the kids would slide down on their sleds. I did not have a sled...no Rosebud.

Once, on a bus on the way to the park, I saw a small blonde girl. She was about my age but was wearing heavy glasses. She definitely had troubles with her eyes. I spoke to my mother, in French, commenting on how strange the girl looked. The girl's mother leaned over to us and, in perfect French, stated that one should be careful of what one says about other people's looks...because others did speak French and it could hurt their feelings. These people became our best friends in New York. The mother, Lucia, and her daughter, Elena Delgado Chalbaud. Her husband was once the president of Venezuela[16] and was finally assassinated by Pérez Jiménez.

One summer, in Central Park, some tough kids, ten or eleven years old, started pushing me around. They stuck pins into me. I had to run away.

First Love:

Her name was Phyllis. She also went to P.S. 6 and we would meet in the Central Park playground. Once I tried to put my arms around her, to tell her of my love, so she kicked me in the head. That's as far as that went.

---

[16] Carlos Román Delgado Chaubaud Gómez, 1909-1950, a career military officer, was leader of the military junta, and President of Venezuela from 1948-50.

VACATIONS

During the hottest part of the summer, we would go to an inexpensive vacation spot in the Catskills for a week. It was called The Spanish Farm Inn. Several refugees from the Spanish Civil War had opened up an old farm-hotel and many Republicanos who lived in New York City would go there for a few weeks during the summer. The children would play in the fields and woods, the women would make paellas or grill lamb chops. The men would drink wine and discuss the Spanish Civil War so loudly that at times it scared the children.

Luis Buñuel, Jeanne, Juan Luis

Rafael, Jeanne, Juan Luis

The evenings were magic because we were not sent to bed, but allowed to play games long after dark. During the afternoons, when it got very hot, we would go to the ice house, a large barn-like building, where, during the winter, the farmers would place great squares of ice cut from the surrounding lakes, placing them tightly together and covering them with sawdust. This material was from the neighboring sawmills. There were always rivulets of cold water seeping from the old barn as the ice melted. We would climb up a ladder and sit on the cool moist sawdust. With an ice pick, an older boy would chip off chunks of ice. They were delicious. The best ice cream in the world.

When it rained, the adults would organize Chinese Checkers tournaments. Everyone played.

During the hot nights, the air would be filled with lightning bugs. We would catch them and put them into glass jars.

While on a walk through the woods, my father lost his watch. My mother went back up the path repeating, "Saint Antoine de Padoue,[17] help me find the watch and I'll light you a candle." Then she looked down and there was the watch. Even though she was an atheist, she went to a Catholic church and lit a candle to Saint Antoine de Padoue.

---

[17] St. Anthony of Padua (1195-1231) was a Portuguese Catholic and a member of the Franciscan Order. He is credited with helping people find lost objects or people.

RETURN TO CALIFORNIA, 1945

When we went back to California, we took the train. Chicago was very cold and a tremendous wind made us dodge from doorway to doorway. The ferocity of the freezing wind made us laugh. With one parent on each side holding my arms, my feet were swept into the air by the gusts and rarely touched the sidewalk.

I remember as we crossed the U.S. by train, reading a brightly illustrated book about King Arthur and the knights of the Round Table, then looking out the window and seeing the interminable prairies of the Midwest flowing past. The stories and images were much more interesting than the monotonous countryside.

I don't remember Rafael being with us, but he must have been. He was only a year old.

California

We lived, for several months, at a friend's place in the San Fernando Valley...a beautiful farm in the country. He was a set designer named Ferrari and his wife Yvonne (who liked whiskey so we called her Yvrogne [drunkard]). They were very nice people and he had a large pigeon coop in the backfield of his house. He loved to eat squab but was kind-hearted and the very act of cutting a pigeon's head off was impossible. So he had his technicians at the studio build him a small but lethal guillotine. When he wanted squab for supper, he would tie up a couple of young pigeons, put their heads into the guillotine, turn away and pull the rope.

LIFE IN LOS ANGELES

Finally we moved to 5642 Fountain Avenue.

Fountain Avenue was a long quiet street of small houses with big front and back yards and hardly any traffic. At the corner of the street was a drugstore-soda fountain where the kids could buy candy bars and comic books and the adults, cigarettes and aspirins.

House in Hollywood, 1946

My father had a job at Warner Brothers dubbing English-speaking films into Spanish. Ours was a small house with a big back yard. This area became the focal point of my activities. There was a large palm tree at the back of this area and a tumbledown gardener's shack that quickly became the Roy Rogers Fan Club (my hero at that time). I had set up an old pup tent in the middle of the yard. My father did his exercises with an iron bar. He would stretch with it, lift it over his head...and throw it...once right through my tent's side.

My father had bouts with sciatica. At times he was bedridden for several days. I would be playing in another room and he would knock rhythmically on the wall behind his head six times. It meant *"Vanvis n'aime pas Papa"* (Vanvis doesn't love Papa). I would yell out, saying it was not true and would run into the bedroom and jump into his arms. He would laugh. *Vanvis n'aime pas Papa.*

In the dining room was an ironing machine. It had a round stainless-steel tube that heated up electrically. My mother would then slip a clean wrinkled shirt or pair of pants into this tube, press the hot circular blade against the cloth and Presto! out would come an ironed article of clothing.

My brother (who was five at this time) had a little friend called Dennis and they were constantly playing at cowboys and Indians in the backyard. Their vocal imitation of guns firing with the following ricochet made my father come out of his room to banish them to the front yard. He couldn't work because of all the "bullets" whizzing around his head.

∞ ∞ ∞

Once, in the Roy Rogers' Fan Club Shack, my brother found an old opened cardboard box of arsenic snail poison. My father caught him nibbling at the greenish powder. He immediately rushed my brother to the hospital where the doctor informed us that it was too late to do anything. The arsenic was very old and had probably lost its potency. But, if Rafael had ingurgitated a large amount, it could prove fatal. Upon getting home my father interrogated my brother.

"How much powder did you take? A pinch?" My brother nodded yes.

"Tell me the truth, did you take two pinches? If you tell me the truth, I'll give you a present." My brother nodded excitedly. Two pinches...and a present.

The interrogation continued. "If you really tell me the truth, I'll give you a big big present."

By the end of the session my brother admitted to having eaten two whole boxes of arsenic.

Finally nothing happened and he did not die...he also did not get his presents.

∞ ∞ ∞

Living on top of the clubhouse and the garage were a gang of pigeons. They reproduced very rapidly. Something had to be done. Using a special cage and corn kernels, all the pigeons were quickly trapped, about 20 in number. They were packed into three crates and we drove out to the desert, about a hundred miles, to release them. It was an all-day outing. We had a picnic lunch and then opened the doors to the crates. The pigeons flew off into the sky.

When we arrived home, they were all lined up on the garage roof waiting for us. I suppose they are still there.

Almost all food during World War II was rationed. At times, even with ration stamps we couldn't get basic foodstuffs. My mother would rush home from her daily trip to the supermarket. A fresh arrival of butter had arrived. Only one-quarter pound bar per customer. Our whole family would gallop to the store. Each one of us would go by the cash register with our bar of butter. My brother was too small to be considered a customer. Later that day my mother would bake a cake.

During the war, meat was often impossible to obtain. Luckily, my best friend's father, who lived down the block, was a butcher. Every now and then he would sell us a choice piece of meat. We were very grateful. My friend's name was Jimmy Grindstaff.

Talking about meat, my father was preparing a paella. Friends were coming over that night for dinner. He was in the kitchen cutting up some pork when he accidentally sliced a small piece off the top of his thumb. The chunk fell into the chopped pork. He dropped the knife and ran to the bathroom to bandage his hand, to stop the bleeding. Later we tried to find the piece of thumb but it had gotten mixed with the small pieces of pork meat. Someone ate the piece of my father's thumb in that evening's paella. We didn't tell our friends of the food supplement.

They say that in taste human flesh is very like pork.

Years later, in Mexico City, Juan Antonio Bardem,[18] Muñoz Suay,[19] and the actor Paco Rabal were to come over that afternoon for a paella. An hour had to be decided upon. My father, a very precise man, had asked them to give the exact hour. A paella has to be eaten exactly 15 minutes after it is ready.

My father knew that Bardem, Rabal and Muñoz Suay had a meeting with Siquieros, the very Communist Mexican muralist. He was also a very talkative man. It was possible that they would start drinking tequila and that Siquieros would begin on his innumerable anecdotes of the Mexican Revolution.

My father was worried.

"Stay as long as you like but we must establish an hour upon which you must arrive. A paella cannot wait."

The problem was discussed and 3:30 in the afternoon was decided upon.

"Don't worry, Don Luis. We'll be there at 15:30 hours on the spot," said Bardem. Rabal also promised that they would break away from Siquieros.

---

[18] Juan Antonio Bardem (1922-2002) is known for his films *Death of a Cyclist* (*Muerte de un ciclista*, 1955) and *Calle Mayor* (1956). Bardem was imprisoned for political reasons while shooting the latter. He was instrumental in bringing Luis Buñuel back to Spain to make *Viridiana* in 1960.

[19] Ricardo Muñoz Suay (1917-1997) was a Spanish director, screenwriter, and executive producer of *Viridiana* (among other films).

The next day, my father started cooking his paella. At exactly 3:30 it was ready. It was big, because these friends were coming over with their wives. It was a superb paella.

Three thirty five...Three forty-five.... Four p.m.

Half an hour had gone by.

At 4:10 the bell rang. The guests had arrived.

We could hear from outside their voices, "Luis, we couldn't stop Siquieros from talking, he just wouldn't let us go...."

When the door was finally opened, the first thing they saw was my father's enraged face. Then they saw that the huge paella was on the floor.

My father spat out, "You wanted a paella...well here it is."

And he jumped into the delicious creation and stomped it into the ground.

How did it end? Finally they made up, started laughing and then they all went off to a restaurant...where they didn't order a paella.

∞ ∞ ∞

Once, in California, while my parents were shopping in the supermarket, I started to fool around with the exit turnstile. Suddenly my neck was caught. The turnstile could only close tighter. I started to choke. The personnel did not know what to do. My father rushed up and broke the turnstile. I was freed. The supermarket director admitted that it was a dangerous turnstile and promised to get it fixed.

Summer vacations: we would go Balboa Beach for a week. My father would rent a small apartment consisting of a bedroom with bunk beds and a kitchen in a block-long wooden building. The kitchen was equipped with an old-fashioned icebox and every day the iceman would come. He would use his ice pick with extreme dexterity and all the kids of the block would fight to get the chips of ice that fell from his horse-drawn wagon onto the street. At times it would mix with the horse droppings. We'd wash it clean. Poor kid's ice-cream. It also was delicious.

Everyday we'd go to the beach. I made friends with some boys who had a tiny motorboat. Once, in Balboa Harbor, we cruised by a small sailing yacht. One of the boys yelled out to the young woman sunning herself on the deck, "Are you Lauren Bacall?" "Yes," she answered. We circled the sailing boat twice. The young woman waved to us in a friendly manner and we puttered away, pleased at having spoken to a star.

Once a Hungarian woman refugee taught my mother to make delicious potato and onion pancakes.

I didn't have any toys so I had to do with what I could find. In the supermarkets I would walk around with my eyes glued to the floor. One day I found a series of plastic price tags that I quickly slipped into my pocket. I played with them for several weeks.

My parents were always broke. Once, when I was walking our dog Mike, I found a purse with 30 dollars and a set of keys in it. My father insisted that we take it to the police station. Which we did. They said that if nobody claimed it in 30 days, the loot was ours. A month later, we claimed the money and my parents bought food and wine for a week.

My father was forced to spend quite a bit of time in bed. His sciatica nerve was acting up and at times he could not even get up. Once I asked him why his back hurt and why he couldn't move. He told me this story:

> When I was little, my father set up a very tall ladder and told me to climb it. Once I had reached the top, he told me to jump. He would catch me. I was scared but he said, 'Trust me, I am your father!' So I jumped and he stepped out of the way. I crashed to the ground and hurt my back. Then he leaned over me and said, 'See, never trust anyone, not even your own father!'

His sciatica was finally cured by a chiropractor, a gentle lady who massaged his back and made him sleep between two cardboard tubes which contained radioactive rocks. Once we put a fresh lettuce between the tubes for two weeks and it did not wilt or rot.

My allowance, when my father had a job, was twenty-five cents a week. Saturday morning I would go to the corner soda fountain-drugstore. Ten cents for a comic book, five cents for a Hershey bar and ten cents for a caramel sundae. Sometimes I would save the money to buy a huge bag of popcorn. During the late afternoon, I would go to the Boys' Club with my popcorn. Every Wednesday evening a 16mm film would be projected. Sixty boys (and some girls) of all ages would see a free Western or comedy. Usually there would be an older couple (16 or 17 years old) who would be kissing and petting in the back rows. At times they were more interesting than the film.

We did not have television at that time. On Sundays we would go to the movies but during the week I listened to the radio. From 4:15 (when I got home from school) until 5:30, there were programs for children. First came TOM MIX. A cowboy. Tom Mix had really existed, had been a rodeo star, a movie stuntman and now he was a radio hero. Adventures, saving the young woman from the burning house etc etc. It seems his body was covered with scars from his many stunts and falls. His sponsor was SHREDDED RALSTON WHEAT CEREAL. Little pillows which fell apart into shredded wheat sticks in the milk.

Then came SUPERMAN..."Faster than a speeding bullet, jumps over a building with a single leap." It was SUPERMAN from the planet Krypton. His disguise was that of Clark Kent. All he did was change from his red and blue tights and cape into his dark suit, put on a pair of glasses and even his girl friend, who worked with him every day, did not recognize him.

THE GREEN HORNET with his faithful partner Kato. His car sounded like the buzzing of a hornet.

The most mysterious of them all, THE SHADOW. The announcer would speak out, "The Weed of Evil bears bitter fruit...who knows, the Shadow knows!" He would sneak around, like a shadow at night and get rid of the nasty people.

Those were the afternoon shows. As I listened, I would draw what I heard. There were no images to spoil my imagination. One of my big disappointments was when I first saw Superman on film. Here was this guy in long red underwear with slicked black hair who would jump into the air and be carried away by a wire. My imagination had been much more powerful and creative...all children's thoughts are rubbed out by television because the images are made by someone else...leaving nothing to their creative process.

In the evenings, and once a week, were a series of adult programs which I listened to...JACK BENNY and his man ROCHESTER. Benny was famous for his tightfistedness. BOB HOPE as I remember, was very funny. But there was one program which struck terror into my heart: INNNER SANCTUM. It started with the sinister sound of a creaking door opening. The stories were of witches and werewolves, of terror. I once had a awful nightmare. I was listening to Inner Sanctum and the story was too frightening for me to go on listening. Much to my horror, I could not turn the radio off. I awoke covered with sweat.

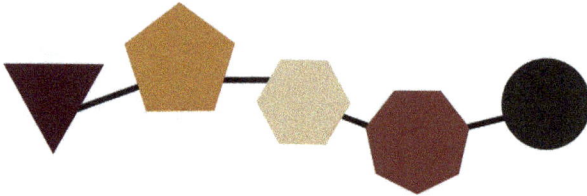

COMIC BOOKS

Between the ages of 6 until 12, my favorite reading material was, or were, comic books.

Superman: I was always astonished that when Clark Kent took off his glasses and became Superman, nobody but nobody (even Lois Lane), recognized him. And what did he do with his suit when he jumped into an empty phone booth to change into the red tights of Superman? In England, they say that because Clark Kent has jet black hair with a "banana," wears glasses and a suit, he must surely be a Pakistani. (In the old days [1950's] and if you had enough hair, you would comb up the front part of your hair, fluffing it out. It would form a big "banana." Elvis at times would make one on his head.)

Batman and Robin: Looking back, I realize that Batman must have been some sort of pedophile. Robin wore extremely tight hot pants or shorts, little boots and a cape. Suspicious.

Captain America: He, dressed in an American flag, fought Nazis. He also had a young kid assistant.

Captain Marvel: In real life he was a young boy named Billy Batson but when he uttered the magic word "Shazam!" a bolt of lightning would strike him and he would become a mighty crime fighter, also with a cape.

Classic Comics: All the great works of literature (adventures) were illustrated in these comics. It was a known fact that many a high school student used these comics for their reports instead of reading the original book.

Roy Rogers: My hero at the time. He had a horse named Trigger and a girlfriend name Dale Evans. Their importance came in that order. He also played the guitar and sang. That's why I learned to play the guitar. Because of him. Years later I heard his songs again and they are the most godawful pieces of music, songs about a patriotic America, about love and babies and backyard barbecues.

The Phantom: He lived in Africa, wore very long purple underwear tights and was a Great White God for the regional Blacks. He had a skull ring and when he punched an evil white man, the mark of the skull was impressed forever on the scoundrel's forehead.

Hanging on a wall of the house was a portrait of my father that Salvador Dalí had done while they had been in La Residencia in Madrid (1923). One day I was carrying a chair and tripped. One of the legs of the chair ripped through the painting. If you ever see the painting (it's now in the Reina Sofia in Madrid), check for a small slit where my father's collar is located. If it isn't there, the painting is a fake. (Note: I saw the painting in the Reina Sofia Museum in Madrid, July 1996. It had been repaired.)

We would take the car and go out to Antelope Valley. There we would shoot my father's .22 caliber rifle, look for insects, and have a picnic. One Sunday it was very hot and we had two flat tires.

∞ ∞ ∞

Since the U.S. school system is not the best, out of desperation, my parents put me into a Catholic teaching institution, the Blessed Sacrament School on Sunset Boulevard. It was run by nuns. I must say that they did teach you to read and write. But, if you acted up, you were hustled immediately to the Sister Superior's office for punishment. Since, by law, the sisters were not allowed to beat you, the punishing nun (usually the Sister Superior) ordered you to roll up your pant legs. Then she would slap a thick ruler into your hand and would order you to hit yourself on your own calf. *Thwack!* Her trained ear could tell if you weren't slamming the skin hard enough. *Thwack!* That sounded better. And so *Thwack! Thwack! Thwack!* until she was satisfied and your leg was a bright red. It hurt. But she didn't lay a hand on you.

Three boys from Blessed Sacrament School, Los Angeles (Juan Luis on right)

The big sexual scandal of 1945 was a Western film by Howard Hughes and Howard Hawks called THE OUTLAW starring Jane Russell. The news came out on the playground of Blessed Sacrament: the nuns had announced it was a MORTAL SIN to see the film. There was one 13-year-old who had risked eternal Damnation and had seen it...I think his father was the projectionist. The key scene was Billy the Kid disappearing under a blanket with Jane Russell in a horsebarn. You could see the blanket undulating up and down. Fifty years later I finally saw the film. The scene: interior of a dark barn, shot with a wide angle lens...which puts the blanket and the characters in a distant corner. They do crawl, if you look very attentively, half hidden by the shadows, under the blanket...and then, Sin of all Sins, the blanket barely starts to move. So many people sent to hell for that little ripple. I wonder if the Church has ever lifted its ban on that film?

Every Sunday, my mother would take my brother and me, by bus, to a cinema called the Hitching Post on Hollywood Boulevard. There, for 35 cents each, we would see a Western double feature. One Sunday, half-way through the second film, sounds of yelling and laughter, bells and car horns, interrupted Roy Rogers' attempt to overpower the bad guys (all dressed in black, Roy Rogers had loud-colored embroidered western shirts). The theater was emptied. Hollywood Boulevard was full of people of all ages and races, singing and dancing. Victory over Japan. World War II had just ended. We had to walk home. The bus service had been interrupted because of the crowds.

END OF WWII, MOVE TO MEXICO CITY (D.F.)

Hiroshima and Nagasaki had been blasted into oblivion and we entered the Atomic Age. To celebrate this, the Atomic Fountain Pen came out on the market. It was the first ballpoint pen. It would bend almost in half without breaking. You could also write underwater with it. A magnificent way to commemorate the death of hundreds of thousands of civilian Japanese.

These pens were sold in a stationery store on Hollywood Boulevard. Great piles of white paper of different sizes and shapes lined the walls. Drawing paper from different countries (of an infinite variety) placed on shelves waiting to be felt, judged...and bought. I became a paper fetishist there, wanting to buy all the goods, and then violate them with pencils, paints, Atomic pens and even charcoal. I enjoy touching the paper. But it ain't sexual.

1946 – Mexico:

Union strikes at Warner Brothers left my father without a job. A film was offered to him in Mexico City so we sold all the furniture, packed our bags and gave Mike, the dog, to a friendly neighbor. I was 11 years old.

The flight from Los Angeles to Mexico City seemed very short, very exciting. My mother was terrified, she had never flown before. My brother and I kept looking out the porthole of the airplane and telling her, "Look how small the houses are down there!" She would just grip the arms of her seat and stare straight ahead.

Our first apartment in the D.F. was facing the fountains of Chapultepec Park. The building does not exist anymore. First impressions: sadness at having left a children's paradise (Post-war Los Angeles without cars, bicycling down the streets without a care, my friends) and now having to live in a rundown apartment and not being able to go out freely. Also, I did not speak Spanish. Sitting many hours at my desk looking out into the street, sad, bored. Then Chapultepec Zoo on Sundays, just a few minutes' walk from our building. There was the armless man who would, with the toes of his feet, shuffle cards, sew, draw and make miniature Mexican *charro* (cowboy) hats out of straw. ...and the bird-trainer whose tiny canaries would jump out of their cages, fire a cannon, offer you a flower and then beak you your fortune from a small box filled with tiny letters.

We would meet other families of Spanish refugees and some became life-long friends. Jackie, La Tica...

∞ ∞ ∞

One day I was playing on the trolley-car tracks. Up ahead of me, a fat Indian lady was waving her arms and yelling something. I did not quite understand her. She looked frightened. I was puzzled. She cupped her hands to her mouth, "*El tren! El tren!*" She pointed over my shoulder. I looked around. Just a few feet away, a trolley was bearing down on me, throttle wide open. I jumped out of the way and that infernal machine clattered past. The driver had not even slowed down. I looked for the Indian lady but she had gone her way...after saving my life. I would like to meet that trolley conductor some day. Probably wouldn't recognize him anyway.

I was enrolled at the new campus of the American School in the Colonia Observatorio. Since my hero had been Roy Rogers,

King of the Cowboys and he was a guitar player...I also wanted to play that same instrument.

My mother asked other Spanish refugee friends for the name of a guitar professor...and one was brought up. Jaime Calpe, ex-Republican Guardia Civil and refugee in Mexico. He helped me pick out a cheap guitar and I started classes on the terrace of his downtown D.F. building. There was only one problem, I wanted to play cowboy music and he only knew Spanish classical and Flamenco. So I learned a little of his and he figured out the simplistic chords of "Detour," "Your Cheatin' Heart," and "Water, Cool Water."

This same terrace was used once for paella contests. After much yelling and arguing on the art of paella making, several of the men chipped in and bought a cheap silver-plated trophy. Then one Sunday morning, their wives bought the ingredients: rice, *chorizos*, shrimp, clams, *azafrán* (saffron). All this was gathered at Calpe's terrace. Fires were built on the roof and each man started his Paella. The guests arrived at 2 p.m. Drinks were passed around. Then at 3 p.m. precisely, the large paella pans were put out on long tables made of boards placed on saw-horses. It was simple. People would taste the paellas...and the first pan to be empty, won! My father was the winner and he cherished that trophy more than the Oscar he won many years later.

∞ ∞ ∞

On Sundays I would go to Cinelandia, a movie house on Avenida San Juan de Letrán. Two hours of cartoons. Nobody had warned me about the nasty men who haunted these establishments. I didn't even know about those people.

Anyway, I was innocently watching Bugs Bunny destroying Elmer Fudd when a man sat next to me. I didn't even notice him. Then his hand dropped on my knee. I just flicked it off. Again the hand adventured its way across my thigh. Again I threw it off. The third time I suddenly jumped out of the seat, his hand fell to the seat...and then I sat down very hard on the unprotected hand. I heard the crackling of little bones, then the pervert let out a gasp and left the theater very rapidly. Finally, when I was a little older, I finally figured out what he wanted. Nobody had ever told me.

NOTE: When cooking with butter, add a little oil.
This stops the butter from burning.

DIFFERENT HOMES, D.F.

1947

Calle Rio Elba-Colonia Cuatemoc:

We moved to Rio Elba, also just a few blocks from Chapultepec Park. It was a smaller apartment and my room overlooked a large, heavily frequented avenue. I was very lonely during this period...didn't have many friends. I would pass the days drawing and painting or, poking my air-rifle out the window through the slates of the Venetian blinds, drawing a bead on an innocent pedestrian. In my head, I murdered many pedestrians. This gave me great satisfaction.

One evening, as we were eating supper, someone threw a small rock through the living room window. My father turned out all the lights and made us lie on the floor. Then he went to get his gun. He looked out between the drawn Venetian blinds. The street was empty. Our assailants had fled. He never found out who had thrown the rock.

∞ ∞ ∞

Then one Saturday night all the Spanish refugee friends came over dressed as if in a Don Juan Tenorio[20] play. They strutted around, big beards, bristling with swords, boots and spouting verse. My brother and I tried on a few hats, capes and especially loved the swords.

---

[20] This play was written by José Zorrilla in 1844 (not to be confused with Tirso de Molina's *El burlador de Sevilla*, 1630).

Costume party in Mexico City, 1947-8
(Luis Buñuel is bearded man in back. Rafael and Juan Luis in front row)

My mother had made a *cocido madrileño* and everyone had brought wine. After supper my brother and I were sent to bed. We could hear them roaring into the night...louder and louder as the wine intake increased...then the poetry was drowned out by discussions on the Civil War. **All** dinners and parties ended that way. The Spanish Civil War.

∞ ∞ ∞

Two good things happened while we lived on Calle Nilo:

1) I started horseback riding lessons. The stables were run by a Spanish refugee called El Doctor Galapatorio ("Galloping

Man"). He just threw me on a horse and told me to go out riding. At that time, part of the Lomas of Mexico City (which are now luxury neighborhoods) were just dry fields and hills. No houses, no people. Each time I went out was an adventure. It was great to go out alone on a horse for several hours every Saturday afternoon. Once, riding along Reforma, I went under a tree. A branch caught on my shoulder, then slammed back on the horse's rump. He shied away, knocking me from the saddle. I fell on my left side. Forty years later: I'll probably have to have a hip implant because of that. (Finally it happened. I did have a hip implant.)

2) I was given a secondhand bike. Since we lived just a few blocks from Chapultepec Park, I would meet other friends from the American School and we would bike all over the forests, lakes, streams and fields which composed this area in the middle of Mexico City.

Just a hundred meters from our home, the first supermarket in Mexico City opened, Supermercado Sociedad Anónima or SuMeSa. It was a tiny thing, but one could get all basic supplies easily. In front of it was a guardian with an official cap. He would help the women carry their groceries to their cars, hold the doors open, help them park, blow his whistle to stop traffic, etc. etc.

One Saturday morning I went to buy a kilo of carrots to feed my horse later that day. I got off my bike and was about to chain it to a tree when the "official" guardian came up, "*Te guardo tu bicicleta, Jefe?*" (Can I watch your bicycle, Boss?). He would watch over my bike and I would give him a "*veinte*" (a copper 20-centavo piece which was the most common form of exchange at that time). So I nodded in agreement and as I went to get the carrots, he got my bike. I never saw it or him again.

By now my father started working so one day he brought me a secondhand 78rpm electric record player. It was great. I had two records "Detour" and "Froggy went a'courtin'." I played them incessantly and drove my mother mad. One day, a friend of my mother's from California brought me several records from her neighbor, Tex Ritter. Now I drove her mad with "Blood on the Saddle," "You are my Sunshine," and "Cool Water" by Bob Nolan and the Sons of the Pioneers.

My friends and I became MONOPOLY addicts. We would have games that lasted ten days. We had to print up extra money. We would play after school.

I had a friend in high school. His name was Mario Vargas Villa. His father was a tough General in the Mexican Army and he would treat his son very severely. He kept a small .25 cal automatic in his bedside table and at times Mario would show it to me. One day he committed suicide with it.

1949

Moved to Calle Nilo (the first three apartments were all within five blocks of each other). We had a parrot called Coco (Coconut, this was a very original name for a parrot [since most parrots were called Coco]). He had the tips of his wings cut and therefore could not fly. We taught him to say "Coco Burro." He also imitated us when we would call our mother. "Mamaa!" In the mornings he would climb out of his cage and slowly make his way down the long corridor which went from the living room to the bedrooms. He would go directly to my mother's bed. We could hear him coming: "Coco Burro, Coco Burro..." he would mutter to himself. Once at the foot of her bed, he would clamber up the sheets and blankets, using his claws and his beak. Then he would gently nibble on her earlobe and whisper lovingly, "Coco Burro."

My mother would then get up and make his breakfast of bread dipped in *café con leche*. Once in Oaxaca, I noticed that a woman fed her parrot green chiles. She said, "*Le hace hablar* (it makes him speak)." I can imagine what he said...

Coco would spend the rest of the day outside on the balcony whistling and singing. When the sun was too hot, he would get under the sheets of newspapers which lined the bottom of his cage. But this parrot had an eagle eye. Four blocks away was the Paseo Reforma and when he spotted my mother getting off the bus, he would start shouting, "Mama! Mamaa!"

> Editor's Note: Juan Luis recalled that once Coco the parrot bit the lower lip of exiled screenwriter Dalton Trumbo, and he bled all the way to the airport. In addition to the parrot, Juan Luis recalled the following pets: a bilingual tucan, a crocodile, two ducks, and the parrot who acted in his father's film *Robinson Crusoe*.

Once a week, down our street, *charros* would drive herds of cattle towards the slaughterhouses. Mexico was then much smaller and the traffic was, in the early mornings, practically non-existent on the side streets. At times the *Guajolote* (turkey) Man would come by, driving a herd of several dozen turkeys before him with a long whip. Obedient creatures. The maids would come down from the apartments, buy a live bird...and slaughter him in the solitude of their own kitchens. In that way one was sure that the fowl was fresh.

It was in this apartment that I really got into books. The last "*locataire*" (renter) had left in a closet about 100 detective novels...good, bad and classic...from Sam Spade and Mickey Spillane to Sherlock Holmes. I read and enjoyed them all.

Joined the school band. I played the guitar, it wasn't electric (they didn't exist at that time) so no one could hear me. Finally the band director, Mr. Beatty, handed me the Sousaphone (Bass tuba). I was the only person who could carry the damned thing. Since I didn't know how to read music or play the instrument, I just imitated the bass drum. Boom boom boom.

CALLE EXTREMADURA & PANTEÓN DOLORES

1951

Interesting phenomenon. We lived in this house for several years yet I have almost no memory of what the interior looked like. One thing comes to mind. My father's room had plasterboard walls. I was walking down the steps, wearing my new cowboy boots. The leather soles were bright and shiny. My foot slipped on the staircase tiles and the heavy boot heel went through the wall and into his room. He wasn't too happy about that.

I became friendly with Juan Larrea's[21] beautiful daughter. He was a Spanish refugee, a writer with whom my father had projects. The daughter was eight years older than I, and our relationship was limited to stealing human skulls from the large Panteón Dolores Cemetery near the American school. She would put a large round box under her skirt, and a raincoat over her shoulders. She looked pregnant. Then we would go to the cemetery to pray for our dearly departed. When we were sure no watchmen were in sight (the Panteón Dolores was immense...many acres), we would go to the *"fossas communes"* (mass graves). All the families who had not paid rent or who had disappeared, had their dear dead ones dug up and thrown into the common trench. There we would sift through splintered coffins, rotting cloth and bits and pieces of bones, eventually picking out a handsome skull. She would slip it under her dress and, with tears in our eyes, we would leave. I think she decorated her room with these grinning

---

[21] Juan Larrea (1895-1980) was a Spanish essayist who lived in Paris and, after the Spanish Civil War, moved to the Americas. His books include *Oscuro dominio* (1935) and *Versión celeste* (1969).

bones. They were better off by her bed than in the commoners' trench.

SCOUTS & SNIPE HUNT

We met Chief Red Fox (a Sioux) who as a boy had been present at Custer's Last Stand. Then he was part of Buffalo Bill's Wild West Show and had toured the US and Europe. When he attended our camp, he was about 100 years old. He then wrote his memoirs, had them published, then died. It was found out a few years later that much of his material had been stolen from other books. Sneaky old bastard. A very funny man and it was great listening to him tell his stories.

As a Boy Scout, with Chief Red Fox in the "Aztec camp," ca. 1950. Rafael on left

The most interesting aspects of the Boy Scouts in Mexico City was that we could choose the climate and topography for our camping trips. Within a few minutes we could be in tall pine country, or else go up to the eternal snows of the Popocateptl. If we headed south, Cuernavaca and Cuatla offered us desert country...a few kilomters more to the south and we'd hit tropical climes.

One of our favorite campgrounds was on the flanks of the Popo, near a village called Amecameca. There we'd set up camp and make the younger Scouts go through their training in First Aid, knot tying, etc. At night we'd play different stalking games.

One of my jobs was to secure the area of dangerous spots: broken glass, slippery banks into the river...and deep wells. Near our camp site was an abandoned well, about 20 meters deep. The bottom was lined with stones and broken branches. Tall, slippery grass lined the rim. It was definitely a dangerous spot. There was some barbed wire laying about, so I nailed it to three trees which grew along the edge to form a crude fence. And then we forgot about it.

That night we decided to play a joke on some of the new boys. A game called The Snipe Hunt. Snipes are small edible birds which run rapidly through underbrush on long legs. We would give the kids large bags, place them in the dark woods with instructions to hold the bag open. They were not to move or make any noise. Then we were to form a line, several hundred meters from them and make a lot of noise. This would frighten the snipes and they would run into the bags. That night we would have a delicacy for dinner around the campfire: roasted snipe. The object of the game, of course, was to abandon the kids in the dark until they got scared. Then, depending on our meanness, or goodness, we would fetch them back to the campsite and everyone would have a good laugh at their innocence. An intellectual Boy Scout game.

We started at 9 o'clock. An older Scout named Pat Mulvey would set the boys up with their bags, then we'd shine our lights at him and he would join us. We'd go back to the campfire, have a coffee, wait an hour, then go pick up the frightened and abandoned kids.

We flashed our lights in Mulvey's direction. He answered and headed for us at a run...in the dark. Then we heard a yell and a dull thump. Someone called out, "The well!" We had circled the well to get into our present position. Mulvey had cut straight towards us.

We rushed, all ten of us, the fifty meters that separated us from that awful hole. When we got there, our flashlight lit up the scene. Mulvey had crashed into one of the barbed wires. It had ripped out from the tree that I had nailed it into that very afternoon. But the other two nails, had held. Mulvey now was balanced on his stomach, like some circus acrobat, between the two trees and about two meters down into the well. Below him, darkness. Our flashlights beams could not reach the rock-filled bottom. We could hear the barbed wires groaning and the nails giving way.

Then we moved very quickly, like a well-trained team. Someone grabbed my legs and started pushing me towards the edge of the pit, then another boy grabbed his legs and so on, forming a human chain. I was pushed down, deep into the well. But Mulvey was hanging too low. I could not reach him. Above me I could see Jerry Lindner fumbling madly with a rope, trying to get it untangled. Again I reached for Mulvey's hand. Just a few inches separated us but it was impossible grasp his fingers. Suddenly the rope whirled pass me and fell into Mulvey's grasp. The boys above pulled him within my reach. I had him. He clambered over me and up the human chain. Quickly we pulled ourselves out and moved to a safe distance from the pit. The skin on Mulvey's stomach had been badly lacerated by the barbed wire. One of the Scout fathers took him that night by car to a hospital in Mexico City to have him sewed up. He was also given tetanus shots.

Then we realized that we had forgotten the younger kids who were still holding the bags. We went to find them, greatly humbled by the experience. They were brought back and informed of the accident.

∞ ∞ ∞

We used to come back from Boy Scout meetings in the trolley car which went up Felix Cuevas and its continuation, Extremadura. One day, two friends and I came back in such a manner. At the corner of Insurgentes and Extremadura, my two friends, Bill Anderson and Richard Kimrey, got off the trolley. Bill started walking towards the bus stop on Insurgentes and Kimrey, without looking stepped out onto the opposite tracks (he was waving good-bye to me) and into the path of a speeding trolley. He was lucky. Those old trolleys had long wooden hand bars on the doors to help the travelers on or off. One of these bars caught Richard on the side of his head and knocked him for a complete cartwheel, He fell next to the track, the wheels of the trolley passing centimeters from his head and body. I jumped off my tram and (this all happened in seconds) saw that Richard was not chopped to pieces, then I looked at Bill Anderson for help. Bill having seen the accident and thinking the worst, was walking away his hands over his eyes. I called out to him and he came back. We picked up Richard, who was knocked out, and dragged him to my house. We were very excited. I did not have the keys to the gate so we started yelling and hollering for my parents to open up (We did not know how badly Richard was hurt).

My father, whose room was on the second floor, came out on his terrace. Seeing two of us holding up the third...and yelling, he concluded, "*están borrachos!*" (they're drunk), and called down to my mother who came out to open the gate.

Anyway, we checked Richard out, called his father who immediately came over to take him to a doctor. Luckily, he only had a bump on his head to bear witness to his cartwheel. It was his lucky day.

San José Perua:

Another time we had gone camping at San José Purua, about a two-hour drive from Mexico City. In Michoacán. We arrived in the late evening. The sun had already gone down. We immediately set up our pup tents and built our cooking fires. But since the sun sets early in Mexico at that latitude, we decided to look around. Not far from our campsite was a hollow, or what we thought was a hollow. We stood on the edge and heard someone playing the guitar down below. I decide that I would jump down. It probably wasn't that deep...But just to be careful, I decided to grab onto a root and lower myself down. I couldn't feel the ground below me. I would wait until morning. We went back to our tents, had another coffee and then sacked out.

The next morning we found ourself camping on the edge of a very very deep canyon. The ground below us was several

91

hundred meters down. Luckly I had not jumped or dropped down into this little "hollow."

But then we found that our camping ground was infested with scorpions so we decided to burn all the grass around us. We started to do this when a *campesino* (peasant) came running up, telling us to stop. He looked frightened. We also were soon frightened. It seems that on that very same spot a cache of dynamite and gun powder had been buried for safe keeping.

We decided to change camping grounds.

Note: Take time out to learn knots.
Even the simplest will help you all your life.

AMERICAN FOOTBALL

I played American football at the High School. During my senior year I was elected football captain. It was during a game against Colegio Militar that I got clipped from behind and from then on I've had back trouble. Football was fun and, since I was always a little shy, it taught me to give and take hard kicks.

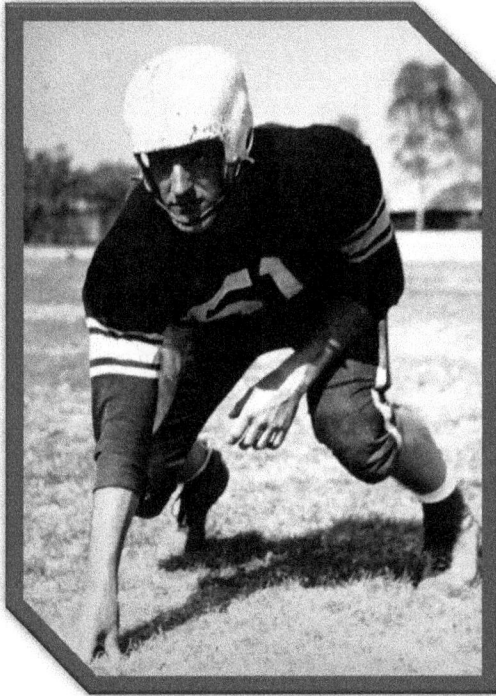

Captain of the American High School football team

During that period, we did not have the football helmets of today. Some were old leather headgear from ancient times. I had my nose broken once. Very painful.

Jerry Lindner, Severne Schaeffer and I formed a cowboy or country music trio. We sang at most of the school gatherings and parties. After four years, people were sort of tired of our intervention. But we enjoyed singing, "Detour, there's a muddy road ahead..."

∞ ∞ ∞

There were moments. One weekend, with Jerry Lindner and another friend, we went camping at a place called Zempoala. The area, at some 3500 meters above sea level, was made up of one huge volcano which had blasted out seven craters~some big, others smaller. These craters had filled with pure clear waters from volcanic springs...and the trout had moved in.

We set up our pup tents in a clear area next to one of the smaller lakes. The whole volcano was covered by a dense growth of tall dark blue-green pine. We built a small fire, and had our evening meal of grilled meat, roasted potatoes (in the ashes) and some tequila for finishers. A couple of Indians, their burros loaded with supplies, stopped by and we asked them over for a drink. They drank silently but the atmosphere was friendly, the tequila relaxed everyone. With a smile and a tug at their sombrero brims, they left us to the night's silence. We sat around, sipping tequila, wrapped in our sleeping bags...the temperature could drop several degrees below zero at that altitude. We turned in early that night.

Jerry was up before the sun came out...5:30 a.m. He served us hot coffee in our tents and by 6 a.m. we could hear the trout striking at the insects that flew close to the water's surface. We piled some wood on the fire to have good embers for cooking our breakfast and walked the several meters to the edge of the lake.

We used flies, and just about every cast brought on a hit. I moved up and away from my two friends to a lonelier spot. Flying a few feet above the surface of the water a white crane was crossing the lake. A scream broke through the morning's silence and a dark mass of feathers and claws slashed through the air towards the crane. The crane ducked to one side and the eagle slammed on its airbrakes to avoid hitting the water. The crane started hightailing it towards the opposite bank. The eagle, with powerful strokes of its wings, gained altitude and again dived towards the other bird. Its tactic, I suppose, was to hit the other bird at a hundred kilometers an hour, breaking its back or neck.

Again the crane ducked away from the attacker and took refuge in some trees. There, the eagle could not get up enough speed to be efficient. It flew away slowly, looking for other prey.

In a while, we met back at the camp. We mixed some flour, dried fruit, baking powder, and water. This heavy stuff was twisted around a green twig (first we tasted the twig to be sure it wasn't bitter) and this stick was punched into the ground near the fire in such a manner that the fresh dough hung over the embers. "Twist bread." When one side is cooked, you simply rotate the branch to one side until the uncooked part of the dough is over the fire.

We put a sliver of good smoked bacon into the gutted trout and fried them in a mixture of butter and oil. Twist bread and fried trout for breakfast ...and Jerry's hot coffee laced with a wee drop of tequila. It was good.

∞ ∞ ∞

In the American High School we had a teacher by the name of Philippe Groesbeck. He had a twin brother who at times would start the class and then the original Groesbeck would walk in...

We were camping one night near the outskirts of Tepotzlán at a Scout Camp At midnight Bill Anderson came to get us. He told us that our great teacher had pulled a young Scout into his sleeping bag. Bill Anderson, Bob White and I pulled little Tommy Green (his father was military attache at the US Embassy) out of Groesbeck's sleeping bag. Ol' Phil was dead drunk and he had dragged the little kid into his sleeping bag in front of a room full of younger Scouts.

White and I went over to save little Green. I still remember his little face at the bottom of the bag. We pulled them both out, and we slammed Groesbeck up against a wall. We were ready to smash him when he fell into a drunken faint. We left him propped up against an outside wall. We went to tell the adult Scout leaders and they told us not to say anything, they didn't want to start trouble. Bunch of hypocrites.

A couple of years later (coming home from college), I heard of Groesbeck's bloody suicide.

Also I didn't like him or his manner of treating his favorites.

VISA FOR U.S., 1953

To get a visa to study in the United States, I had a private meeting with the U.S. Consul at the American Embassy. He looked very stern. I was sitting in front of his desk. There was a large file marked "Buñuel-Secret F.B.I. Files." He looked me up and down coldly, then flipped open the file.

"Your father attended a leftist political meeting in 1932 in Paris."

"I wasn't even born then."

"Hmmm, yes..." He looked a little startled, then waved another report. "Your father went to a Communist meeting in 1929..."

I interrupted, "I wasn't even born then."

He seemed bothered, "Yes, but your father, in 1935..."

"I was only one year old."

He seemed very distraught. It was impossible for him to associate me with the Communist Party no matter how hard he tried.

Then I brought out my Ace card. A week earlier I had won the American Legion Outstanding High School Student Award. This prize was given automatically to the Football Captain of that year by the American Legion Post of Mexico City. The American Legion was made up of ex-soldiers, veterans of all the wars in which the U.S. had participated.

The Consul broke out with a big smile when he saw the big bronze medal and the certificate, "Oh! Oh! That changes everything!" And he immediately stamped my visa. But first I had to swear not to assassinate the President of the United States. I told the Consul that I would be studying and would not have time for trips to Washington. This was no laughing matter, he said...so I swore not to go lean on Mr. Eisenhower.

CABARETS IN MEXICO

High School graduation: The boys rented tuxedos and the girls had on long gowns. The graduation ceremonies took place in the Palacio de Bellas Artes in downtown Mexico City. It was very fancy and the girls all had small bouquets of flowers. Then we went on a two-day binge where we hit all the nightclubs of Mexico City. We even took a watered-down version of Speed (amphetamines, pills which are used to take away your hunger) to stay awake.

The nightclubs (discoteques did not exist) in Mexico at that time had good live orchestras...a mambo and chachacha 8-piece band, and during the breaks, a small jazz combo would take over. But above all, these clubs were created with a sense of humour. There was the CATACUMBAS (Catacombs). A monk would greet the partygoers at the door and the decor, built to remind you of early Christian catacombs, was lit by a black (ultra-violet) light. Your teeth and the white of your eyes would flash eerily in the dark. If you and your date were lucky enough to have a fresh sun tan, then your skin would glow with a beautiful golden sheen.

As you sat in your cubicle, a fake spider would drop down in front of your date, sending her screaming into your arms. Then the head monk would come by for the Tour of the Mummies. Along the walls of the club were several upright coffins. The guide would lift up a dusty shroud, exposing the leather-like face of an ancient mummy from Guanajuato. He would explain how the dry air of that northern Mexican town had perfectly preserved the dead man's features. He would hold his dim flashlight close to the cadaver's face and ask your date to lean forward, to see the remarkable preservation of the skin. Of course, as she warily leaned forward, the other waiter who was wearing the mummy mask, would jump out at her, sending her again screaming into your arms. The mummy would then disappear into the gloom after you had greased his palm with a few pesos.

At EL TURCOS (The Turks), the decoration was different. Instead of booths or tables, you had little oriental tents of different sizes for one to four couples. There were large pillows to sit on and a small table in the middle for drinks. The whole place was almost totally without lights. Very cozy and discreet.

Usually the last drink was at the Plaza Garibaldi, at the TENAMPA. It was a very large bar containing about fifty tables and booths. Great lurid murals of Mexican ranch life adorned the walls. The music was provided by five mariachi groups, all playing at the same time and at different tables. If you were smashed enough, your table would do the singing. Mingled with all this were several dozen prostitutes.

As the customers walked in, they were immediately frisked for weapons by two sinister-looking individuals who wore 1930's suits and hats. The women were never touched. Tequila and *ponché* (punch) were the favorite drinks but whiskey could be had at a much higher price. The evening wore on and, when a group felt itself too rowdy, or too drunken, they would call over EL HOMBRE DE LOS TOQUES. A simple fellow in a dark blue suit would walk over carrying a car battery with two wires. Everyone at the table would hold hands and the wires would be given to the two members of your party at the extreme ends of the table. The man in the blue suit would then blast out a double jolt of electricity that would flash around the table through the guests, quickly sobering the party. Shaken, we would pay him two pesos and leave the Tenampa.

Once, years later, we drove down and parked in the Plaza Garibaldi. We were about to get out of the car, when a large group of mariachis surrounded the car and offered, for a small price, to serenade us. I, being a smart aleck decided that they should play a classical piece: "The Poet and Peasant Overture." With a smile, they launched into that wonderful piece. A miracle! No, the *charro*-dressed mariachi played to perfection this classical piece. They were members of the Bellas Artes Symphony Orchestra who, on their free nights, to make a little extra cash, would put on the wide-brimmed *charro* hats and play to the tourists. We all had a good laugh.

The evening would end where the D.F.'s electric trolley cars spend their nights: the trolley barns of Indianilla. There the famous stands or "*puestos*" of the Caldos de Indianilla would be full of customers. The trolley car drivers and engineers were arriving for breakfast, after which they would hustle out their trams to begin Mexico's workday transportation. But also, all the late-night revelers and drunks and whores and workmen would also descend for the famous *caldos*...thick, filled with fresh vegetables, chile, chopped onions and cilantro and white chicken meat, served with hot hand-made tortillas, the *caldo de gallina* (chicken soup) was the best in the world after a night of drinking...or working. Then some would go home, take a shower and go to their offices, others, the lucky ones, to bed.

Note: If you ever have to touch an electrical wire, for any reason, in an emergency, always touch it with the back of your hand. If you were to touch it with your fingers, or your palm, the electricity might contract the muscles of your hand and you would be stuck to the live wire.

Lindners' House:

My best friend at that time was Jerry Lindner. He was a total musician...played the guitar and sang, played the trumpet, the piano, the banjo, whatever instrument he could get his hands on. We formed a little cowboy band...Jerry, Severne Schaeffer and I, all with guitars...and would play at parties, high school meetings. Eventually, the band shifted to Dixieland. Since I was to handle the banjo and didn't know how to play that instrument, I tuned it to the lower four chords of the guitar and in that way helped with the noise.

During our senior year in high school, on Saturday nights I would stop by Jerry's house. We'd have a drink and then go out on dates. Milton Lindner, Jerry's father, would be in the kitchen, home after a hard day as the Agricultural Attaché at the American Embassy. All he cared about was cooking. As we were leaving, he would be putting on his white chef's apron, mixing his first drink and preparing giant shrimp or getting pork meat ready for smoking. He also made his version of Camembert and different "*eaux de vie*."

After taking our dates home around two in the morning, we'd go back to Jerry's house. I would spend the night there. As we quietly let ourselves into the house, Mr. Lindner would be cleaning up the kitchen and having his last drink. The next day's meal would be all laid out and ready for the stove. We'd have a nightcap and he would lead us through the secrets of his art.

The parties at Jerry's house were always very animated with Jerry's mother playing the piano and singing New Orleans songs.

RANCHO DEL CHARRO

The Rancho del Charro was a small bullring dedicated to *"charreadas"* or rodeos...there the Mexican cowboys would do their *"suertes"*: bulldogging, lasso work, bucking horses and bulls, etc. The best place to watch all this was under the stands. There, decorated with old bullfight posters, was the bar...rough cement, a long bar and several tables. If you got there early enough, you could get the prize tables, the ones that were situated near a long narrow slit that looked out onto the plaza itself. While having a beer and/or a tequila, you could be within an arm's reach of the bucking broncos or the bellowing bulls (alliteration). Their mad hooves would kick sand and dirt right into your face and it was important to keep your glass under the table if you wanted a clean drink. The atmosphere was charged and we really enjoyed the *charreadas*.

Once we walked in an hour early to assure a good table. At the bar were two very drunk *charros*. Each was pulling straight from individual tequila bottles. Both were carrying pistols...38 caliber revolvers. They were having an argument as who was more "macho." At first we laughed to ourselves about their discussion but suddenly the logic got very serious. One pulled his gun from its holster, cocked it, and put it against the other man's temple and asked him to do the same. Now these two idiots stood there, each holding their cannons to each other's head. The first man spoke through his big mustache. "I'm more macho than you are...therefore you can pull the trigger first!" The second man disagreed, "No, I'm more macho...you pull the trigger first!"

By this time we were all under the table. If one of the idiots did pull the trigger, and both were so drunk they could hardly stand, the shock of the explosion would probably make the other person twitch his trigger finger...A wild bullet could hit one of us. Finally two waiters sneaked up on them, grabbed the guns away and threw them out of the bar. We all felt better and could enjoy the *charreada*.

Note: After you have handled a gun, always, before putting it away, wipe it clean with a soft oiled cloth. The hand exudes a natural acid which stains the gun metal and eventually leaves rust marks.

CERRADA FÉLIX CUEVAS

1953

Cerrada de Félix Cuevas 27-Colonia del Valle

My father asked Republican-in-exile architect Arturo Sáenz de la Calzada to build our house. Both had lived, while students, at the Residencia de Estudiantes in Madrid during the 1920's. I heard Calzada ask my father, "How would you like the house to be?" My father mentioned it could be made out of red bricks ...to resemble the Residencia.

House on Félix Cuevas (now a cultural center)

Our house was the second one built in the Cerrada. The first house belonged to the Giral family who were members of the Spanish Republican government-in-exile.

Across the street (which wasn't yet paved) was a *pulquería* where masons and construction workers would go for a drink after work.

Editor's Note: *pulque* is made from *maguey*, a large cactus, and cannot be purchased at a regular bar.

One evening, a man and a woman, completely drunk, made love on the sidewalk. I was not present. But several mothers hid the act from their children by locking them up in their houses.

The street was of dirt and gravel, not yet paved. When I came home from college the first time, a new home awaited me.

∞ ∞ ∞

One night a procession went by the house...a Saint, a priest and several hundred faithful carrying candles. I decided to follow them. The procession went down into a small *barranca* (ravine) at the end of the street and over to a field where a little church stood...about 300 meters from our house.

I followed them into the inner courtyard of the church. And then the "slaughter" began. Men and boys, poised on top of the courtyard walls suddenly pointed and fired hundreds of rockets and firecrackers down into the crowd. It was an ambush in the true sense of the word. Women and children were screaming, flames were coming at them from all sides, crackers exploding in their faces. I made a rush, along with some sensible members of the procession, for the courtyard door and squeezed out into the safety of the field. By the screams of terror and the laughter coming from the interior, I could tell that everyone was having a great time.

This church still stands today but it is in the middle of a very pretty park whose outstanding features are a great variety of trees and flowers.

Skull with Flowers (Juan Luis Buñuel)

OBERLIN COLLEGE, OHIO

Leaving for College (Juan Luis, Jeanne, Rafael)

I was very happy to get back to the United States. I had left that country when I was ten and a half years old and remembered only the ideal world that the U.S. offered a child. Now I was nineteen. I was quickly disillusioned about the United States.

College photo, age 19

The first shock came when I witnessed the McCarthy hearings on television at the college snack bar. The place was crowded with students and faculty members. When I saw what was going on, my first reaction was that of laughter. It was a soap opera and very serious people were saying outrageous things...Eisenhower was a communist, the U.S. colleges were infiltrated by communists, etc. But I quickly shut up when I saw the audience's faces. It seemed that Oberlin was next on the House Un-American Activities list. All the professors were worried and would watch the hearings on television. That the intellectuals of a huge "free" country like the United States should be held in terror by an alcoholic madman seemed to me unbelievable. Finally he accused Eisenhower of being soft on the communists. That was a bit too much. And cirrhosis got him. There was a sequence in a magnificent documentary, POINT OF ORDER, made years later (Emile de Antonio director, 1964) of an insane McCarthy sitting alone in the huge hearings room, muttering into the microphone, "Point of order, Mr. Chairman, point of order...The Communists have infiltrated every part of American..." etc., etc., ad nauseum. It seemed like a bad film. But it was true.

Note: Never trust a politician...or a very religious person. Anyone who knows the Truth should be avoided.

My dormitory was an old broken down two-storey building made of pasteboard that had been built during World War II to house Navy students who were on government grants. They would go on to become officers.

From the very first day, I encountered many young men and women of my age. Something happened which was entirely new to me. Each person had his own interests and points of view and this was freely brought out and discussed. My intellectual life at the American High School had been severely limited by my group, which I was, of course, a part of...but we spoke of football and music and girls and Boy Scouts...very seldom did we speak of literature, history, philosophy or science. Suddenly we were all thrust together, our minds churning, the professors heaping on work...It was great...but difficult for an untrained mind.

At night, after classes and studying at the library, we used to have "bull sessions" to talk and exchange ideas which would last until the early hours of the morning. I think that is where we exercised our little brains the most...and it was where we had the most fun.

Talking about untrained minds, I first saw Charles Fitzgerald one early morning. Classes started on the hour and most students had left for their 8 a.m. class. I was sitting at my desk preparing for my 9 a.m. class. As I looked out the window, I saw this big fellow come running out of the dorm. It was 7:59 and he was obviously hurrying to his 8 o'clock. He grabbed his bike, threw his books into the basket, jumped on, started to peddle furiously...and the front wheel came off. He crashed into a tree and the bushes around it, arms and legs tangled with the wheels and spokes of the bike. Furious, he stood up, grabbed the bike and with one mighty throw, smashed it against the guilty tree. Then he stomped off to class...to which he would be late.

Near Oberlin was a steel milltown called Elyria. Saturday night, the young workers would booze up. Their sport was to beat up the faggy Oberlin students. Obviously a class war. They would cruise by in their old chopped and channeled Chevrolets and Fords, usually falling upon some poor Conservatory student coming back to his dorm after four hours of violin practice. Charles and I, both of the wrestling team, decided to form a two-man vigilante committee. Saturday nights we would stalk the campus and come help the poor piccolo student. We'd show those bullies not to fool around with Oberlin students.

And it happened. One Saturday evening, around ten o'clock, we heard a car squeal to a stop across the main square and insults thrown at our effete musician. We charged across the square and arrived in time to out-yell the four "townies" who were about to commit the crime. "Oh, yeah," they growled, "we'll go get some friends!" "Go ahead, you cheap punks!" we retorted, "We'll still beat the shit out of you." With a curse, they roared away in their late '40's Chevy, double exhaust pipes spewing flames.

We were victorious. Our chests filled with pride. The piccolo major thanked us and disappeared into the Conservatory. We strutted about, ready to take on another carload of toughs. And then we heard it. The menacing roar of many duel exhausts...a symphony of chopped and channeled cars. Looking across Tappan Square, and to our right and left, the streets seemed to be filling with evil-looking motor vehicles. We counted at least 12 cars coming to our rendez-vous. Charles, who was a better mathematician than I, quickly spit out the statistics. "Twelve cars, with at least four guys in each vehicle...that makes 48 steelmill toughened hoods." My only statement was,"Feet, get moving!" We plunged into the shrubs on one side of the square, burst through on the other side and made it back to our dorm in seconds flat, probably breaking all 200-yard records. They didn't even see us!

Sunday morning was a time of leisure. We would usually have a late breakfast in the town café which happened to be situated right on the path where the young freshmen girls would be going towards the different churches. We would hijack a couple of girls, drag them into a café (THE PEN AND PENCIL), buy them a cup of memorably bad coffee and a doughnut...and instill the seed of doubt in their mind. We were highly trained in religion and logic. The minutes would pass. The girls would nervously ask the hour. We had previously set our wristwatches back. Then we'd order another coffee and attack the very structure of their religious belief. We were not prejudiced. Catholics and Jews would fall to our cudgel logic. But the most delightful to attack were the Protestants ...so innocent and credulous. And by the time we would release them, trembling and unsure of what to think, the religious services would be over.

Years later I received news from a couple of those girls, sisters. All our work had not been in vain. They eventually had become atheists. The little seed of doubt which we had planted had blossomed into a mighty non-believing tree.

One Sunday we scandalized the campus. The Methodist church, located on a slight rise in the center of town, was covered with snow. So was the broad lawn in front of it. Charles and I could hear the boring choir repeating the eternally stupid song which emanated from that building on Sundays.

We quickly stamped out, in huge letters, THERE IS NO GOD, on the snow in front of the church...and then retired, unseen, to the coffee shop across the road. There was no proof that we had done it, but we were under suspicion for many months after.

Charles Fitzgerald, and other friends lived in a small dorm. Capacity: about 15 students. I lived right next door where I rented a room from Miss Zearing, 91 years old, who had been a founding member of the WCTU (Woman's Christian Temperance Union), she was probably still a virgin. This morally righteous and muscular group of "femmes" would, armed with axes and sledgehammers, crash into some unsuspecting bar or saloon and destroy the place with well-aimed blows: whiskey bottles, beer barrels...everything would perish under their moral indignation.

Anyway, Miss Zearing would discreetly leave little pamphlets on my pillow for my enlightenment: "The Demon Rum," "The Devil in the Bottle," etc. She was suspicious and thought that I partook of alcoholic beverages. She was right. But it was a silent hypocritical war. I, in turn, would leave pamphlets on atheism and well-known free thinkers in her parlor on Sundays when she was receiving some of her friends for the insipid tea she served. I also left a booklet: "How to Mix 500 Cocktails."

On the other hand, we had Christian Raiders from a girls' dorm that was situated a hundred yards away who, every Sunday morning, would stomp by in their high heels, yell at us and sing religious songs. They were trying to make us go to church. Sunday morning to us was sacred...but in another manner. The only day of the week when we could sleep late!

We were very correct. First we pleaded with the girls. To no avail. Then we threatened. They were ready to be martyrs. But they didn't know with whom they were dealing.

The next Sunday we put on a miracle play: The Crucifixion of Christ. We set up a large cross and crucified each other. Charles was the thin Christ and I was the Fat Christ. Gwen

114

Judd, a friend of ours (whose father was a minister), played both Mary Magdalen and the Virgin Mary. It was a success. We were even called into the Dean's office...to be chastised but we claimed religious freedom and our way to exhibit it...and the girls from the Christian Virgin Mary Dormitory never came back again.

> Editor's Note: Juan Luis pointed out that they always sought the advice of law students in advance of such events to be sure they knew their rights.

Mock crucifixion (Juan Luis on cross)

30 years later, Gwen Judd went to a party in New York City. She danced, talked with some friends, had a few drinks and went home at 2 a.m. She had a headache. She went into a coma and when she woke up, she was completely paralyzed. A virus. Poor Gwen. Her nickname was The Turtle.

Charles' nickname was The Octopus.

Mine was The Fox.

TRIP TO FLORIDA (1956)

On the East coast of the United States there is a tradition: during Spring vacation all college students go to a beach in Florida. It is called Fort Lauderdale.

Charles had an old 1947 Ford and we decided that we would join the thousands that gathered at that beach and in the famous Elbow Room, a beer bar, for the week-long party.

We left one early morning. Charles, my ex-roommate Ron Messner, Sharon Haight (Charles' girlfriend at that time) and Jan Falkenberg, a Swedish baron-to-be, who was a foreign student at Oberlin, and myself. We would drop Sharon at her home in Atlanta, Georgia and then continue the trip. Three days and two nights of steady driving. But, since there were five of us, we would switch around and in this manner, the trip would not be too tiring.

Then it happened. Three o'clock in the morning, in southern Tennessee, going through a winding road in the mountains somewhere near Fort Knox. Charles and Sharon asleep in the back seat. Falkenberg driving...Falkenberg who had never driven a large American car before. Ron sitting next to him. I was by the window. And suddenly, on a sharp curve, Falkenberg lost control of the car. It swung across the road. He jammed the wheel over to right us but it was too late. We shot out over the edge of the road and down a thirty-meter cliff. It seemed that the car would never stop. We did two end-over-end flips, and three normal rolls. The sound of steel ripping like paper is still in my ears.

One of the headlights burst immediately, but the other illuminated the whole fall. We just silently held on. No one screamed. We crashed through small trees (which broke our fall and finally saved us) and landed upside down, a few meters from a deep river. At first the silence was broken only by the sound of one of the wheels still spinning. My first reaction was to reach out and cut the car's ignition system. My side of the vehicle had been crushed. It was impossible to stick my hand out the window. Another few inches and my neck would have been broken. We were completely tangled in the cubicle: bodies, blankets, maps, suitcases, books (Oberlin students always take books with them). Still, no one said anything. Then we went around with names, "Sharon?" "O.K." "Ron?" "Yup." "Falkenberg?" "I'm all right!" "Charles?" He kicked me in the head. "Let's get the hell out of here!" There was the smell of gasoline everywhere.

But the problem was that we could not move. Most of the windows were so crushed that an exit was impossible. Charles said, "My window's intact, but I can't open it. But there's a foot against it. Whose is it?" He pinched it. It was mine. "Start kicking!" It took me ten minutes to get all the glass smashed out and another ten to untangle ourselves and get out of the car.

We clambered up the side of the mountain, and joining arms, laughing and joking, made our way up the road. A mile later we found a closed garage and gas station. We settled down under the porch until the attendant arrived that morning. As we waited, we were all suddenly struck by what had happened. I started to tremble. We were all in a state of shock. It took me a few years before I could be at ease in a car. I'm still not.

Finally, the attendant arrived. He got out his tow truck and we guided him to our precipice. "Jesus God," he whistled through his teeth. "How many were killed?" We all smiled up at him. During the fall, the trunk had broken open and all our baggage had been strewn about the forest. I found a shoe thirty meters from the car.

He gave Charles $25 dollars for the wreck and we hitchhiked to Atlanta, Georgia where Sharon's parents were kind enough to let us spend the night there...and to shower and get the broken glass out of our hair and skin. From there we broke up into two groups. Ron and Charles, Falkenberg and I...it was easier to hitchhike that way. We decided to meet at a friend's house, Ed Weldon, near Miami.

We had several more adventures: a drunk driver picked us up and drove incredibly fast, scaring the bejesus out of us. In another town we got picked up by the police. They didn't want any hobos in town. But the captain was of Swedish origin and Falkenberg immediately started yakking with him in their native language. They bought us coffee and doughnuts. Over the radio we heard a police report saying they had picked up two bums, one of them was big and tough and roared a lot. "That's Charles!" we insisted and they were brought in by a police car and we were all given more coffee.

Finally we made it to our friend's house near Miami. He drove us down to Fort Lauderdale. Of course, we were completely broke and could not, even if we had found one, afforded a motel. And then we were shocked by the mass of drunken stupid students that were gathered on the beach. Thousands...tens of thousands. We had a quick beer at the Elbow Room and hitchhiked out of town to a deserted beach called Boca Raton...which is now the site of a very luxurious hotel. There we set out our sleeping bags and skin-diving equipment. The beach was long and silent and empty.

It was lined with coconut trees. The problem of eating became an important factor. We had very little money. In a nearby town we found the "grand opening" of a supermarket...a free loaf of bread was given for every purchase. We went in and bought salt (one loaf of bread), ketchup (another loaf of bread), oil etc. etc. So now we had enough bread for a few days. Charles went spear fishing and we picked coconuts which lay strewn about the beach. For the next few days we had tomato soup (ketchup in hot water), fish (fried or steamed in seaweed) and all possible manner of coconut meat...raw, fried, boiled etc.

One night, we were sleeping quietly when a car drove up and parked just a few feet from our camp. The driver had not seen us. We probably looked like a bunch of logs surrounded by garbage (our equipment). I woke up and looked at Charles. He also had been awakened. In the car a man started to make out with his girlfriend. Then they started arguing. Finally the girl jumped out of the car. She did not have a lot of clothes on and was furious. He had probably made an indecent proposal to her. She refused to get back in the car. But it was cold outside. He just sat in the car and smoked cigarette after cigarette. The girl started to shiver. Charles and I did not move. Finally she got back in the car and the windows quickly steamed up.

The next morning we awoke before they did and started to build our breakfast campfire...about 20 centimeters from their car. When they awoke, we greeted them with a big smile and offered them coffee. After all, we were family, we had shared their night. They were embarrassed and left quickly.

∞ ∞ ∞

To get back to Ohio, we looked in the ads of the local newspaper for Drive-Back Services. We found one fellow who wanted his car driven to Chicago. We would get the car, stop by Oberlin and, since it had been Falkenberg who had driven us off the cliff, he would drive the car to Chicago and then hitchhike back to school. We went to an address in Fort Lauderdale and picked up a large white...Cadillac. We drove back to Ohio slowly and safely...but at times allowing ourselves a drag race in the night with small-town hoods whom we would encounter in the many villages we passed through.

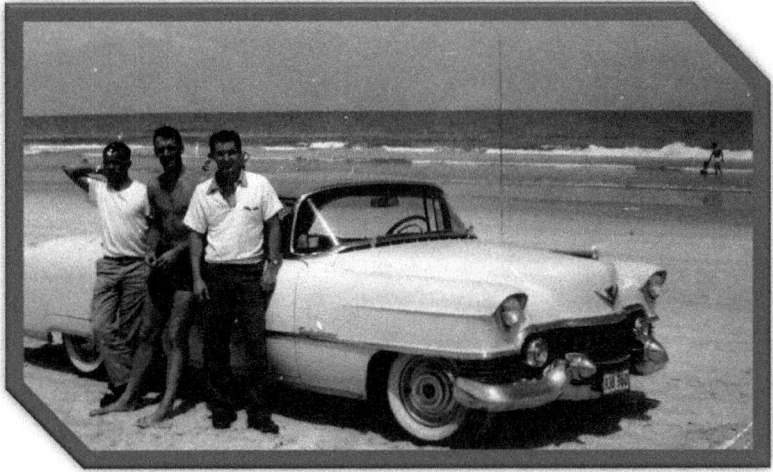

The drive-back Cadillac (Swedish friend, Charles, Ron Messner. Photo by Juan Luis)

TRIP TO TEXAS

That summer I returned to Mexico with Charles Fitzgerald and accompanying us, Ernie Atwell, a black philosophy student from Texas who had red hair and orange skin. We took the Greyhound bus from Ohio and we would go all the way to Mexico City with a two-day stop in Dallas at Ernie's house. While waiting for our bus in the Cleveland depot we met an old cowboy who was just loafing around. We struck up a conversation with him. "You know, boys," he informed us, his Texas twang ringing through the bus garage, "Cleveland's a big town. There's a lot of whars around!" For him, a town was considered big if it had a large prostitute population.

It was a two day and two night trip to Texas. We sat together in front of the bus, discussing final exams, history and philosophy courses and general gossip of the college. When the bus finally arrived at the Mason-Dixon line, the bus driver asked all 'colored folks' to move to the back of the bus. This was the law. Ernie obeyed and we meekly followed him to the back. How politically ignorant and unconscious we were. But we had been in the middle of a long drawn-out conversation on Kant and it did not bother us too much. Soon some rednecks got on and started to heckle us when they saw two white boys sitting in the back with a black guy. "Nigger lover...etc. etc." So Charles stood up, stretched his one meter 96 centimeter frame out all over the narrow aisle of the bus and walked forward. Since they were sitting, he towered over them. He bared his teeth and growled. That quieted them down for the next hundred miles. There they got off.

We did not have any more trouble until we got to a small Texas town where we had a half-hour rest stop. It was very hot and we longed for an ice cold soda. There was one drugstore by the bus station so we headed for it. But suddenly Ernie pulled back. A sign said "No Colored People Allowed!" Charles and I didn't understand this. It was ridiculous. Ernie understood and tried to pull back but, since he was smaller than both of us, we picked him up and walked into the drugstore. We got served, much to our friend's terror. Suddenly the police appeared. A big fat Stetson-wearing sheriff wanted to know what was going on. He wore large mirrored sunglasses and a .45 caliber automatic hanging from his belt. He could look out at us but we couldn't see his eyes. Well, we explained to him that we found the sign on the drugstore window foolish and we wanted to know why Ernie couldn't have a coke. The sheriff looked dumbfounded. He had never faced two white guys with a "colored folk."He didn't seem to know what to say. During this conversation Charles kept looking into his mirrored glasses and making horrible faces. Finally our bus announced its departure. We said good-bye to the small crowd that had gathered and jumped on the bus. I asked Charles what he had thought to accomplish by making faces at the sheriff. Well, he answered, since he couldn't see the policeman's eyes, he figured the policeman couldn't see him. I shudder to think what would have happened just a few years later when the Civil Rights movement started in the U.S.

In Dallas we lived in the black neighborhood a couple of days, had a great time and reached Mexico City without any further incidents.

∞ ∞ ∞

Talking about crossing the border, once in Nuevo Laredo, Mexico, an immigration official said that I couldn't go back into

Mexico unless I had a medical certificate and that this certificate could only be obtained in San Antonio, Texas, 800 kilometers to the north. I knew what he wanted and he knew that I knew so I played the game. "I must get to Mexico City immediately because my mother is dying." "Right at this moment she is dying?" he asked. "Yes!" "What a tragedy, please follow me," he replied and led me to his private office. He respectfully begged me to sit down and stamped my passport. I thanked him. Then he opened a drawer of his desk and pulled out a small cheese, placing it in front of himself. He looked at me wistfully. "A beer would go very well with this 'botana' (appetizer)." So I gave him the price of one beer...I bribed him with five centavos! We left the best of friends and he called me "Jefe!" (Boss).

Brian Nissen had a similar experience with most probably the same man. He had gone to San Antonio to renew his visa at the Mexican Consulate and was taking the bus back to the D.F. In Nuevo Laredo the immigration official said, "There's one problem. Where is your permission from the United Kingdom to come into Mexico?" Brian was astonished, "Since when does England give permission to go into Mexico?" The official smiled, "It's a new law." Then he stood up. "Just one moment." He left the room. A few minutes later he came back with a broad smile, "Everything is all right! I called London and they have given you permission to enter Mexico!" Brian jumped up, "What? Who gave permission? The Prime Minister? The Queen?" The Official stamped the passport, "No problem, everything is in order." He handed Brian his papers. Brian thanked him and was about to leave when the official held up his hand, "One moment...there is a small charge." "What?" The man smiled, "Yes, you must pay for the phone call to London!" Brian burst out laughing and handed him a few pesos. They both shook hands.

Then it was Brian's turn. Down the road was another immigration checkpoint where another official usually ripped you off for a few more pesos. Brian told the man, "Do me a favor, I've no money left. Please call your *compadre* down the road and tell him I'm broke." "*Como no* (no problem)," answered the man, reaching for the phone. He dialed. "José, there's an Englishman coming on the bus. Let him go by...*ya le pelé!* (I've already skinned him!)"

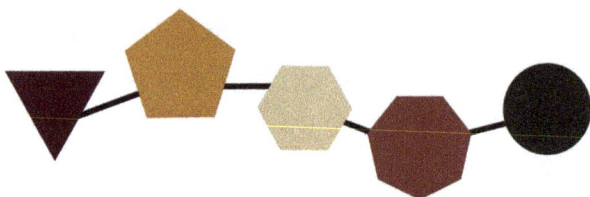

ACCIDENTS

1) 15 years old and riding up Reforma in Mexico City. There were about seven of us on horseback. There was a *pirule* tree with low-hanging branches, and we went under it. A branch stuck on my shoulder and then snapped back, whacking the horse on the rump. He jumped to the right, catching me off balance. I fell to the ground, hitting my left hip on a rock. That has always hurt. (Years later, because of this fall, my hip is in bad shape.)

2) In a football game against Colegio Militar (military high school), I was clipped (hit from the rear) by a big tackle. It hurt my back ...and it still does many years later.

3) Ohio. With the wrestling team. We were going to a meet at another Ohio college. It was the middle of winter and the turnpike was frozen. Suddenly we hit a part of the road which was sheet ice. Our minibus went out of control, spinning...but we were going so slow that there seemed to be no danger. And then I looked up. A huge trailer truck was bearing down on me. It was out of control. I could see the driver looking straight into my eyes, almost excusing himself. He could do nothing. Luckily for us there was another huge truck parked on the side of the road. We were crushed, but very gently, by the two behemoths. But it was my left hip again that received the impact. I limped for about two months and the insurance company gave me $100 so as not to claim more in the future. I was thankful for that sum of money. At that time my father did not work very much. I used some of that dough to have my laundry done at the automat...usually I did all my laundry by hand. It was the same hip as the one I hit from the horse fall and it still hurts.

4) The famous over-the-cliff-in-Fitzgerald's '46 Ford while on a trip to Florida.

FILMING

DON QUIXOTE + ORSON WELLES

1957

June: Graduated from Oberlin College.

July: Short documentary films with Barbachano Ponce.[22] Re-edit one-hour Russian science films into three-minute spots for editing practice.

July: Oscar Dansigers,[23] a producer, offers me a job as assistant director with an American director. At first I refuse. I know nothing about cinema. And I would probably return to college to get a Masters in English Literature. He insists, I speak Spanish and English. Just stay close to the director and translate whatever he orders. Finally I agree. Some spare cash is always welcome. Dansigers tells me to be at the Hotel Prado the next morning at 7 a.m. and ask for Orson

Welles.

August: DON QUIXOTE with Orson Welles. Mexico City, Cuatla, Cuernavaca.

---

[22] Barbachano Ponce (1925-1994) was a Mexican film producer, director, screenwriter and novelist.

[23] Oscar Dansigers was a Russian émigré producer who worked in Mexico on such films as Luis Buñuel's *El gran calavera* (1949) and *Los Olvidados* (*The Young and the Damned*, 1950).

The film starts in the patio of a colonial palace which has been turned into the Hotel Cortéz in downtown Mexico City.

Orson is having breakfast and reading a large copy of *Don Quixote*. A little blonde girl runs up, Patty McCormack,[24] and says, "Oh, are you Orson Welles, the famous film director?"

Patty McCormack and Orson Welles

He admits that he is. Then the little girl sees Cervantes' book and says, "I saw this man the other day." It turns out that this girl's name is Dulcie (Dulcinea) and that she has seen Don Quixote, and has followed him on some of his adventures.

------

[24] Patty McCormack (b. 1945 in Brooklyn) is known for her sinister role in *The Bad Seed* (1956), and later played the role of Pat Nixon in *Frost/Nixon* (2008).

Patty McCormack

One afternoon, we were shooting on the roof of the hotel Cortéz. Charles Fitzgerald came for a visit. He had just bought a set of bongo drums. When Orson saw Charles with the drums, he called him over and gave us a magnificent performance of a Latin-American beat.

Every morning, we would gather our small crew and head out, with Orson's car in the lead, to see what he would find, what he could improvise. He rode up front, I would sit in the back. We'd talk...or rather, he talked, because I did not have much to say, until suddenly, he would point his cigar at a field, a copse of trees, a series of broken-down adobe huts or a mass of wrecked cars and we would unload the camera, the dolly, the reflectors, and the day's shoot would begin.

One day on location near Cuatla, I spotted a hole in the ground near the camera. Someone might step into it, twisting his leg or her leg. Then I promptly forgot to give orders to have it covered up. Welles stepped into it and sprained his ankle quite badly. This was my contribution to TOUCH OF EVIL which he shot right after QUIXOTE. His evil character is enhanced throughout the film by a well-defined limp.

After shooting, we would go drinking at a bar on the square in Cuernavaca. A Cuba Libre for me, a bottle of vodka for Orson. He would ramble on. Having no knowledge, or interest in cinema, most of his conversation was lost on me. I felt like a fool. His voice was so powerful that, even when whispering, people at the other side of the room turned around.

Shooting outside of Cuernavaca, Welles finds an abandoned junk yard full of old cars. There he has Don Quixote (Francisco Reiguera,[25] a Spanish Republican refugee), dressed in battered armor, sit and strut among the rusting cars.

---

[25] Spanish actor Francisco Reiguera (1899-1969), a refugee from the Spanish Civil War living in Mexico, also performed in Luis Buñuel's *Abismos de Pasión* (*Wuthering Heights*, 1954) and *Simon of the Desert* (1965), as well as films in which Juan Luis participated: *Viva María* (1965) and *Guns for San Sebastian* (1968). Juan Luis wrote that Reiguera "really thought he was Don Quixote."

Francisco (Paco) Reiguera as Don Quixote

Jack Drapper, an American cameraman (who lived in Mexico and who was not too fast in lighting the scenes — Welles called him Flash Drapper) sets up his lights. Welles wants the scene to be dramatic but doesn't know exactly how to do it. In the meantime, I put a heavy red filter on my black & white still camera and snap away at Don Quixote. Several days later, I show the pictures to Orson. With a curse he looks at the bright white clouds and very dark sky the red filter has created. He calls Drapper, asks him why didn't he suggest those filters. They get into a fight. I moved away discreetly. Later Drapper looks at me in an unfriendly manner.

∞ ∞ ∞

Welles hated his nose. His body was large and imposing. His proboscis was small and pugged. Every day before shooting, he

135

would sit in front of a mirror and build himself a wax beak. Some days it would lean to the right, on other occasions it would droop forward. Never the same. The scriptgirl would come up to me: "It's leaning too much to the left. It's green. It'll never match yesterday's scene." She was scared to go up to him, so it was my job to convince Orson to let the make-up lady straighten up the monument.

∞ ∞ ∞

September came along. Welles stopped the filming for five weeks. He had to go back to Hollywood for new financing. So, having nothing better to do, and two friends (Ron Messner and Charles Fitzgerald) from Oberlin visiting in Mexico, we decided to head for Acapulco.

> Editor's Note: In a 2005 phone interview by Peter Tonguette, published in the online *Bright Light Film Journal*, Juan Luis reported that Orson Welles "sort of improvised a lot. He'd see something he was interested in, a Mexican hut or a town or a field. He'd stop and then we'd shoot. Get the horse down from the truck and have Don Quixote ride by...To my knowledge there was no script. In the evenings, Welles would edit the film and do the dubbing. He dubbed both Sancho Panza and Don Quixote, giving Don Quixote an Oxford accent and Sancho Panza a Cockney accent."[26]

---

[26] Also in that interview, Juan Luis reported: "I saw Orson Welles many years later in Paris at the studios. I said `Hi, Orson! What...' And he stopped me. He said `Yeah. What ever happened to *Don Quixote?* Well, Francisco Reiguera...died, the horse died. Akim Tamiroff [Sancho Panza] died...'"

ACAPULCO AND END OF *QUIXOTE*

September: Acapulco. We rented a house with a swimming pool and paid for it by inviting international students picked up on the beach for a party. We advertised, "For one dollar, all you could eat and drink. Plus a party." 30 or 40 students would fork over their dollar. We'd pay our five-dollar rent. With the rest of the money we'd buy five gallons of rum, icecubes, potatoes, mayonnaise, sliced ham and bread. A perfect supper for hungry college students. Potato salad, ham sandwiches, cokes. The avocados we'd pick from the trees, along with limes for the Cuba Libres.

Acapulco with friends

Note: If a bee or wasp gets you, pull out the barbed stinger and quickly rub the swollen area with lemon juice while beating, either with two fingers or two sticks, around the injection point. This is a cure given by a Tahitian friend when we lived in Los Angeles during the forties.

Among the group formed by our nightly "fêtes" were two sisters from Arizona. At night, the rum substituted for breathing. Since we had to give a party every night to pay the rent, it was not to our interest to drink too much. We'd water our drinks down with lime juice and...water. But the other guests would drink as much as they could. So did one of the Arizona sisters who, by the fourth night, had become infatuated by us. One night, we were all in the pool. It must have been 4 a.m. She kept swimming towards us, trying to grab what she could. Since she looked like trouble, we avoided her as best we could. Finally, she jumped out of the water trying to head us off before we got into the deeper end of the pool. The tile was slippery. What happened had to happen. She slipped and smashed her head on the tile. A great gash now decorated her forehead. Blood flowed into the pool. It looked like we'd had a shark attack. She started to scream hysterically: "Charles and I were Greek gods!" she stated. Greek gods? Then she began to rip at her wound with her fingernails. Mexican rum does strange things to Protestant *gringas*. We held her down, patched her up with surgical tape (I always carried a small first-aid kit for such occasions). Finally she passed out. The next day we put her on a plane back to Arizona.

"Greek gods?"...or maybe, as Charles said, "God-damn Greeks." We weren't too sure what we were. There was Ron (my ex-roommate from Oberlin, from Chicago), Charles (my friend from Boston), and our *lancheros* from Caleta beach (they ran the *lanchas* [barges] for the tourists): Balín (always running around like a lost bullet), El Muerto (his nickname originated when someone stabbed him in the stomach and left him for dead), El Alacrán (his mustache curled up like a scorpion's tail), Señorita Papaya and Señorita Tortilla (this described their mammary glands quite efficiently)...anyway, we were all having fun. Usually around four a.m., as the party was dying out, we'd start getting hungry. Near us was the Hotel Caleta. First we'd invade the swimming pool, diving right in as if we were guests. Then, we'd nosily head for the kitchen where the morning breakfast's *pan dulces* (pastries) were stacked up on large trays. If anyone asked questions, we'd give a room number (305) and tell them to bill us. Then we'd disappear in a cloud of crumbs and alcoholic fumes.

Our world was not yet invaded by drugs. One night during our get-together, someone walked in with a shopping bag full of Acapulco Gold Marijuana. Supposedly the best in the world. Nobody even batted an eye. I think the bag was throw out with the morning's garbage.

Then one of the parties got out of hand. Not in an evil manner. But we all had bongo and conga drums and maracas and guitars. We were pretty loud...loud enough to merit a visit from the army. Three soldiers walked in and told us to calm down. The neighbors were complaining. They pointed their rifles at us. But we were in such a good mood that we took the rifles away from the military invaders and started strumming them like guitars. They looked frightened but we quickly convinced them that we meant no harm. They each had a couple of Cuba Libres and then we quieted down the "*fête*." We didn't want them to look bad in front of their officers.

Since we had just graduated from college, all our courses were still fresh in our minds. We had developed during the past four years, a way of argumentation which was not classical, to say the least. We called it Cudgel Logic. It consisted of using logic and good sense in an argument, but presenting it by yelling and roaring, and eventually laughing. He who yelled and stomped the hardest would usually win. Joining our group, and also becoming a strong habituée of the Demon Rum, was a young philosophy professor from Harvard, several years our senior, whom we had picked up at Hornos Beach. At first he tried to introduce cold reasoning into our discussions. Poor thing. Eventually we got him to admit that *Oedipus Rex* was a comedy. "When you see someone slip on a banana peel in the street, you laugh, his fall is funny! But to the chap who breaks his backbone on the hard cement, it isn't humorous at all!" He would sip his rum, "Yes, well..." So we would roar, "Then Oedipus murders his father and marries his mother. To him, Tragedy. To us, high Comedy!" Finally, after several liters of rum and being pounded from three sides by masters of Cudgel Logic, he would admit that it was a comedy. Eventually he broke down, and one day, in a drunken stupor, asked if he could join our gang. We were shocked that a Harvard professor would act in this manner. We cruelly banished him to another beach.

∞ ∞ ∞

During the day we would go to Pie de la Cuesta. This beach was famous for its huge waves. As these monstrous hills of water would raise high above the ocean's surface, we could see sharks swimming through them. The effect was that of watching fish in a bowl...a very large bowl. These waves were created because the ocean bottom, at that point, was very deep, and then suddenly rose up to the beach.

Our idea was to catch sharks and sell the meat to the fishermen as bait. Early in the morning, we would go to the public docks to buy buckets of turtle blood (they slaughtered those poor reptiles every morning at the docks), and great chunks of sailfish meat. We had large shark hooks which were attached by chains (the shark could not bite through the chains) to heavy fishing line.

The turtle blood was thrown into the waves to attract the monsters, then one of us would wade into the water as far as possible, spin the meat-laden hook over our head and throw it into, or over, the wave. Getting out before the tons of water crashed down was always a gut-wrenching process. Then, on the beach, the rest of the gang, between five and ten friends, all holding tightly to the line, would be ready to haul the thrashing monster up onto the beach. We never caught any sharks. Filthy creatures. Didn't trust us.

Why Mermaids Never Grow Old (Juan Luis Buñuel)

A month later back in Mexico City: Welles can't finish his film, has run out of money and time. Also he has a starting date for the of filming of TOUCH OF EVIL. Last day of shooting. Orson is very sad. He leaves the set (Hotel Cortéz patio) and goes across the street to the Alameda Park. He sits on a bench and cries. I put my arm around his shoulders and try to confort him. Finally he thanks me, shakes his head and we go back to the Hotel Cortéz to wrap up the film.

December: Go up to Oberlin to see Lee Childs (her parents were missionaries in Angola but she wasn't at all religious). Then we drive down to Florida for New Years.

1958

Trip to New Orleans on way back to Mexico City. Jerry Lindner had shown me how to keep the rhythm with a pair of spoons, so I played the spoons with some of the bands on Bourbon Street.

LITTLE GIANTS

February to May: LITTLE GIANTS: Film with Hugo Butler and George Pepper (both were refugees in Mexico from the McCarthy witch hunts)[27] We spent about two months in Monterrey, Mexico. It was a documentary-feature about a group of small Mexican Little League baseball players who had won the World Series in the United States. Very small Mexican kids, coming from poor families, they had beaten the well-fed American kids. The U.S. players, between 9 and 11 years old, were easily twice the size of their South-of-the-border counterparts. At first, the Mexican kids were scared of their size, but Zurdo, the tiny, but tough, left-handed first baseman, turned to face his team and yelled at them, "We don't have to carry them, we just have to play against them!" The Mexican boys just happened to be superior ball players. They were excellent. These kids came from the poorer neighborhoods of Monterrey. Some had worked in "*casas de puta*" (whore houses), fetching water, beers and clean towels. They were tough. During the filming, many times I had to take knives away from them.

Since they had won the Little League World Series, the presidents of both countries, Mexico and the United States, had received them. They were cheered and honored, parades were given in their honor. And suddenly they were sent back to their

---

[27] This *Little Giants* film (*Los pequeño gigantes*), starring Ángel Macías, Francisco Aguilar, and Claudio Brook, is not to be confused with the 1994 film directed by Wayne Dunham, starring Rick Moranis and Ed O'Neill. Hugo Butler (b. 1914 in Calgary, Alberta, d. 1968 in Hollywood), also wrote *Lassie Come Home* (1943), *The Southerner* (1945), and Luis Buñuel's *Robinson Crusoe* (1954) and *The Young One* (1960).

slums and forgotten. They found themselves without decent schools and later on, without jobs and went the way of most slum kids: rackets, drugs, gangs.

∞ ∞ ∞

We went to Texas to reconstruct their first games and spent several weeks in McAllen. One Sunday afternoon, we left McAllen and went out to a hamburger joint (McDonalds didn't exist then) on the highway just outside of town. There we met a man, a tall handsome Texan with his daughter. They were eating burgers because his wife was playing poker, couldn't cook for them that day. He invited us to his ranch. His vehicle was a brand new 1958 Cadillac, but completely beat up. He would buy a new one every year and use it as a jeep. His ranch was a fruit and vegetable spread. He had water on his property...in that region, water was as valuable as petroleum.

He showed us a large heart-shaped lake which he had created in the middle of the desert. In the middle of this body of water was a small island upon which stood a small neo-classical Greek temple. He had built this pond for his card-playing wife so that she could water-ski. His best water-well was called the Jax Well. One night, he and several friends, had been driving around and getting drunk on Jax beer. At one moment, he had to urinate. It was at that spot that he decided to drill for water...and was rewarded by the greatest flow of H_2O on his property.

The heat in Monterrey was terrific. My room did not have air conditioning. The bed sheets were so hot that I had to take a warm shower (there was no cold water) and lower myself slowly, soaking wet, onto the sheets so as not to burn myself.

One day the director, Hugo Butler, awakened me at midnight. He needed the costume of a Mexican general for the next day's shooting at 8 a.m. I was stumped. Where to find a Mexican general at that time and then convince him to lend me his uniform? There was only one answer. I went to all the whorehouses in Monterrey, found my drunken general, had a couple of drinks with him and finally he lent me his uniform. I was to go by his residence at 7:30 a.m. and get it from his ordinance.

July: Filming of NAZARÍN. Went as observer. Also studying the filming was a Cuban student, Alfredo Guevara,[28] later to become head of the Cuban film industry.

Nazarín (Paco Rabal in center)

---

[28] Alfredo Guevara Valdés (1925-2013) created the Cuban Institute of Cinematographic Art and Industy (ICAIC) and helped found the International Festival of New Latin American Cinema in Havana.

VOYAGE TO EUROPE

New York: At that time it was cheaper to go to Europe by boat than by plane. A one-way ticket from New York to Le Havre cost $100. So I took the French liner S.S. Flandre that September for Le Havre.

There was something magical about feeling the boat pull away from the New York dock. Suddenly you were in a little world that had not existed a few minutes before and that you would have to endure...or enjoy for the next five or six days.

Wonderful breakfasts, playing ping pong or shooting skeet off the bow of the boat. Then the apperitif hour at the bar, lunch where you had a huge menu and could ask for any extras...wine was free.

The afternoons were spent working out in the gym, or reading in the library. Then tea time on deck, wrapped in a blanket, a trio playing Vivaldi...and again before dinner apperitif, dinner, then movies, or theatre, or gambling. The night ended up with long walks on deck or dancing to live orchestras.

Of course there were the storms. At that time I did not get seasick so I would stay on the top deck, in the bow of the ship and watch the huge waves crash over the boat.

The last evening was always Gala Night. If there were any famous singers or actors or dancers on board, and if they were willing, they would put on a show for the passengers in the ship's theatre.

On one such trip, an old Buster Keaton was making the crossing in First Class. I saw him sadly looking out to sea from my perch on the second-class deck.

On board, on this my first trip, was a group of British airmen going back home after training in the U.S. Much drinking and laughing...and singing the popular Italian song "*Volare*." Also there were about 18 Basque shepherds returning to Spain, with their nest-egg, after working 15 years in the United States. They were always dancing. Since we were continuously laughing and spawning trouble and fun, a very rich man invited us all to the First Class cabaret to liven up the atmosphere. Champagne for everyone. A storm was brewing and the ship began to sway. This made us laugh, and we would time our dancing with the rocking of the boat.

The Basques were all dancing, the English pilots were quite drunk as they charmed all the snobish long-gowned women (who after several drinks, weren't all that snobish). We were a success and our host was happy. First Class very quickly lost its dignity. A very quiet girl, who had been a silent member of our gang for the past few days, suddenly started drinking all the glasses at our table. Then, with a scream, she jumped up, pulled her dress over her head and started doing a rumba on the dance floor. Some people were shocked. I was elected to take her out on the open deck for a breath of fresh air. She was so drunk that her legs could hardly support the weight of her body. The storm was now blasting the ship from the starboard side. Even I had difficulty keeping my balance. She insisted that she was pure and good. Then her face contorted. She raged and cried. She hated her mother. Then she passionately wanted to make love. Suddenly she would break away and try to jump overboard. She wanted to commit suicide because she was bad. As I struggled with her, the boat was lurching about.

150

The storm was taking on serious proportions. I looked for help. A French sailor walked by, saw me with this writhing woman in my arms, smiled, gave me the O.K. sign, then disappeared. I tried to call out to him but the wind drowned my shouts. Finally she passed out. I had to carry her down three decks. Because of the storm, we bumped from side to side as we made our way down the narrow corridors. I kept slamming her head against doorknobs. She was very heavy. Some people should learn how to drink. Finally I found her cabin and knocked. The door opened and she promptly vomited all over her cabin and her roommates. I admitted to cowardice and disappeared rapidly.

The next morning we sailed into Plymouth Harbour. I joined a small group of people on deck huddled together against the cold. We were all smoking cigarettes. In this group were two girls, history graduates, from a U.S. university (I will not reveal the name of this hallowed center of learning). I decided to test their knowledge. "Look, girls," I pointed to a large rock or island in the middle of the bay. "Plymouth Rock! That's where the Pilgrims landed in 1492!" "Oh," they exclaimed, and started to take pictures of the infamous rock. I left and made my way to the bar which had just opened. One of the British pilots was there and I told him of my latest adventure. "That's nothing," he said. "Some American chap, this morning, asked me if Australia was next to England." We both toasted U.S. Higher Education.

Got to Paris on the 20th September, Le Havre, exactly 20 years to the day (20 September 1938) of our departure. Tante Georgette and the Moscos come to greet me at Gare St. Lazare.

The Moscos were the neighbors of my mother's family when they lived in Paris after World War I. Dr. Moscos was of Greek origin. One of the Moscos sisters had been my mother's best friend. Another sister had been Sylvia Beach's assistant in her famous Shakespeare and Company Book Store in Saint-Germain-des-Prés during the 1930's She helped James Joyce in the publishing and binding of his POEMS PENNYEACH. She gave me a copy of the book.

Juan Luis at Notre Dame Cathedral, ca. 1958

(photo by Juan Luis)

48 RUE MAZARINE

My Tante Georgette lived at 48 Rue Mazarine, corner of Rue Guéneguad. She lived alone. She had had a serious beau (a Spanish painter, Vicens) during the 1930's but he disappeared during the Spanish Civil War. He ended up in China and by that time Tante Georgette had become an old maid and had dedicated her life to her mother...my grandmother...who died several years later. Georgette, an "expert *comptable*" (accountant) and fine secretary, was left alone. She became a wine alcoholic. At first I thought that if I drank all her wine every day, she would slowly snap out of her alcoholic life. Even Charles Fitzgerald, when he came to visit, in 1958, helped me drink her "*gros rouge*" (cheap table wine). We drank everything in sight. She was delighted and would bring out her hidden bottles. Charles and I were becoming alcoholic. Finally I gave up and she continued in her liquid ways, living in her dark first floor apartment in an interior courtyard, in Saint-Germain-des-Prés. The sun never reached this apartment.

My first night in Paris, I went for a midnight drink at a corner bar where a big burly fellow was throwing empty beer bottles at two scared-looking, young, and burly women. He claimed they were lesbians. I did not know if I should react. He would throw a bottle and a couple of insults at the girls, then they would discuss the situation. The bottles were not hurled with anger. He was almost indifferent. Finally nothing happened.

I met again Lucia and Elena Delgado Chalbaud. Had not seen them since 1945 in New York. Lucia gave me an old Volkswagen Beetle. I also went to see Ionesco plays on Rue de la Huchette with her. What impressed me most about Paris was not the buildings or the general atmosphere, but the reaction of the public that night of the Ionesco play. ***They understood !!***

I met mother's brother, Oncle Gaston. He was a barber in Ménilmontant, Rue Pixérécourt. He had fought in World War I. He liked, as Georgette did, a nice bottle of red wine...well, more than one. He also liked to tell stories that never ended. Most of his stories were adventures where he was the hero. They were all lies. Finally it all went very bad for him. Before, the average working man (Ménilmontant was a working-class neighborhood) went to the barber once every two weeks, just to keep his hair trim. But with the mode of long hair brought on by the Beatles and others, they ceased to be regular visitors.

Gaston had married Berthe, a much older woman. Georgette whispered to me that Berthe had claimed to be pregnant and he, being a good man, had married her. It turned out that she wasn't. Later they had a son, Georges, and a daughter, Denise.

Berthe did the clients' fingernails in the barbershop.

MONACO BAR AND TRIP WITH CHARLES

There were two places where I hung out for several years: The Monaco Bar, near the Metro Odéon, and the Louvre. A small, unassuming "café" where travelers, musicians, bums, writers and painters from different countries would gather at all times of day or night for a "demi" of beer or a coffee. Not having much money those first few years, I became friends with Alex, "the only Scottish cowboy in Paris." I knew Alex for many years and never saw him eat anything. He drank beer. He was extremely thin and had a deep Scottish accent, except for when he sang...then his voice would acquire a Texas twang. He sported a goatee and wore a beat-up Levi jacket and pants. A large tattered cowboy hat neatly fit the back of his head. He would sing in the streets, along the banks of the Seine or to the people standing in line waiting to get into the cinema. I was his look-out. At that time the police did not allow "panhandling." As they came up the street, I would call out to Alex, "The Fuzz!" and we'd hightail it around the corner.

Alex would slam away at his guitar and sing. I would pass the hat around...and then we would retire to the Monaco. Alex would keep just enough for that night's cheap hotel room...and we would drink the rest.

∞ ∞ ∞

I was also friendly with a street-chalk painter (I don't remember his name). He would draw huge religious paintings on the sidewalks, usually near a popular cinema. People would drop coins in a cup if they liked his rendition of the Pietà or Christ on the Cross (the agony he would put on J.C.'s face was magnificent). When I needed money, I would drop by around eleven in the morning. I knew that by this time he would want a coffee. He would indicate a region of the painting, Christ's thigh or the Virgin Mary's left breast. "Fill it in, slowly, with this color." Then he'd empty the money cup and head for the nearest café. Very diligently I would work away at the holy anatomy. With a bit of luck, people would drop coins into the mystical artist's cup. Thirty minutes later, my friend would come back. He'd take half the money (for the chalk used) and I got the rest. This was called "painting-sitting." Some days were good, some days were bad.

∞ ∞ ∞

I was the only one at the Monaco who had a car. Lucia Delgado's old VW Beetle. One day, a couple of black guys asked me if I would drive Richard Wright, the American writer, to the American Hospital in Neuilly. He had to go for some blood tests. Richard lived up the street. We went to his book-filled apartment. He had a small suitcase ready, he would only be spending the night, just a few tests. But he looked worried.

A few days later I learned of his death. Sad. He was one of the first writers to depict and analyse the life of the blacks in the U.S.

∞ ∞ ∞

On rainy days, the best place to visit was the Louvre. As the rain rattled against the window I would spend hours just walking around the dusty *empty* halls. There were very few visitors present. Maybe a lonely painter making a clumsy copy of a David, a forlorn American tourist who couldn't wait to get out...and me. The incredible luxury of silence. On your right, the Mona Lisa. Quiet, beautiful and delicate. On your left the Winged Victory of

Samothrace of which an American had made, after staring at it for several minutes, a historical comment, "It'll never fly!"

But above all, you were alone with all these paintings.

The Egyptian and Greek rooms, the plundered treasures of past civilizations. One day a group of 14-year-old French students were being lectured on Greek classical statuary. Two girls seemed fascinated by the well-proportioned buttocks of an Olympic discus thrower. One girl turned to her friend and said with a smile, "Is this what they call a Greek profile?"

∞ ∞ ∞

Simone Signoret introduced me to (screenwriter/poet) Jacques Prévert. Some mornings I would go up for coffee and cigarettes at his house above the Moulin Rouge. Then we would walk around the streets of Montmartre and he would ramble on, stories, jokes, and all the inhabitants would wave to him or greet him in a very friendly and simple manner. We would stop for lunch in the little bistros of his "*quartier.*"

He would get angry when his daughter would go off to school. She was getting, he complained, a bourgeois education. She later turned to drugs.

Charles Fitzgerald was to be Yves Montand's English teacher but he had to go back to Boston and it didn't work out. Yves wanted to learn English for his singing debut and film career in the U.S.

Charles and I took a trip to Hamburg. There was a gambling casino there and Charles knew a foolproof manner to win at roulette.

Before we left Paris it was important to get new license plates for the old VW Lucia had given me. We wanted to leave that evening but there were no stores open that late to get license plates. The police officer told me that it was legal to make your own plates. So I found a piece of wood of the right size and shape...and my oil paints. It was a beautiful and artistic license plate...with its red flowers and yellow butterflies.

When we got to the Belgium border, the French customs official stopped us and, pointing at my plates, asked "What is that?" I answered that they were my license plates. He touched them. The oil paints, freshly applied, got all over his hands, and then onto his uniform. He was furious. He told us to go on, refused to be bothered. "Let the Belgians take care of you!"

The Belgian border guards didn't even notice and waved us on. That night in Brussels we tried to steal several plates from French cars to create our own new set...but we were too scared. The next day we went to a specialized store and had a set made.

We went up through Holland and stopped in Edam to buy cheese and wooden shoes...*des sabots* (clogs). We wore our "*sabots*" in the tiny Dutch towns and crowds of children followed us. Charles' shoes looked like huge wooden barges and we both rattled around the cobblestone streets.

We found a huge hoop on a Dutch dike and Charles lashed it to the back of the VW. It stuck up about a meter above the car.

We finally arrived in Hamburg. Crowds would gather around our hoop-decorated VW. They had never seen such a badly treated car, with its license plates smeared with paint. All the German cars were impeccably clean. We had our oil changed in one garage and noticed that people would tip the mechanics with cigarettes. Germany was still getting over World War II.

We finally made it to the Hamburg Speil Casino. Charles had a sure-win plan at the roulette wheel. We would be millionaires. Charles lost all our money in seven minutes. We had just enough money for the gas back to Paris.

ZARAGOZA AND FAMILY, CALANDA

SPAIN (for the first time):

That Christmas I went to Zaragoza to meet my father's family. The last time I had been with them was in 1937. I did not know what an aunt or uncle or cousin was...

Editor's Note: This picture was taken after the family crossed the border into France since Luis Buñuel would have been arrested in Spain at that time.

The Buñuel family
Back row: Alfonso, Alicia, Margarita, Leonardo, Conchita;
Front row: María, Doña María, Luis.

Uncles and Aunts of the Buñuel family:

Pedro Christián, son of Tia Conchita, came to the Zaragoza train station to meet me. I was 24 years old, he was 19. We struck it off immediately. He took me to my grandmother's apartment on the Avenida Independencia...a large many-roomed apartment dating back to the late 1800's. There my grandmother, La Madrina, now senile, lived and was cared for by her two sons: Alfonso, the youngest, an architect, and Leonardo, a doctor and radiologist.

TÍO ALFONSO: I did not get to know Alfonso very well...he died two years later of cancer, but I remember a large, powerfully built, warm man who resembled my father surprisingly. He would take me on walks around Zaragoza, pointing out and explaining the different types of architecture of which I was totally ignorant...architecture influenced by Christian, Jewish and Arab cultures. He also loved to plant trees and had done a heroic task in Calanda by planting and caring for trees from different regions of Spain and the world. He also did beautiful and strange collages from turn-of-the-century magazines and newspapers.

Some people thought he was a homosexual. He did leave his belongings to a young man in Madrid.

TÍO LEONARDO: The kindliest and quietest of all the brothers and sisters...and the handsomest. He had studied medicine and then become a radiologist because he couldn't stand the sight of blood. It would make him faint. But his real love was the country...and guns. (This seems to be the great love of all men in the Buñuel family. We **all** love and have guns!)

Sometimes, he would gather up Pedro Christián, Carlos, Alfonsito (Tía Margarita's sons), and me, and we would drive out to the empty moonscapes outside of Calanda. There, perched on a cliff overlooking a dry gulch, we would first roll cigarettes, smoke and talk about guns. On a bright clear summer day it was impossible to go there without sunglasses. The glare of the sun off the white rocks made it painful to look down. But this small canyon was populated with echoes waiting to be released. Tío Leonardo owned a Colt Automatic .38 which he cared for with love and respect. During the Franco regime, it was very difficult to obtain cartridges. He himself had saved 12 from the Civil War. That day, he had brought **one** bullet with him. After we had smoked several cigarettes (from a tobacco he called "*caldo de gallina*" [chicken soup] it was so good), he would pass the unloaded pistol around. We would aim, fondle it and pretend to shoot. Then he would load the pistol, aim at a distant rock and fire. We knew why he had picked that spot. The echoes were freed! That one explosion resounded a dozen times. Twelve shots for the price of one. Quickly we would pass the gun around again but this time to smell the powder. The wine *bota* was brought out, a jar of black olives, and the day was complete.

We've kept the tradition: Whenever possible, I sneak bullets into Spain and the cousins meet near Calanda, now in an abandoned railway station. But this time we have several boxes of shells, and we spend the whole morning shooting at old pans and cans and bottles and drinking wine from the *bota* and eating black olives...thank you, Mr. Hemingway, for the literary style. Diego even came once to carry on the tradition. Later, I was pleased to read that Lord Byron and Shelley and his wife Mary used to do the same thing in Switzerland. They would load up a picnic with wine, bread, sausages and guns...and spend the afternoon shooting at targets. Intelligent people.

Right after the Civil War, Leonardo had bought a Fiat Topolino, the smallest of cars. He would drive proudly off with his wife, Tía Matilde and his daughter Cuchica to visit the countryside and spend long weekends around Aragón and the Basque country.

But since the car was so small, everything they took had to be reduced. Three socks per person. At night the left foot sock was washed and the next day the right foot sock was passed to the left...in that manner they always had a clean sock every day. Toothbrushes were cut in half to make more space for the small *bota de vino* (wine bottle) he carried. (I was given a Fiat Topolino in Paris, a rich American friend didn't want to be bothered by it any more..it was quite old. I was very happy to have the car. I got in and the damned thing wouldn't start. After three days of trying, I finally sold it to a friend for 50 francs. "Good luck with that pile of junk!" He got in the car and called out. "The valve which allows gas to get to the engine has been pushed down. No wonder it doesn't start." He flipped the switch and roared off. Since the car was so small, I had trouble squeezing into the driver's seat and had inadvertently flipped the switch down with my knee.)

∞ ∞ ∞

When Leonardo decided to take Matilde (a big Basque girl) as "*novia*" (girlfriend), he took her to a cider bar in San Sebastián. They opened a bottle of cider and drank. Leonardo then said, "The glass is better than the cider!" and proceeded to eat the glass. This seduced her and she agreed to become his wife.

During the Civil War, Leonardo, being a doctor, was forced into the Franquista Army. If he did not obey, there would be a reprisal against his/our family. Friends told me that, in the trenches, with canon shot flying overhead, Leonardo, after having drunk a bit too much *aguardiente* (unmatured brandy), would stand up and try to hit the canon shells with his head, like a football (soccer) player trying to slam a ball into the goal. He even mentioned that, after having finished off a relatively large amount of *aguardiente*, he was walking back towards his tent when suddenly, and mysteriously, the ground rose up in front of him, hitting him in the face.

Years later, when Leonardo was dying of cancer, he thought about committing suicide with his gun. But the idea of shooting himself in the head and the gun dropping from his lifeless hand and landing on the ground, scratching itself, put a stop to that.

He devised another plan. He would invent a complicated rigging of wires and strings which, when he fired the bullet into his head, would slip the gun from his hand and leave it dangling in the air in the middle of the room, unharmed. But then, he explained, his wife Matilde would come running in, screaming, and then would take the gun down, leaving her fingerprints on the polished blue steel. That wasn't the problem, no one could accuse her of murdering my uncle. No. But everyone knows that the sweat on human hands leave marks on gun steel that eventually will rust. The idea that his gun would have rust marks horrified him. So my poor uncle died a sad death in the hospital.

TÍA MARÍA: The religious mystique. She carried a heavy solid gold medal with Christ engraved on it. It was the *Medalla de la Buena Muerte*, Medal of the Good Death...what does that mean? It means that when you die and have that medal on you, you'll have a good death, go straight to Heaven. She was a light epileptic and had a tendency towards drink. Everyone watched out that she did not ingest too much alcoholic beverage.

She boasted that she knew all of Wagner. She had all his operas in 78 rpm records but they looked strangely new to me. My father claimed that she had never heard the music or read a book in her life.

During the Spanish Civil War, when bombs were dropping around them, she refused to go down into the cellars of the building in which they were living. She did not want her husband, Vicente (El Tío de la Mancha -he had a huge red birthmark on his face, thus the title La Mancha) to see the female neighbors erotically attired and scared to death in their nightgowns and night caps. My uncle was scared stiff, but she made him sit on the edge of the bed and pray as the bombs dropped around them.

After the war, she subscribed to *Elle* magazine. All my aunts spoke French...they had been educated by "Mademoiselle," a private tutor. Anyway, the female members of the "*haute bourgeoisie*" of Zaragoza read *Elle* to know what was happening in "la mode de Paris." But, as soon as the magazine arrived in her apartment, she would cut out all the panty and lingerie ads. In that way, El Tío de la Mancha could not see and appreciate the youthful French models in their skimpy attire.

∞ ∞ ∞

She had two children, a boy and a girl. She bragged to my cousin Pedro Christián (who was a doctor) that she had always been frigid. She turned to her husband who was sitting nearby and asked, "*No es cierto, Vicente?*" (Isn't that so, Vicente). He answered with a sad grunt. Then she stated that she had made love only twice in her life: once for each child, Aurora and Luis Fernando. My cousin asked, "What about that natural abortion, at two months, you had in my hospital in the year 19xx?" "Well," she answered, "Three times!"

166

∞ ∞ ∞

One Christmas Eve we all sat around the *mesa camilla* (a warmer under the table filled with hot ashes or burnt olive pits) at the Madrina's house and drank cognac and coffee and told stories. Pedro Christián had warned me that at midnight something would happen which would interest me. At about 12:15 a.m. my Aunt María said, "Guess what I saw yesterday in my closet?" Everyone pulled back in horror. My aunt reached out and her hand became a monstrous spider, crawling between the little cakes and the cognac glasses. "Yes, it walked like this..." Her hand stumbled over its own finger and the spider came to life. The inevitable question came up, "What color was it?" the other aunts asked. "It was 'color de patata' (potato colored)!" And everyone screamed with terror. Then we spoke about spiders for the next three hours. It happens that way every Christmas eve.

Another time, she was describing a spider that she had seen. She begged a pencil and some paper so she could draw the beast. Someone handed her a folded newspaper. She spread open the newspaper page and then declared, "It's not big enough!"

Black spider painting by Juan Luis (gouache on paper)

Tía María would sit besides me at these, and other, family reunions. When my other aunt would bring in the refreshments (cognac, wine, beer, and a soda) for the epileptic sister, Tía María would grasp my arm with her claws and look at me pleadingly. I would reassure her. She relaxed. When possible, I would discreetly place my glass of beer near her and she, with incredible skill, would pour the whole glass down her throat in a half-beat of an eyelash. No one ever saw her do it. I always limited her intake to two glass and with that she would be satisfied.

∞ ∞ ∞

Her apartment was very large, but it had not been painted since the Spanish Civil War. The heat had been cut off from most of the rooms.

Some radiators, if leaned against, would rattle and almost fall over. All this to save money. But, in the living, or living rooms (they had two), she had an incredible collection of gold-plated furniture and carved chests. A veritable fortune. Yet they would pass most of the day warming themselves at a cheap *mesa camilla* and drinking chamomile tea.She had a nun working for them...a dried-up creature who probably was out for a bit of the inheritance. She looked like a leathery old crow. But Tía María outlived her. In fact, by 1999, Tía María was still alive, lying in her bed like a mummy.

Once I was invited, with my daughter Juliette (who was five at the time), for a drink. My aunt informed me that she had some cookies for my little girl. When we got there, Tía María sent the nun out to get a quarter-liter bottle of cheap Valdepenas wine for me. For Juliette, she brought out a huge cookie jar. She lifted the top off and pointed the opening towards my daughter. The little girl reached her whole arm into the jar and pulled out the entire contents...one cookie.

But El Tío de la Mancha had his revenge. He had a lover. He would give Tía María a beer (that was the only way he could leave the house without recriminations) and scuttle out the door. One cousin saw him walking guiltily along the streets of the slum neighborhood around the Basilica de la Virgen del Pilar. She started following him. Then, another cousin who was buying knives in that neighborhood saw his cousin following their uncle. So he followed them. El Tío de la Mancha headed for his lover's apartment and, after hesitating, bought her five pesetas worth of grilled chestnuts. A grandiose present. The first cousin never knew the second cousin had followed them.

In that neighborhood was located the best knife store *in the world.* Hand-made horn or wood-clasped folding knives, long butcher knives, small delicate steak knives whose handles were made of Boj...a harder-than-steel boxwood which grew in the water-starved hills of Aragón, straight razors (which I was incapable of using because of the fear it instilled in me when the glass-sharp blade approached my throat), small blades for castrating pigs, stickers for killing bulls, knives with blades that were wider than they were long for skinning lambs, and deadly knives which would "clack" menacingly as you opened them. There was one knife which was barely half a centimeter thick yet the blade was a good 20 centimeters long. I wanted all of them and each time I went to Zaragoza, instead of going to the Virgen del Pilar for a prayer, I would go to that shop for a knife.

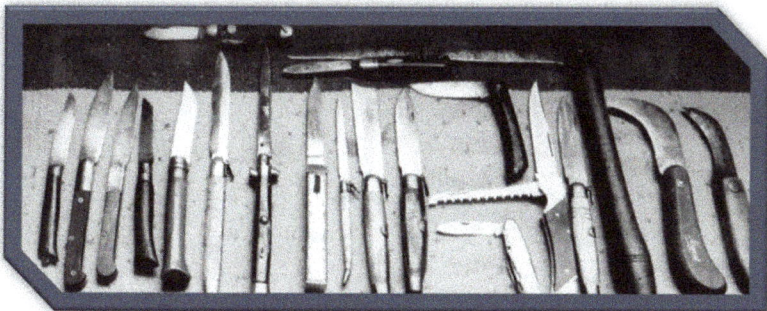

Part of Juan Luis' knife collection

TÍA ALICIA

La Tía Tanqué (Aunt Tank) as I used to call her. The most bourgeois of all the brothers and sisters, she was as wide as she was tall. She would come crashing into a living room and suddenly throw herself head first over the back of a sofa, do a double somersault and land spread-eagled on the rug...when she was over 60.

She would join religious organizations to help out in church sales and raffles. She was also a great poker, canasta and bridge player, and her obsession with cards was overpowering. Once at a church sale, she was installed at a small table at the entrance and was to sell holy images of saints to the faithful. Disaster! The images were exactly the same dimensions as playing cards. A friend started talking with her, and as the conversation became more interesting, Tía Alicia's hands started to twitch and to react normally to the card-sized objects in their grip. Much to the horror and indignation of the attending audience, Tía Alicia started shuffling the holy images with such speed and dexterity that, as the legend goes, many saints changed sex that day.

∞ ∞ ∞

Years later, in 1973, in Calanda, I was waiting for my film crew. We were to film the drums of Calanda, my first film.

It was 11 p.m., they were driving down from Paris and I was worried. The ceremonies started the next day at noon. They had to get there to have a night's rest because the next day we would be shooting for 24 hours without a break. I was staying at Tia Alicia's house (which before had been the huge Buñuel family house on the square of the village). We were both leaning over the balcony nervously looking up the street. My aunt could see that I was very worried. Then she said, "I will say a prayer and, if they get here before midnight, will you convert to Catholicism?" I thought a minute and answered, "All right, I accept, but on the condition that, if they come after midnight, you become an atheist." She thought a minute, then said, "No!" I, of course, could not accept an unfair exchange and also said, "No!" The crew finally got there at 12:15 a.m. My aunt smiled at me, relieved that she had not accepted the contract.

∞ ∞ ∞

Alicia had a daughter, Alicita who had given birth to two brutish twins. When the two boys were eighteen, and weighed each a hundred kilos, they practiced a favorite game with their mother, Alicita. She would run down the long hall of their apartment as fast as she could. She was built like her mother. As she ran by, the boys would step out of different doorways and slug her as hard as they could on the arm. She was tough enough to laugh at them.

Later, one of the twins became a banker. I put a sum of money into his bank and let it sit for a couple of years. I figured it would make a little interest. It didn't. My loving cousin had appropriated all the interest. The other twin was decent enough but since they looked so much alike, it was difficult to tell the thieving twin from the honest one. As Pedro Christián so aptly put it, "*Ellos saben cual es el hijo de puta.*" Translation: Only they know which one is the son of a bitch.

Alicita was also very nervous about trips. If the train for Madrid or Barcelona was to leave at 3 in the afternoon, she would be at the station five hours before departure time, nervously walking up and down, looking at her watch every few moments.

Alicita was also very bourgeois and liked to compare Zaragoza to Paris. Once, in 1960, sitting in my grandmother's apartment, Alicita looked out at the Paseo Independencia and saw a car drive by. At that time there were hardly any cars in Spain. This was the second car in fifteen minutes. "It's like Parisian traffic," she proudly stated.

When she first came to Paris, I set up a rendez-vous with her in a bar full of prostitutes located near Place Pigalle. On purpose I arrived 30 minutes late. She thought the bar was very chic and Parisian.

TÍA MARGARITA

Blond, beautiful, tall, strong, she was my mother's best friend and companion whenever they met in Spain. Her first husband, father of Carlos and Kuki, died at a very young age. She remarried Alfonso de Lucas who fathered Alfonso Junior (Alfonsito).

I have seen her climb three flights of steps with a case of champagne under each arm. She also was obsessed with spiders. Once, when going into a country café-bar after having been for a walk in the mountains, she saw a man looking at her with curiosity. As she approached, the man pointed towards her chest and started to say," Madame, you have a..." Tía Margarita let out a cry of terror, grabbed the man's hand and started slapping it on her generous bosom. The man was shocked. When Tio Alfonso finally stopped Margarita's hysterical screaming and calmed things down, an explanation was offered. The stranger had intended to say, "Madame, you have a beautiful brooch." Tía Margarita, coming in from her country walk, thought the man was going to say, "Madame, you have a spider on your bosom!" and she was using his hand to chase the arachnid away.

When she was little, she used to go up to her father, who would be sitting in the cool inner patio, and start introducing into his open-necked shirt all the knives and forks she could find. Each time she would do this, her father would sit there patiently, until there was no more room for any more knives and forks.

My father maintained that she also, like Tía María, had never read a book in her life...but she was one of the best cooks I have ever known. Dietary fact: Tio Alfonso, her husband and a film set designer, was a product of Spanish cooking. He hated raw (salads, tomatoes) or fresh vegetables. He **always** ate fried foods. Always! And he **never** drank water. Just wine or beer. As I write this he is over 85 years old and walks five kilometers a day at a pace that tires the strongest of men.

Note: To make a good rice "a la Mexicana," first fry it in oil where two heads of garlic have already been browned. Then add the exact double in water (plus a drop more) and one or two chicken bouillon cubes. Once the water starts to boil, DO NOT TOUCH THE RICE until it is cooked.

TÍA CONCHITA

The most beautiful of the Buñuel girls, ethereal, not of this world, yet her humorous eye was on everything, ready to interpret, to analyze and to laugh. Even at 65 she was pushed into a doorway near Madrid's Puerta Del Sol and elegantly told, "*Gallina vieja hace buena sopa*" ("With an old hen you can make good soup").

When she and her sister Margarita would get together, telling stories of their childhood, imitating a mass and the preaching of the priest, they would have us laughing for hours. It was a vision of life on another planet, another culture, both desirable and awful. What luck that we did not live during that period...yet we missed something.

PEDRO CHRISTIÁN GARCÍA

Pedro was Conchita's youngest son. She had four sons. All became doctors. In Spain, during the Franco period, and depending on whom you knew, you would be a doctor or an engineer. The influential person they knew happened to have friends in the medical school. Pedro became an anesthelogist. He also loved cemeteries and the first thing he would do when arriving in a strange city was to look up the burying grounds.

176

Once he took me to visit the Basilica of the Virgen del Pilar. The Virgen supposedly appeared on a pillar and that is where she is now, on a filthy pillar which has been worn down by millions of people kissing it. Nearby, and attached to the ceiling of the Basilica, are several bombs which had been dropped by the godless Reds during the Civil War. A miracle then occurred. The bombs crashed through the ceiling of the Basilica and landed at the feet of the Virgen. They did not explode. Oh Miracle! As Pedro Christián says, the real miracle is that each bomb has a delicate aluminum propeller attached to its nose and, as they came crashing through the hard roof tiles and cement of the Basilica's roof and landed on the stone floor, they weren't even bent. *That* is a miracle!

In Paris, Pedro found, in the St. Sulpice church (of Huysman's fame) and behind an altar, a small box of consecrated wafers. He naturally stole them and brought the sacred little box back to the house. There we invited Anita Fernández, who is Jewish (but not a believer) for lunch. We fed her sandwiches made of Consecrated Wafers, buttered and with ham. In this manner, she sinned against two religions but nothing happened.

LEONARDO GARCÍA BUÑUEL

Pedro's brother and Conchita's eldest son. Probably the kindest man I've ever know, apart from his namesake, Tío Leonardo lives in Phoenix, Arizona and works for the sheriff's office as a forensic psychologist.

CARLOS DE LA FIGUERA

Carlos was the son of Tía Margarita, and brother of Kuki, from a first marriage which had ended in the sudden and tragic death of the two children's father.

Carlos was strange, to say the least. When Juliette first met him in Calanda, the first thing he did to impress her was to eat a rock, grinding it down with his powerful teeth and jaws. He would also bend coins with his teeth and would, now and then, eat a glass.

He inherited a large sum when his father died but spent it all in bars and restaurants in two years. Then he ran away from military duty and, to avoid being arrested, became a parachutist in the Spanish Foreign Legion. His face was a mass of scars. For example, while standing at attention in the Legion, his sergeant said that he did not like Carlos' haircut. Carlos retorted that he also did not like the Sergeant's hair-do. Without a word, the sergeant reached over, pulled Carlos' machete from its sheath and slashed him across the face. Another time, an officer broke all the bones in our cousin's nose with the butt-end of a rifle...for insubordination.

Once, while in Barcelona, Pedro Christián received a call from a hospital. Carlos had been in a terrible auto accident and was in the hospital with a fractured skull. Pedro rushed to the hospital to find the establishment in a uproar. All the doctors and nurses pleaded innocent. They had been incapable of keeping Carlos in bed. He had gotten dressed and had jumped out of the first-floor window. Being a parachutist, he knew how to jump and fall. Pedro finally found him taking a shower in his apartment. He was famous for jumping out of first-floor windows.

Whenever in Barcelona, on the day of my departure, I would wonder at exactly what time my train was to leave. Carlos would pull out a little pad in which he had careful noted <u>all</u> the train and airline schedules. Then he would nervously hurry me out the door and into a taxi...even if my train or flight was four hours away.

Carlos could be very delicate with women. Once, in Sitges, he was in love with an American girl. He had invited her and several friends to have strawberries and cream at a corner café. At one moment, there were no more strawberries and the girl in question said, "Oh, how I wish I had more strawberries!" Carlos leaned over, popped his nose into the cream and gallantly offered it to the woman.

He was also capable of walking up to a girl with very long hair, grabbing a handful and blowing his nose into it.

He would put out cigarettes on his forearm and once put one out on his forehead.

The last time I saw him was in his apartment. We drank a little cognac and had a coffee. He was playing with his baby daughter. It was time for me to go. He accompanied me to the elevator. As I got in he said, "I can run down faster than you in the elevator!" We were on the 9th floor. So I pressed the "down" button and he raced off. I could hear the slamming of his shoes as he ran faster and faster. When I got to the ground floor, I stepped out of the elevator and looked around, "Carlos! Carlos?" Nobody in sight. He had run out the door...and kept going. Nobody saw him again for six months.

He was an alcoholic. Once when I visited Tía Margarita, she was very happy. "Carlos is not drinking any more!" Then she told me to go to the refrigerator and help myself to the white wine. I poured myself a glass but it looked strangely clear. I tasted it...90% water. Carlos had gotten there before.

He died, in a hospital, of cirrhosis and other excesses.

Anyway, on this first trip to Spain (after Zaragoza), I went to Madrid and lived in Tía Maria's son's old apartment at the Puerta del Sol. Met Pepe and Domingo Dominguín.[29] Spent New Year's Eve at Domingo Dominguín's apartment on Calle Ferraz. Muñoz Suay was present. Domingo Dominguín's daughter, "La Patata" (Carmen), would yell insults to Franco's motorcade from the sixth-floor terrace. "*Les gritó y se van echando leches!*" (I yelled at them and they left, "as if they were spitting milk from their mouths"). She was four years old.

---

[29] Domingo González Mateos (better known as Dominguín) was a Spanish bullfighter born in Toledo in 1895 whose career began in 1918. He is the father of the *toreros* Luis Miguel, Domingo and Pepe. He continued to be a strong support of bullfighting until his death in 1958.

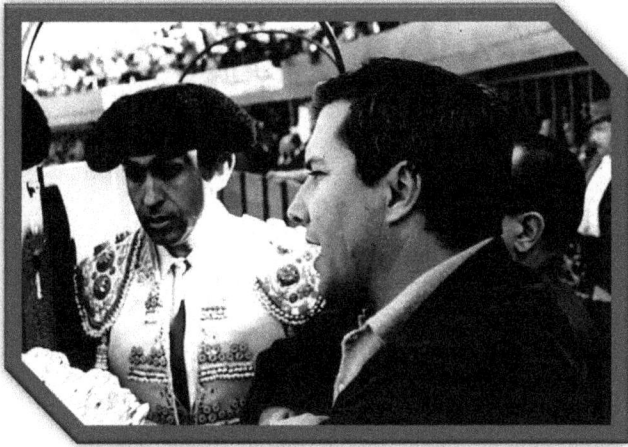

Domingo Dominguín (on right)

Coming back to Tía Maria's oldest (and only) son, Luis Fernando. He was an architect and had been living with a woman for nearly 30 years. At that time, it was impossible to get a divorce in Spain and this woman, *"esa mujer"* (that woman) as Tía María would call her, had left her husband three decades ago. Poor Luis Fernando was a very devoted man but because they were living out of wedlock, his mother had never wanted to see *"esa mujer!"* Her name was Carmen and all she was interested in was money. When she was in her seventies she dressed like she was twelve years old. You would see, from far away, a young girl dancing up to you and then the shock of seeing this hag with golden pigtails talking about money...

They had an incredibly luxurious apartment (in reality, two apartments joined together) in Madrid and she proudly showed it off, exclaiming, "And there's no kitchen!" They had a 24-hour cafeteria on the ground floor of the building.

CALANDA I went there to prepare the ground for the filming of my first film, the documentary CALANDA. The town had one *posada* (rustic inn) with five rooms. I called on the innkeeper and asked him to reserve all five rooms for me. He stared at me a minute, then shook his head, "No!" he growled. I insisted, argued, asked for an explanation, were the rooms already rented? He would not give me a reason. "No!"

I was desperate. My crew was arriving in a few days and I had no place to lodge them. In haste I went to see the *alcalde* (mayor) of the village. He listened to me, then left the room. Several minutes later he was back, all smiles. "You've got the rooms." I was astonished. Why didn't he rent them to me before? "The answer was quite simple." said the mayor. "He had never rented all of his rooms at the same time and wasn't about to start now!"

At that time there was only one phone in Calanda. It was situated at the post office. One could also send telegrams from there. Once Charles had to send an urgent telegram to New York, something about his business. The post mistress read the telegram, figured out the cost and then looked up at Charles, "No, I won't send it." "Why?" asked Charles. "Because it costs too much. Send a letter." It took us 15 minutes to convince her that 1) it was an important message, 2) a letter took too long and, 3) it was Charles' money and he could do what he wanted with it. Finally, and with a grumble, she sent the telegram.

THE CONTRESCARPE

Back in Paris:

At night I would hang out at the Place de la Contrescarpe. There was a café there, the Contrescarpe, run by Arlette (the actress) and Mel Howard. They welcomed singers and comics to put on their acts. If the audience reaction was favorable, they would ask the personality to come back the next night. Many were just starting out: Barbara, Bernard Haller (the Swiss comic)...they were paid 20 francs a night. Mel Howard eventually became a big producer on Broadway in New York. CATS, etc.

Behind the bar, André Schwarz-Bart, the writer, handled the drinks.[30] I got a job as bouncer. I was paid two "demis" of beer a night. The bouncing was limited to an Algerian chap who came in every two weeks. He would stand at the bar very quietly. As soon as I spotted him, I would start moving in. It was too late. He would yell out, "I'm a man!" and bite into his beer glass. Then, with the bartender, we'd hold him down and take the bloodied broken pieces of glass from his mouth. Then we'd escort him to the door. Never any resistance. Two weeks later he'd be back, healed and ready for another mouthful.

One night, a Mexican friend of mine, Severn Schaeffer (we had gone to the American High School together and, along with Jerry Lindner, had formed a Western music trio), and I decided to sing Mexican songs to the habitués of the Contrescarpe. Fate had

---

[30] André Schwarz-Bart (1928-2006), of Polish-Jewish ancestry, was the son of parents who were sent to Auschwitz. He joined the Resistance movement. He is known for his novels *The Last of the Just* (*Le dernier des justes*, 1959), and *A Woman Named Solitude* (1973).

it that Jerry and I were both wearing heavy thick white hand-knitted Mexican sweaters (made in Toluca). We started off with two popular numbers, "La Cucaracha" and I forget the other. Before we launched into a third melody, a dark-haired girl sitting directly in front of us eyed our matching sweaters and asked in a loud humorless voice, "Which of you two plays the girl?" That stopped our singing career right then and there.

The Place de la Contrescarpe was known for its "*clochards*" (bums, tramps). They would gather there at night, drinking from their liter bottles of *vin rouge*, eating baguettes and garlic sausage, laughing, singing and arguing. Then they would fall asleep on the benches or in the gutters. Every now and then, a police "*panier à salade*" (slang for police van) would pick them up, bathe them and shave their heads (for the lice), give them old but disinfected clothes and then turn them loose again. During the winters they would all go to the Côte d'Azur for the balmier climate.

One summer night we witnessed a glorious battle. Two men (a little bit under the wagon) fought for the love of a woman. Charlemagne, 89 years old, pulled a knife on Le Chinois, 78 years of age, who defended himself with a broken bottle. There was blood everywhere. Finally the police had to intervene. All this for the favors of La Belle Héloïse...she was a blushing 82 years old.

I was especially fond of the hot-blooded Charlemagne. He always had funny anecdotes. I would give him the cheap Gauloises which I smoked and could afford. One day he asked me for "*un clou*" (a nail...for the coffin) but I was out. He then gave *me* a new pack of Pall Malls which he produced from the many folds of his filthy clothing.

There was also Albert, who wheeled all his belongings around in a supermarket caddie. And sitting majestically on top of his junk, was a little white dog with a big pink ribbon around its neck. Whenever there was a big traffic jam in Saint-Germain-des-Prés, and the cars were loudly honking their horns for many blocks, it would invariably be Albert, with his caddie and dog, in the middle of the street, weaving back and forth, drunk, waving a finger about, putting it to his lips, telling the cars that they should not make so much noise. Usually the police would drag him out of the way.

"La Reine du Pont Neuf." A fearsome, 65-year-old woman, huge, wearing six pairs of skirts, seven sweaters, five jackets, eight hats, three pairs of shoes (big, big shoes, then smaller...and smaller). Her face was smeared with make-up...a huge red mouth, the lipstick almost coming up to her eyes. She carried unrecognizable trash in her arms, an immense bundle which was always falling apart. Wherever she stalked, she left a trail of trash and garbage. She polluted the atmosphere. And from her mouth, blasphemies...her dialogue was dedicated to outraging God. She never left the Pont Neuf. She was magnificent. Paris should build a monument to her memory next to that of Henri IV on the Square du Vert-Galant.

There was an abandoned area near the old Bibliothèque de Paris, an area a big as a small village. Before it had been a textile factory and emporium. It was comprised of a series of tiny streets with small apartment houses where the textile workers lived. The front part of the structure was a huge "magazine" where the bolts of cloth would be laid out for the customers to paw over and to buy. There was only one entrance, a huge wrought-iron gate. The whole place was eventually abandoned, the workers put out of work and the gates welded shut. It remained this way for many years. But an enterprising gangster type managed to find a way in and it became a *clochard* hotel. He would, for a small sum (for the *clochards* not so small) rent them a room and the secret of how to enter this little town. I visited these rooms after all the *clochards* had been moved out forcibly by the police.

∞ ∞ ∞

One of the members of the non-*clochard* gang who hung out at the Contrescarpe was a nice quiet blond girl. 'Zabeth was her name. She always hung back as we roared and argued. Timid. Then one night, the word went out. We were all invited to have dinner at her place. Again spaghetti and tomato sauce with several liters of cheap red wine and the eternal baguettes. Nobody complained. Most food is very good, especially if you don't have to pay for it. The address was on the Right Bank. We expected the usual white-walled studio with the sink and the gas stove and the paper plates.

When the zoo (we were like jungle animals, different and wild: beards, weird make-up, leather jackets and pants, long hair before the Beatles, mini-skirts before Carnaby Street, sandals and boots, barefooted) arrived at 'Zabeth's address we stood in the street with our jaws unslung.

Before us was a building which had the air of the Élysée Palace. We were greeted at the door by costumed men in wigs and silk stockings (liveried footmen, they were). We walked through spacious living rooms, all in Louis XIV furniture. In the back gardens, trimmed shrubs and trees surrounded fountains and marble statuary. A wooden platform had been raised. La Chunga, a famous Flamenco dancer during the fifties, was performing barefooted with her group.[31] A few feet away, several lambs were being roasted on spits. That night we ate on solid gold plates.

'Zabeth's name was...Elizabeth de Rothschild. We were sadly tempted to take some of the golden cutlery. But 'Zabeth had always been decent and quiet, and until that night, unassuming. So we didn't take any of the golden silverware. It was a good party and a change from the spaghetti and tomato sauce.

Café Select (photo by Juan Luis)

---

[31] La Chunga (literally, "the difficult woman") was the name used for Micaela Flores Amaya, born in 1938 of Andalusian Romani parents who were immigrants in France. She appeared in several Hollywood films, thanks to the help of Ava Gardner. In addition to her flamenco dancing, she was also a painter of *naïf* art.

At the Café Select in Montparnasse, Suicide Sam hung out. Always sad, always ready to make the big move to another country, he'd always end up at the Select, nursing his "demi" all afternoon and night.

Why Suicide Sam? Every six or seven months, he'd have a great depression. Then, during the first part of the week, he'd call between 10 and 15 friends, inviting them to his house for a Saturday night party. Saturday morning he'd call again to be sure that everyone was coming. When he was sure, he'd commit suicide (gas or pills) ten minutes before his guests would arrive. Then they would break the door down, air the room out, take him to the hospital.

Conversation at the Select the next morning, "Sam committed suicide last night." "Oh?" "Yeah, he'll be here at 5:00 this afternoon to tell us about it." Suicide Sam.

THE YOUNG ONE (*La joven*), GABRIEL FIGUEROA

1960

I flew from Paris to New York to meet my father. I was to help him, since his hearing was not good, to find actors for his next film which was to be shot in English and in Mexico. The producer was George Pepper and the screenwriter was Hugo Butler. Both, living in Mexico at that time, had been forced to leave Hollywood due to the McCarthy Un-American Activities investigations. George Pepper was a small, kindly, smiling man who smoked his cigarettes from a filter holder. He had been a friend of Einstein. Hugo Butler was a big burly man, with five children that he hustled around in a ten-year-old black Cadillac. All these children went to the American High school in Mexico City and, though younger than I, had been my schoolmates.

Both these men had already worked with my father on the writing, producing and shooting of ROBINSON CRUSOE, and I had already worked with George and Hugo in a documentary fiction called LOS PEQUEÑOS GIGANTES, shot in Monterrey, Mexico.

Work was scarce and in those days everyone had a hard time making ends meet.

George and Hugo got my father interested in the idea of making a film which dealt with the racial unrest manifesting itself in the United States at the moment. The big problem, in making such a film, was to find locations in Mexico that looked like the United States.

They wanted to release the film in the United States but because of their anti-McCarthy stance and their exile in Mexico, they changed their names. George Werker was to be the producer's new title and Hugo took on the name of H.B. (Hugo Butler) Addis.

We were in New York to look for actors. Zachary Scott was to have the main role of the gamekeeper Miller.

In Mexico, Claudio Brook, who later played the role of Simeon del Desierto and who spoke perfect English, would play the role of the pastor. Bernie Hamilton, brother of the musician Chico Hamilton, played the part of Travers, a black clarinet player. In the script, he was unjustifiably accused of raping a white woman.

Zachary was an incredibly kind man, ready to please, ready to laugh. He worked hard but he put the same energy into enjoying himself. His wife, Ruth Ford, had been a friend of William Faulkner and was also an actress.

Two characters were left: Evie, the "young one," and the racist redneck, Jackson.

We borrowed an office in New York City and started seeing actors and child actresses. Most of the girls, who had to be about 14 or 15, childlike, yet with a certain physical sexual maturity, looked like 28-year-old women.

One day, an actor came in for the role of Jackson. He was accompanied by his daughter. He was a gentle man and did not have the slightly brutal look the character had to have. My father was sorry...but was his daughter an actress? She was young, but just at the right age for the role of Evie. Her name was Key Meersman. The father was overjoyed and Key was retained for the role. An interesting fact: Key is a strange name for a child. Her ancestor was Francis Scott Key, the man who had written the national anthem of the United States of America. "Oh, say can you see, by the dawn's early light..."etc. etc. ad nauseam. And thus her name, Key.

The Young One (Bernie Hamilton and Key Meersman)

The role of Jackson was given to Graham Denton who looked like a brutal redneck, but was a warm, funny and totally non-racist person.

In the evenings in New York, we would go to the Plaza Hotel bar for the traditional dry martini and end up having dinner in a small Italian restaurant in Greenwich Village...a restaurant which during the Prohibition was a speak-easy. The Mama of this establishment had recognized my father from the old days and would prepare special dishes for us.

One day, we had forgotten to wear ties. When we arrived at the Plaza Bar, we were kindly but firmly escorted to the exit.

Other evenings we would go to old friends' homes for dinner, ex-members of the Spanish Republican government. Demetrio Delgado de Torres would always have a bottle of California wine ready. There the conversation would move away from the racial problem in the U.S. and deep into the Spanish Civil War. As the conversation got louder and louder, I would slip away with his daughter, Inés and her husband, and we would go to the Five Spot in the East Village to listen to Thelonius Monk at his piano... at 25 cents a beer.

One night Zachary Scott invited us to his home for a typical New York cocktail party. He lived in a building called "The Dakota" which was used for the filming of Polanski's ROSEMARY'S BABY and became the site of John Lennon's assassination.

"*Le tout New York*" (all the artsy people in NYC) was there, including Andy Warhol and some of his circus animals. At one moment, I was sitting on a bed, talking with a friend. On the bed were all the coats and capes of the guests. Suddenly I felt someone trying to pull out a coat upon where I was sitting. I excused myself and got up. A very beautiful woman of about seventy smiled and tried to get the wrinkles out of her coat. It was Greta Garbo.

∞ ∞ ∞

Once back in Mexico, I got together with Julio "Nacho"Villareal, my father's long-time assistant and friend, to find locations that might look like a small island off the coast of the state of North Carolina. For reference, we got pamphlets from the Department of Tourism at the United States Embassy.

Finally we decided on three exterior locations. The coast and the island would be shot at the Laguna de Tres Palos, 20 kilometres south of Acapulco. There we found a rugged beach. The problem was to avoid any tropical vegetation. We did not want, during a projection of the film, for some holier-than-thou botanist to suddenly yell out, "That Fungus McCarthius Stentorium only grows in latitudes 2000 kilometers to the south!"

The gamekeeper's shack was built very near Mexico City, a place called Contreras, on the flanks of a volcano. But we limited the shooting to a small brush and pine-tree area. (Naturally this variety of pine tree did **not** grow in the Carolinas.)

The third spot to find was where Evie gets baptized. It was a clear river fed by a spring, also near Mexico City. BUT, there our respect for the feelings of botanists went out the window. The spring was surrounded by thousand year-old Ahuehuete trees. The Ahueheute is a very large tree which only grows in Mexico and was sacred to the Aztecs. But the public was so riveted by the scene, that we received no letters of complaint.

The interiors were shot at the Churubusco studios in Mexico City.

Zachary Scott came down a few weeks before the first day of filming. He had bought clothes in the United States which would be satisfactory for the role of a gamekeeper. But we had to look at the problems of makeup, aging of the clothes, haircut, etc.

One Sunday, Zachary rented an old Mexican trolley car, installed a bar, loaded it with a group of Mariachis and we started rolling around the city, drinking and playing Mexican songs. We would stop to pick up startled voyagers, serenade and offer them a drink, and then take them home. Since by renting the trolley, we had the right to go where we pleased, we zigzagged the rails of the City until the sun came up.

The Director of Photography was Gabriel Figueroa, who did many of my father's films in Mexico. Gabriel was Mexico's best cameraman and had become famous making El Indio Fernández's post-war idyllic films which showed a completely false vision of Mexico, with María Félix dressed as a simple Indian lass against a background of cacti and clouds. But Gabriel had a great sense of humor and he was good and FAST. Enough qualities to become my father's favorite technician and friend.

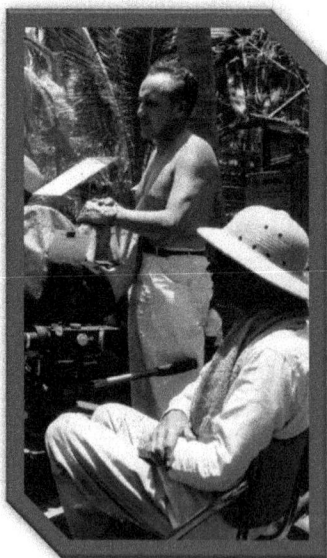

Gabriel Figueroa and Luis Buñuel filming *Fever Mounts at El Pao,* 1959

While the construction crew built Miller's cabin near Mexico City, we went down to Acapulco to film the exteriors. We stayed at Las Hamacas, a favorite hotel of cinema crews. At that time Acapulco was a clean and not too crowded resort city and port. Not the filthy garbage can it is today. At the Hamacas there was an open-air bar next to the swimming pool. Also, belonging to the hotel and jutting out into Acapulco bay, was a 30-meter jetty. At the end of this pier, there was a *palapa*: platform with a roof made of coconut palm leaves. Several tables, canvas easychairs and a nice bar made the place very comfortable. A constant light breeze transformed it into one of the coolest places in Acapulco. There, in the evenings, after the day's shooting, my father would mix our Picon-Bière-Grenadines or just plain beer. It was too hot to drink dry martinis.

On this same jetty, in 1959, during the filming of LA FIÈVRE MONTE à EL PAO (*Fever Mounts at El Pao*), we would have evening drinks with actor Gérard Philipe. My father would mix the cocktails, strong as usual. They would drink a little and then red splotches would appear on Gérard's face. After such a drink he would always complain of not feeling well, of being dizzy. We would laugh at him, saying that he could not hold his liquor. Several months after the filming he died of a liver cancer. He had given most of the salary of LA FIÈVRE to the Cuban Institute of Cinematography.

Gérard Philipe

We had a production manager, a refugee from the Spanish Civil War, called Salazar. His best friend was Nestor, my father's chauffeur and personal assistant. They had known and worked with each other since Salazar's arrival in 1940.

One morning on location near the Laguna de Tres Palos, Salazar, being a good Spaniard, was blowing his mouth off in a rather loud manner. Mexicans, who speak with a low calm sing-song accent, say that Spaniards speak "*golpeados*" (loudly, like blows). The Spanish way of speaking, to the Mexicans, resembles a mixture of a machine gun and a jack-hammer.

Anyway, Salazar was yelling about a lost pencil. His voice was directed towards Nestor who, after 20 years of friendship, did not even pay attention. A native of the Laguna dressed in white cotton pants and shirt, walking by, heard this loud aggressive voice and, pulling a large knife from his belt, headed for Salazar. He paused in front of Nestor for an instant and muttered, "*Te lo mato, hermano!*" (I'll kill him for you, brother!).

By this time, Salazar was climbing the nearest palm tree. It took Nestor 15 minutes to convince our native well-wisher that the "*fuereño*" (foreigner) had not meant any harm and that they were good friends.

Since my father was slightly deaf, I was the go-between for Key Meersman and him, since she did not speak Spanish. She was very innocent and did not really understand the story: the illicit love affair between an older man and a 14-year-old girl...which I find makes the story more believable. We are convinced of her innocence.

I murdered a rabbit in one sequence. Miller goes out hunting for his supper. Suddenly he sees something. MEDIUM CLOSE-UP of a rabbit munching on some grass. Suddenly a bullet rips through his heart. He dies.

I was standing behind the camera. The director called out, "Camera!" and then "Action!" I lifted the .22 caliber rifle and put a bullet into the rabbit. It was not a cruel death...and the crew ate him roasted over a charcoal fire with some chili sauce and hot tortillas. He had a useful existence, not like many two-legged creatures who wear uniforms and walk around the world carrying guns.

Another animal was killed during the shooting of the film. A chicken. We had constructed a chicken-coop and, one night, we set up the camera and lights. Everyone backed away so as not to scare the chickens. Then we turned a raccoon loose amidst the poultry. He looked around, curiously, then calmly walked over to a chicken, grabbed it by the neck, and started eating its head, as one eats a carrot stick. We were all very impressed.

∞ ∞ ∞

One day, on the set of Miller's cabin, an elderly man and his wife came to visit. His name was Torsvan and his wife Chema. They were both friends of Gabriel Figueroa. We chatted pleasantly between takes and, as the sun got hotter, they bid us good-bye and took their leave.

Years later, as I was filming LA REBELLIÓN DE LOS COLGADOS (*Rebellion of the Hanged*, 1954) in the state of Oaxaca, the same lady came on the set. Her husband had died. And there I found out that Torsvan was in reality B. Traven, the German author who had written LA REBELLIÓN DE LOS COLGADOS, and also THE TREASURE OF THE SIERRA MADRE, filmed by John Huston with Humphry Bogart. Gabriel Figueroa had been the cameraman and became a friend of Traven. Traven had never wanted publicity and had fought all his life to hide his identity.

∞ ∞ ∞

THE YOUNG ONE covered several interesting aspects:

1) The bad guy wasn't really bad. It was just society that made him think that black people were not human. He has a long conversation with Travers in which he explains that

he really did not dislike blacks...but that their problem was that they thought they were human beings. That's where their trouble originated.

2) Travers was not all good either from an American point of view. He was a jazz clarinetist and smoked pot in front of little Evie.

These two facts were probably what stopped the film from even being a mild success in the United States at that time. It seems that they burnt an effigy of my father in the streets of Harlem. I do not know if this is true.

Gabriel Figueroa, when my father started working with him, was Mexico's, and one of the world's, best directors of photography. At the beginning the relationship between both men was a little tense. Gabriel was used to being the master on the set when it came to making artistic decisions with the camera. On LOS OLVIDADOS he was not shooting the pretty side of Mexico. I remember being on location for the last scene of NAZARÍN. It was a typical Mexican country road lined with *magueys* and *pirule* trees. In the distance was a great view of the Popocatepetl and the Ixtaccihuatl, the two dominant and snow-covered volcanoes in the valley of Mexico. Naturally, Gabriel said that the perfect place to shoot the scene was with the two volcanoes as a background. My father immediately turned his back on the volcanoes and said they would shoot against some nondescript trees. By this time, they had become friends and the matter was dropped. But during the filming of LOS OLVIDADOS, the discussions came to a head and Gabriel asked, "Why did you take me as director of photography?" And my father answered, "Because you are very fast." The artistic question was never brought up.

They worked together in good humor and were *always* joking. Gag after gag. The whole day was spent in seeing what joke could be found in each situation.

At times my father's hearing would worsen. So Gabriel would stand by his side and, when the scene was over, he'd gently tug the director's sleeve. Then my father would call out, "Cut!" and the actors would take the break.

Gabriel would *never* come to the rushes. He told me once that on his first film as director of photography, he saw the first day's rushes and fainted. From that moment on, he would call the laboratory, ask his friend, a technician in charge of development, if the negative was in good state...and that would be it. Eventually he would see the film. But he kept short splices of all his negatives and in this way built up a very important archive of all his films.

As far as their private friendship was concerned, they would see each other off the set once or twice a year...for drinks and dinner at each other's house. Not more.

In 1980 I did the television production LE JOUEUR D'ÉCHECS DE MAELZEL, adapted from a story of Edgar Allan Poe, and asked Gabriel to work with me. The reasons were: 1) He was fast and I only had ten days to do the film, 2) I liked Gabriel very much and looked forward to working with him, 3) I knew that the photography would be good and, very importantly 4) his presence on the film guaranteed that the work at the laboratory would be done with great care. Gabriel was a professional and he worked with me as he did with my father or Houston or any other director.

I think that Gabriel was one of the world's great Directors of Photography for black-and-white films. He had his own style. I am not familiar with his color films.

∞ ∞ ∞

THE YOUNG ONE was invited to the Cannes Film Festival. I went along to help with press conferences, organize publicity. At our hotel, my next-door neighbor was Henry Miller and my father and I would dine with him every night. Always smiling, always broke. One evening he came up to me. He was very worried. "Got a hot date tonight.. don't have any money, don'tcha see? What'a my gonna do?" I didn't have any money to lend him...and I really didn't know how to help. The next morning he came down to breakfast, a smile on his face. "So?" I asked. He leaned forward over his croissants and café au lait. "Got a bottle of *vin rouge*, don'tcha see, and a blanket and we went out on the beach!" He leaned back happily. He was in his late sixties at that time. We never did talk about literature.

I like the atmosphere of a gambling casino. Cannes has a casino. My method is: how much would I spend if I went out to dinner, had a few drinks and then went to a movie? I take that amount of money, and only that, and go gambling. That evening I announced to my father (he always went to bed at 8:30) that I was going to the Casino. He blew up. Gambling! I would become an addict to the roulette wheel. My whole future would be ruined by that turning wheel. I assured him that I would not take much money and left him grumbling in his coffee.

By chance I met some friends and, instead of going to the Cannes Casino, we went to what was probably the world's first discotheque, The Whiskey à Gogo, also situated in Cannes (before all night clubs had live orchestras or combos). We drank a few drinks, danced and I was back at the hotel very early.

The next morning at breakfast my father was in a very bad mood. "You didn't go to the Casino last night?" I finally got the story out of him. He had been so worried that I would ruin my life that he had dressed and gone down to the gambling establishment. Since the atmosphere was pleasant, he decided to wait for me. He stood near the roulette wheel. No harm in placing a little bet...and then another. After having lost several hundred dollars he beat a retreat cursing me. I should have gone down to save him.

1961

One Saturday, I went to the Plaza Mayor in Madrid to look at the knife stores which are situated under the Arcos de Cuchilleros. There were a hundred variations on the clasp knife...of bone and steel and ivory and horn...everything a knife lover could wish for. I found one pocket model in the form of a crucifix. The blade would hide away in the main body of the Cross. I showed it to my father that night and he decided to build a scene around it. He took a great close-up of the Cross becoming a knife.

Then the VIRIDIANA scandal exploded. The censors struck. Several years later I went back to the same store. I wanted to buy another crucifix knife. "We've never carried that kind of merchandise!" stated the indignant owner of the store. It was my turn to be indignant. "Whadaya mean! I bought that model in this very store four years ago!" The man looked scared. He motioned me aside and whispered, "O.K., O.K., don't get angry. We received orders from the police to stop producing those knives and throw the others away." One close-up in a film and an industry is penalized.

In Zaragoza, around the Basilica of the Virgen del Pilar, the tourist junk shops sell small metal reproductions of the Virgen, plaster Basilicas and ...ashtrays upon which the Face of the Virgen del Pilar has been faithfully reproduced. An ashtray! Should I destroy an industry? Scene: a man smokes a cigarette. Someone calls him. He looks around. Where can he put out his cigarette? Big close-up of the ashtray. A glowing cigarette butt enters the frame and the Virgen's face is squashed with the burning tobacco. The face is now blackened and filthy...three hundred people are immediately thrown out of work in the ashtray factory.

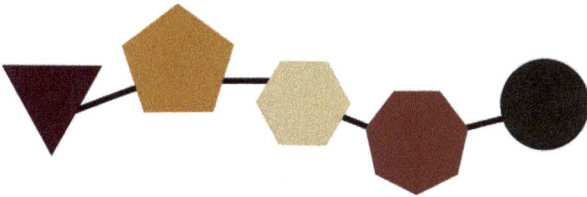

INTERLUDES

WE MUST NOT WEAR OUT THE STONE STEPS

One day, coming home from school, my brother and I found that the front door was closed and locked. We had to go around the driveway, walk by the small garden and finally come in through the kitchen door. We found this strange but were enlightened when our father said, "If we all keep coming in through the front door, we will wear out the front steps of the house."

This did not seem logical, since the steps were made of a very hard stone. For us to wear that material down would take several thousands of us constantly walking in and out during a couple of centuries.

But we did not complain though it was a pain in the— to go all the way around the house to get in.

Sure enough, a week later we found the front door open to passage. No one asked for the reason and life returned to normal.

DESTROYING CHARLIE CHAPLIN'S CHRISTMAS TREE

In 1930, my father was visiting Hollywood. He had a contract to observe filmmaking at the MGM studios.

One day he ran into Charlie Chaplin, who had seen UN CHIEN ANDALOU and they had become friends.

Chaplin said, "Luis, I'm having a Christmas dinner tonight. Why don't you and Eduardo Ugarte come over?[32] There is one condition though. Everyone has to bring a present wrapped in gift paper. We mix and put our presents under the Christmas tree. At midnight we pick a package and everyone has a surprise present."

My father agreed but later, with Ugarte, and after a couple of drinks, they decided that the concept was too bourgeois. Christmas, Bah!

The following plot was worked out. They would bring the presents, place them under the Tree and then, during the dinner, at the height of merriment, my father would pull out a handkerchief and that would be the signal for....

They arrived early, had many drinks and at dinner, when all was well, my father pulled his handkerchief from his pocket and waved it. Then he and Ugarte got up, rushed to the tree, knocked it down, and stomped it and the presents to powder. All was destroyed.

Chaplin, furious, threw them out.

A few days later, Chaplin met my father.

Without mentioning what had happened that night, he invited my father and Ugarte back to his house for a dinner a week

---

[32] Eduardo Ugarte (1901-1955) was a writer, director of films, and anti-Fascist organizer during the Spanish Civil War. He helped Federico García Lorca found the traveling theatre troupe La Barraca. With Luis Buñuel he wrote the screenplay to the film Don Quintin el amargao. He died in exile in Mexico.

later. The two Spaniards were curious about the lack of commentary on their brutal attack.

The evening arrived and they knocked on Chaplin's door. When it was opened, they discovered a large, beautifully decorated Christmas tree in the entrance.

Charlie came up to them, "Luis, Eduardo...please knock the tree down, stomp on it and then we can have a peaceful meal."

They all laughed and went on to have a good supper.

They did not knock down the new Tree.

Brush Your Teeth with Coca Cola

We arrived in Mexico City during the summer of 1964. It was hot yet every afternoon we had cooling rains which lasted about an hour. But it was dangerous. According to my father, the rainwaters would overflow their rivers and creeks and gutters and then mix with the faucet water which was...the drinking water. Water, tropics, broken canals and gutters...this all meant AMEOBAS!

Therefore, until we were organized, Coca Cola would be our main source of drinking water. We could take showers as long as we did not get any water into our mouths. We could not brush our teeth with water....we had to use Coca Cola. There is nothing like Coca Cola and toothpaste. It created a multicoloured foam which would dribble down the side of our faces. Very hard to control. And the mixture of Pepsodent toothpaste and Coke was unforgettable. It was horrible. A company called Electropura said their water had been treated by electric shocks which killed the amoebas. This saved us. Finally we relied on that and boiled water.

SHOOT A BULLET INTO THE PALM OF YOUR HAND

A favorite hobby of my father was to make his own lead bullets and to load them himself. It's a very rigorous process. Each bullet head must have so many ounces of lead; each bullet must have the exact amount of grains of powder.

With too much powder, the bullet tends to rise at first. It all depends how far you are shooting.

Not enough powder, the bullet drops.

Also, a gun barrel has rifling inside it to make the bullet turn as it leaves the barrel. In this manner, the bullet can cut through the air. But the barrel is slightly narrower at the exit. This forces the relatively soft lead to turn better as it bites through the air.

This information is important to understand the following event.

One day my father called me into his room where he was making bullets, and said:

> I think I have solved my problem. I had a dream (when I was younger) about firing a bullet into my hand. But it had no force and only flopped into my palm. Theoretically this is possible. If I put in a large number of grains of powder, the lead bullet will travel miles. But if I put in a very small and precise amount of powder the bullet should just plop into my hand. The one main difficulty is that if I don't put

enough powder into the bullet, the lead missile will stay stuck in the barrel of the gun, not having enough force to overcome the narrowing of the barrel. Too much powder, it'll go through my hand.

He pointed to his desk upon which rested a small pillow, a thick magazine and a sheet of paper.

"According to my calculations, the bullet shouldn't even go through the piece of paper."

He placed the pillow, then the magazine and then the thin piece of paper on the floor, one on top of the other.

He aimed the gun. BOOM!

The bullet went through the paper, the magazine and the pillow, gouging a hole into the wooden floorboards.

He smiled, "I'm glad I didn't shoot it into my hand."

IF YOU TELL MY FRIENDS, I'LL KILL YOU

Hollywood, 1945. The American school system was pretty bad and my parents were so desperate that I get a decent primary education they finally decided to put me in a Catholic school. It was situated on Sunset Boulevard, not too far from my house...a short bus ride. I was ten years old.

All my class was going to take their First Communion; all my friends and acquaintances would take Jesus as their savior.

The day before the great occasion, the priest said to us, "Tomorrow you will be taking Jesus into your mouths. In the morning, before coming to church, I want you to go to your father and get his blessing."

The next morning, dressed in a secondhand white suit (we didn't have enough money for a new suit) I went up to my father, as the priest had instructed, and asked him for his blessing.

He grabbed me by the lapels, lifted me off the ground and snarled, "If you tell any of my friends about this, I'll kill you." He released me and I went off to church, not understanding what had happened.

Years later I understand and find that he was right in doing what he did. I understand and O.K. his action.

Abajo Christo, Viva La Virgen María!

(Down with Christ, Long Live the Virgin Mary!)

In our house in Mexico City we had one room designated as a bar. It had a long Mexican sofa, two easy chairs, several other chairs and small stools. On a crowded day, we could get up to ten people in that room. Usually there were four or five.

One day I came home and found my father mixing dry martinis for a group of four Dominican monks (dressed in dark suits. In Mexico holy men must dress in everyday suits). I commented that it looked like the ending of his film TRISTANA where Fernando Rey is entertaining two priests. My father was furious, "Not at all. They were drinking hot chocolate." And he handed me a Dry Martini.

As the evening, and the Dry martinis wore on, the conversation went towards a theological nature. The monks asked, "Don Luis, what do you think of Jesus Christ?"

"Un *majadero!* A ridiculous man who is trying to fool you, making statements which cannot possibly be followed." He went on and on until the monks did not know what to do.

Then he said, "But the Virgen María!" and then he went on to give a lecture about Mary, her ways, her miracles, her brilliant influence on the world.

Now the priests were totally dazed and finally left, not knowing if they had been with a saint or Satan.

Luis Buñuel's study, Mexico City.

Editor's Note: I was surprised to see a painting of the Virgin Mary in this photo of Luis Buñuel's study. Here's Juan Luis' explanation: "It was given to him as a joke because my father always bad-mouthed Jesus and exalted the Virgin Mary."

Luis Buñuel with dry martini, at his house in Mexico City, 1982.

Recipe for a Dry Martini

To make the **Buñuel Dry Martini,** the correct ingredients are:

1.   A good dry gin.

2.   Noilly Prat...a French dry white wine.

3.   Angostura bitters.

4.   Small pickled onions.

In your cocktail shaker for one person, put in a healthy shot of gin. Add half of a small shot glass of Noilly Prat and a couple small drops of Angostura.

In your Dry Martini glass (which has been kept in the freezing compartment of your ice box), drop in a couple little onions. [You can tell what century I am from by the use of "ice box."]

Then in your cocktail shaker put in a dozen ice cubes and shake violently.

Serve and never have more than two dry martinis.

By the way, the aperitif Maritini must never be used. Much too sweet.

SHOOTING A PISTOL IN HIS LIBRARY

I bought in Cleveland, Ohio an ingenious device. It was made of cast iron, about the size of a big book but weighing 10 kilos. It was hollow and the inside was constructed like the interior of a seashell. It was a bullet trap. You could fire a heavy .38 calibre pistol into it. The bullet would be caught and rendered harmless by the trap.

My father set the object in his library, between books on Surrealism and history. Then, sometimes in the morning or afternoon, when he was bored, he would squeeze off a couple of shots. Sometimes he would miss the bullet trap and some original signed poetry books by García Lorca would receive a few holes.

One late afternoon, Octavio de Alba (who was the editor of *Cinemundial*, a daily film newspaper) had come over for the 6:00 aperitif. My father would question him about the local cinema gossip and usually we had a couple of dry martinis. Then Octavio said, "I bought a new dog yesterday." My father asked, "What did you name him?" Octavio answered, "Juan Negrín." At that moment the phone rang. I picked up the receiver.

"*Bueno?*" I heard a startled voice question, "Juan Luis?" "*Sí, quién habla?*" (Yes, who is this?) There was a pause, then, "Juan Negrín...desde Nueva York! (from New York)"

Now it was our turn to be startled. He continued, "Rosita said that she knew you were all gathered in the bar in Mexico and that I should call to say hello!" We were all dumbstruck and didn't even try to explain this phenomenon.

Rosita Díaz was a Spanish actress married to Juan Negrín, a Spanish refugee surgeon who lived in New York. She was also my brother's godmother...and a bit of a witch...she was also very beautiful.

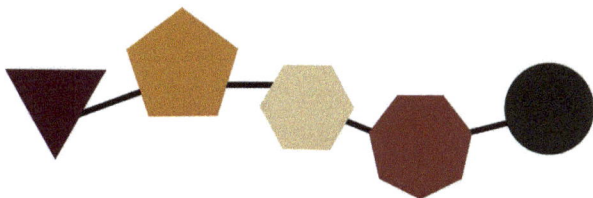

VIRIDIANA

Speaking of Censors, they were not at all happy with the original ending of VIRIDIANA.

Last Scene: Paco Rabal is sitting in his bedroom. The maid, played by Margarita Lozano, has become his mistress and is fussing around the room, cleaning, putting away clothing. Suddenly there is a knock at the door. Viridiana has come to give herself to Rabal. The young man quickly throws out the maid and takes Viridiana into his den. No! shouted the official Censors of the Franco Regime. It's immoral, he is living in sin with one woman, throws her out to live in sin with another. No! A thousand times No!

What if, suggested my father, Rabal has all the doors open and is playing a record. He invites Viridiana in to play a threesome game of cards...the lights are on, all doors open. Fine! said the Censors. Nothing hidden, all very moral. And that is the ending of VIRIDIANA. The three of them playing cards, rock music is blasting out on an old record player. Rabal looks at his cousin with a smile and says, "You know, Viridiana, I knew we'd end up playing cards together."

Ending of *Viridiana*

Knowing full well that if they ever saw the ending there'd be trouble (because between something written and something filmed, there can be a different universe in the intention), we decided to sneak the negative out of Spain. I left one early morning with the negative of VIRIDIANA by train, the Rápido to Barcelona. There I was to meet Domingo Dominguín and his bullfighters (apart from being a film producer, he also had several bullfighters under his tutelage). We loaded the negative into the back of a mini-bus, piled all the *capote* (capes), swords, *trajes de luces* (matadors' suits), etc. on top of them. The matador, his *quadrilla* (the four men who help the matador), Domingo Dominguín and I crossed the Spanish-French border. The Guardia Civil and Customs' men shouted after us, "*Suerte, Torero!!*" (Good luck, matador!).

Juan Luis with bullfighter Pedret in Lunel, France

We got to Lunel, France, and immediately checked into a hotel. Then I spent the next two days watching the preparation for the *corrida*: the choosing of the bulls, visiting friends, the ceremony of dressing the matador. After the *corrida*, I took the night train to Paris with VIRIDIANA safely in my compartment. Once in Paris I turned the negative over to a film laboratory where a positive copy was made. We mixed the soundtrack of the film at the same lab.

VIRIDIANA was invited to Cannes by Favre Le Bret, the Secrétaire Général of the Festival. It was a personal invitation by Le Bret to my father. We all went to Cannes to handle the press, sales and just to generally loaf around and see films. To our surprise, the film won The Palme d'Or. Favre Le Bret called me into his office to announce the news. He would give the prize officially, on stage, to a Spanish minister who happened to be in Cannes at that moment. I argued that the film had been a personal invitation and that it did not represent Spain at all. Someone else should pick up the prize, Sylvia Pinal or Paco Rabal, the actors, Alatriste the producer...anyone, but not an official of the Franquista government. No, no, Le Bret retorted, it's too late. The Minister will pick up the prize.

As soon as the word went out that VIRIDIANA had won the Grand Prix, a certain Padre Fierro, a Spanish priest who was the correspondent of the *Observatore Romano*, official newspaper of the Vatican, yelled SCANDAL! Such an unholy and blasphemous film could not represent Spain. As the word spread through the political strata in Madrid, the Minister who had been so smiling and proud to receive the prize in front of the cheering audience, got immediately sacked. Poor thing. The Sin of Pride.

For many years the film was prohibited in Spain and many tourist agencies got rich outfitting voyages from Barcelona and San Sebastián for shopping tours into France (Perpignan and Biarritz)...and to see VIRIDIANA.

It seems, as the story goes, Franco saw the film ***twice*** and said, "What's all the noise about?"

Luckily for all Spaniards, he died.

∞ ∞ ∞

Years later (1978) we were filming EL OBSCURO OBJETO DEL DESEO (*That Obscure Object of Desire*) in the parking area of the Atocha train station in Madrid. Fernando Rey came up to me, smiling:

> I was in the make-up room getting my hair done when this little man in a dark grey suit walked in. 'Mr. Rey?' he asked. When I nodded, he introduced himself, 'I am Padre Fierro. I was the writer in the *Observatore Romano* who started the scandal on VIRIDIANA. And now I've come to beg your forgiveness.' I stared at him for a full minute and had him thrown out of the room.

Well done! No forgiveness for repentant priests.

GARRET-RUE MAZARINE

When my aunt Georgette died right after the filming of VIRIDIANA, I left her apartment and moved to a maid's mansarded room on the sixth floor. Six flights up with no lift. The toilet was one flight down...with broken window panes. During winter you'd have to think twice before getting out of bed to go to the bathroom at night. Anyway, my room had running cold water which was a luxury. Whenever friends would invite me to dinner, I would ask them, "Do you have a shower?" If the answer was positive, I would arrive half an hour early, with a bag containing clean clothing, soap, shampoo and a towel. If my friends did not have bathrooms, and at that time in Paris very few people did, I would go to the public Bains-Douches on Rue de Buci. For three francs, you could take a shower. The owner of the establishment would shake his finger at you, "Remember, you have five minutes!" As you stepped into your stall, the owner would set an automatic timer. Just about everyone would try to sneak dirty clothes into the shower, to wash them in the hot water. They later could be dried at home. The suspicious owner of the Bains-Douches would stand on a small stool and peer over the door. "Ah, hah," he would shout triumphantly, "Caught you wasting water!" and he would charge you an extra franc. His wife would be peering into the girls' shower stalls for the same reason.

I finally found, at the Bazar de l'Hôtel de Ville, a portable shower set which I installed in my tiny room (the ceiling was so low that my knuckles were always bloody. As I would pull on a sweater over my head, my fists would rub up against the roughly painted ceiling). The shower set had a small gas heater (bottled gas which I lugged up every other week), a large, square plastic bucket in which you would stand, and a rod to hold up the shower curtain. You'd turn on the hot water, soak your body, turn everything off, soap up and then rinse off. Total time: three minutes. If your shower lasted any longer, the plastic bucket would overflow...But what a luxury. A shower every day.

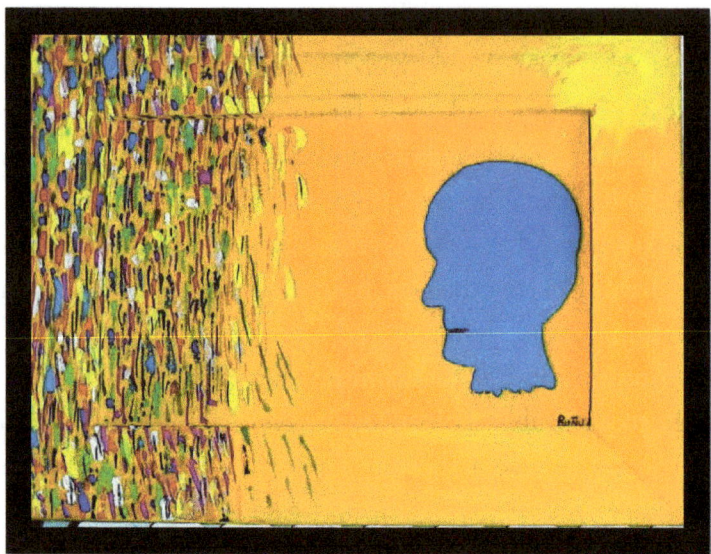

Rain (Juan Luis Buñuel)

LES HALLES

At night, when I couldn't sleep, or if I woke up at 3 or 4 a.m., I would put on a warm sweater and my old leather jacket which I had bought at les Puces-Porte de Clignancourt, and would walk over to Les Halles.

The streets would be lined with huge pyramids of cauliflowers and mountains of lettuce and cases of fruit and the smells of the vegetables and fruit and meat, and the cries of the sellers and buyers. You'd get run down by the "*diables*," little electric carriages used to transport all these goods through the narrow streets. There was a very long and narrow butcher shop where the meat was flung through the air like footballs to the customers who couldn't manage to squeeze into the shop. And an all-night café where, at 5:00 in the morning, a butcher covered with blood would be having his supper and discussing politics with a mink-covered blonde woman who was slurping her *soupe à l'ognion*. Outside the prostitutes would be discussing how to keep warm and still be attractive on a cold and rainy winter's night (woolen underwear and oversized shoes lined with newspaper).

SMUGGLE OUT FLN AGENT

1961

I was working on a film with Jacques Doniol-Valcroze[33] as Second Assistant Director. This was during the French-Algerian conflict. One day, on the set, I was asked to step aside. Three friends had come to see me. There was a problem. The daughter of a well-known French ex-minister, Pierre Cot, one who had helped the Spanish Republic during the Civil War, was in trouble. She had been helping the Algerian F.L.N. (Front de Libération Nationale),[34] smuggling money into France from Switzerland to pay and maintain the different underground groups. A friend had seen her name in the French police Most Wanted Files. Treason was the charge. If they caught her, she might get capital punishment or life imprisonment. She had to be taken out of France quickly. Why me? I asked. Because I was not known by the French police due to the fact that I was legally living in Mexico at the time. All the other friends were under surveillance because of their political tendencies at that time. There was one problem. If we were caught, I could get a heavy prison term. I agreed to help their friend. They gave me instructions.

The next day, at about 6 p.m., I took a cab to an address in Saint-Germain-des-Prés. I asked the driver to wait for me at the

---

[33] Jacques Doniol-Valcroze (1920-1989) was a French actor, screenwriter and director, and co-founder of the *Cahiers du cinéma*.

[34] The National Liberation Front (in French, Front de Libération Nationale, FLN) was established in 1954 in Algeria and continued until 1962 (when the French government signed the Évian Accords which agreed to a cease-fire with the FLN). Full independence from France followed.

corner. I climbed three flights to the given floor and gave a coded knock at the door. Immediately the door was flung open and a young woman came out. We were to pose as lovers. We went out into the street arm-in-arm. I instructed the cab driver to take us to the Gare de Lyon. We were to take the train, an overnight trip, to Menton in southern France. We did not have tickets. Since at that time, FLN terrorists and extreme right-wing agents were blowing up different parts of Paris, the train station was over-run with policemen, in uniform and civilian clothing. We knew the train was to leave at 8 p.m., so we walked around, my arms around her shoulders to hide her face. Suddenly someone thrust train tickets and some money into my jacket pocket. It was a well-known film director who quickly moved away. Two minutes before departure time, we hopped aboard the train for the Côte d'Azur and made our way to a reserved First Class cabin. Once inside, I locked the door. I don't know how she felt, but my heart was thrashing about, like some washing machine that had gone mad, sloshing and slamming about. I thought it was going to blow up.

The train left on schedule. We were almost fainting from the strain. Since I had picked her up, we had not exchanged one word. Finally, after we had been traveling for over an hour, I stood up. My mouth felt like the Sahara desert...well, like the Algerian desert. My first words to her were, "If the police know we're here, then they know we're here. I'm going to get some water. Do you want to come?" She just shook her head. I can't blame her but my thirst was too much.

I left the cabin...we had agreed on a secret knock for her to let me back in. I finally got to the bar wagon and ordered a beer. I had ordered a second one when I suddenly saw him. A grim ugly man looking at me, with beady eyes, studying every movement I made. That was it! The Police...they had followed us! We were through! 30 years in jail! The guillotine! He was an evil-looking bastard. Then he turned away and started to talk to another suspicious-looking character. To get back to our cabin, I had to push between them. As I walked by, would they slam the handcuffs on me? I forced my way through the crowded wagon. Everyone was having an aperitif before dinner. As I passed them, I heard my evil policeman say, "And I sold 170 dozen pairs of stockings in Perpignan in one week!" I almost laughed out loud in relief. A hosiery salesman! I went back and bought bottled water and sandwiches for that evening's supper.

The steward made up the beds, but that night we did not sleep or lie down. We sat up all night. We were scared...even after the salesman incident.

Early the next morning, we got off at Menton, a beautiful little town which I was in no mood to appreciate. We made our way directly to the nearest Bar Tabac by the station and called a number which I had memorized in Paris. A voice answered, and, without even asking my name, asked, "Where are you?" "Corner tabac by the train station!" The person hung up without saying anything else. Within a few minutes, a car roared up and we jumped aboard. We had a fast ride down the coast to Monaco and then down to the marina. There, a large open cockpit motorboat was waiting for us. It was entirely made of varnished wood. A beautiful craft worthy of this adventure...like a bad Hollywood film. Another friend took over. He would pilot the boat. We cast off, heading out to sea...where a storm was blowing up. The wind became stronger, and the waves broke over the bow. Within a few minutes we were drenched. It started to rain. Our pilot headed the boat towards the Italian coast, towards Vintigmiglia. There, on the rocky coast, we scrambled ashore and he was off into the storm, back to France. We clambered up the mountainside until we got to the road. We were in Italy...safe. Now we finally smiled at each other. Then we walked several kilometers into Vintigmiglia to an indicated café where we were met by another friend. I was given another train ticket, Vintigmiglia-Paris and my partner went off immediately to Rome.

The next day I was on the set at 9:30 a.m.

CAMBODIA (1961)

I was offered to do a film as assistant director and language coach (in English) on a French film to be shot in Cambodia...at Angkor Wat.[35] I immediately agreed. Three months filming in the Temples of Angkor! This is what I liked about cinema...being able to go to places where one would never be able to go (unless one is very rich) and to **work** there. Your relationship with the population is completely different. You are not a tourist. You get up at dawn, work hard with their technicians and go to bed tired, after having a couple of beers with your co-workers. They invite you to their houses and you invite their families to dinner.

Angkor Wat

---

[35] The great temple complex of Angkor Wat in northwest Cambodia (Kampuchea) was the historical seat of the Khmer dynasty that ruled between the 8th and 15th centuries. It was "rediscovered" by the French about 150 years ago. Now it is threatened by jungle growth (particularly fig and banyan trees), by earlier periods of war and looting, and by the influx of tourists.

Angkor was more than I could imagine. Temples and pathways and bridges growing out of the dense jungle...wild monkeys in the trees watching us film (they seemed bored). At one moment I caught a three-meter python in the main temple. Instead of a car I used an elephant. They turned out to be very delicate creatures. Their trainers, or *mahouts*, had to be with them all the time, washing them, scratching them, or fussing about if they had a tiny scratch. When we had to cross a river or stream, the elephant would raise his trunk and plunge into the water, at times almost submerged but breathing through his scuba gear. They were kind and friendly creatures.

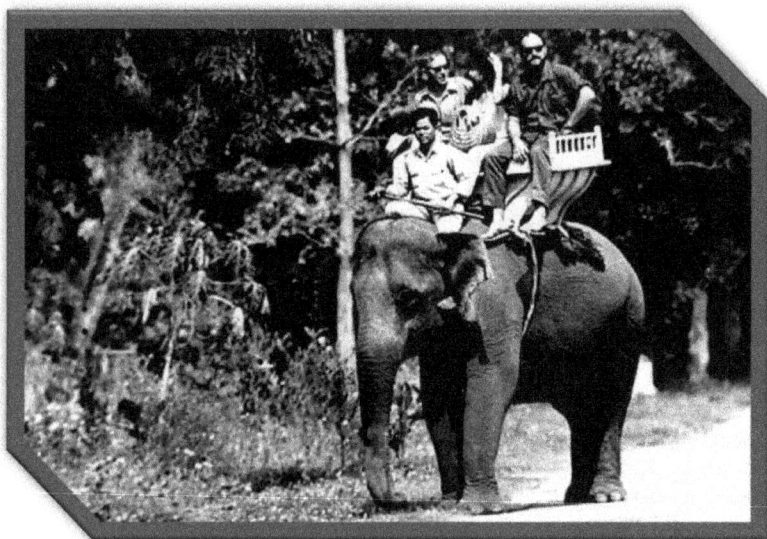

Juan Luis, assistant director, on elephant.

One day, while filming in a banana grove next to a large natural pool, the Cambodian sound engineer yelled out, "Nobody move!" Since it was so hot, everyone wore shorts and rubber flip-flops. When that cry went out, we understood immediately. We had been warned. There were poisonous snakes in the jungle, and one, bright green, was in a striking position just a few inches from Edmond Sechan's (our head cameraman's) bare ankle. We froze. The sound man carefully moved around, a short machete in his hands. Sechan's forehead was covered with great drops of sweat, and it wasn't from the heat. Our man moved in, and with a quick movement, decapitated the beast. Then, picking up the snake with the tip of his machete, or *coup-coup* as they were called, threw the dead creature into the jungle pool. Hardly several seconds had passed than two turtles swam out, one grabbed the snake by the tail, the other by the other end. They started pulling, each one more hungry than the other. We immediately came up with the axiom: The shortest distance between two turtles is a dead snake.

Back in Paris:

Having lent my garret on Rue Mazarine to a friend while I was in Cambodia, I was forced to spend several nights in a cheap hotel near the Odéon metro when I returned. Sixth floor walk-up, no bathroom, naturally, and the sheets were changed every two weeks. One night, at around 2 a.m., I was awakened by the sound of two men slapping a young girl about in the room next door. The walls were paper thin and I could hear every slap and punch. "*Salope!*" (Bitch). Slap. "Ay (tears) *aïe, tu me fais mal!*" (You're hurting me). This went on for a while and I was getting nervous. A Spanish *caballero* (gentleman, *chevalier*) had to intervene. The incident which finally forced me into action was the sound of some small object snapping. "*Ma brosse à dents!* (My toothbrush!)" she yelled. The bastards had broken her toothbrush.

I decided to act. I would scare them. Dressed in only my underwear, I charged out into the dimly lit hallway and, with a roar, I smashed both my fists into their door. The door, dating back to the 16th-century, worm-eaten and half rotten, split in half and fell into their room with a crash and a cloud of dust. Two little *"minables"* (hopeless jerks, cowards) were staring at me, frightened out of their wits. I must say that it was an impressive entrance. They scooted past me and down the staircase, followed by the young lady who muttered, as she passed me, "Why don't you mind your own business...." The other clients came out of their rooms and congratulated me. The Honor of Womankind had been upheld!

SONATAS

In Mexico, I worked as a *stagiare* (intern, lowest assistant) on Bardem's SONATAS. Acting in the film were Fernando Rey, Paco Rabal and María Félix.[36] María couldn't stand Rabal, and neither could Paco stomach María. For the big love scene, María ate onions and Paco smoked big fat cheap cigars. It was a disaster.

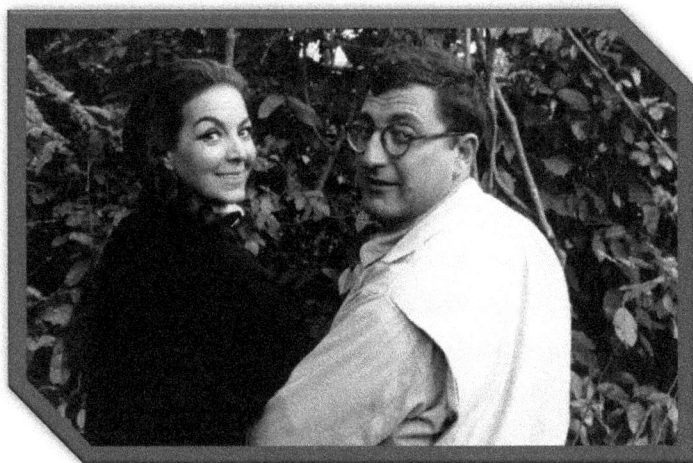

María Félix and director Juan Antonio Bardem

One night María Félix was bored. We were in a small hotel in the jungles near the magnificent pyramids of Tajín, and the incessant rains of a Norte had not let us out in three days. María

---

[36] Mexican actress María Félix was known for her roles in *Doña Barbara* (1943), *Río Escondido* (1947) and for her work with European directors (Jean Renoir, *French Cancan*, 1954, and Luis Buñuel, *Fever Mounts at El Pao*, 1959). Her sutobiography, published in 1993, is entitled *Todas Mis Guerras* (*All My Wars*). She has been celebrated by artists, including Jean Cocteau, Diego Rivera, Octavio Paz and Carlos Fuentes.

decided to invite several of the "amigos" to a game of poker. I was third assistant *stagiare* and my total pay was about $15 a week. We sat around the table and María dealt. I found myself with three kings in my hand. Wonderful luck! I started the bet: "Five pesos!" María smiled. She reached out and dropped a handful of bills on the table. "Ten thousand pesos!" I was furious. "María, I'm just a *stagiare* and what you get for living expenses for one day is ten times my monthly salary. How do you expect me to keep up?" "Juan Luis," she purred, "if you don't know how to play..." I left the game.

TLALOC

He was the Aztec god of Rain. Jerry Lindner had found out where a huge statue or monument to him, carved by that ancient culture, could be found. We took a train (Jerry, John Cole and I), hiked a couple of kilometers, and found him lying on his back in an abandonned quarry. He was about 15 meters long and weighed several tons. That afternoon we had our sandwiches sitting on his stomach.

Picnic on Tlaloc, Aztec god of rain

Years later, the new museum of archeology was opened and he was chosen to guard the entrance to this same museum. The day he arrived in Mexico City, in a huge trailer surrounded by hundreds of people and police, a tremendous thunderstorm broke out over the city. Tlaloc, God of Rain, was coming home. Up Insurgentes, then the turnoff on Reforma to the Museum in Chapûltepec Park where he now stands. There was lighting and gales of wind and the traffic in Mexico City was stopped for several hours.

Tlaloc let every know that he was there.

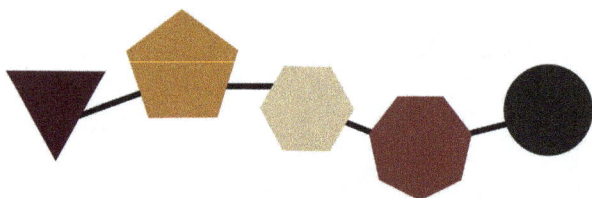

ANTS

I've always been fascinated by ants and have had several happy and not so happy encounters with them.

1) **Cuernavaca 1952:** I was working, during my summer vacations, as a sports instructor in a camp for children of all ages...children mostly from the American colony in the D.F. The instructors and counselors used to sit outside, once the kids were in bed, and have a nightly tequila. Sticking out of the wall was a bare light bulb which used to attract the night insects. And there we would observe Don Pedro, our friendly scorpion. At precisely 10 p.m. he would come out and, with great intelligence, wait for the unsuspecting moths and grasshoppers. He didn't bother anyone and since he did not move from that spot, he was of no danger to the children.

One night he didn't show up. We were worried. So we had another tequila, deciding that we would wait up for him. Then we heard the children screaming...and I suddenly noticed that the floor was starting to move...millions of ants. We rushed to the children's rooms. The floors, ceilings and walls were covered with ants. Some had been dropping down on the kids, biting them. So, we rounded up all the children, and hopping madly to avoid getting bitten, we got them out of the house and on to an ant-free hill near-by.

I approached carefully and saw that there were three armies of ants having a very bloody war...Big red ants against smaller dark ants. The big one would lie in wait behind a rock, jumping out suddenly to rip an opponent apart. If pieces of a leg or thorax were forgotten, the very small black ants would rush out to recuperate the tidbits.

But as long as this war lasted, there was no way we could get back into the house. The Mexican cook and her helpers showed us how to do it. They took powerful and cheap laundry soap, dissolved in buckets, making suds. Then they began swabbing down the whole house. Within half an hour all the ants had disappeared.

2) **Puerto Vallarta:** With Diego, we had been skin diving in the wonderfully warm Pacific Ocean. We flopped up onto an empty beach, white sand, blue water etc etc, to rest. Flowing out of the jungle was a small fresh-water creek. Since it was very hot and the sun seared our skin, we decided to walk up this stream, and thus, under the jungle covering, we could be relieved of the blasting sun. It was cooler, and we washed the sea salt from our parched skin. We wandered up a hundred yards or so from the beach. Suddenly we heard a strange crackling sound and there, before our amazed, and curious, eyes were millions of red ants...Marabunta. They were on the march, eating and ripping into everything that was in their path. And we had the exceptional opportunity to observe them from a very close position...because we were standing in the stream. They couldn't get to us. And so for about an hour we watched and marveled. A stream of creatures, as wide as the creek we were standing in, flowing in the opposite direction, going to the new location of their future home. Not one of these insects led or commanded. Who decided where they were going and where they would stop? Another proof of the non-existence of God.

3) **Cambodia:** We were filming on the eastern coast of Cambodia. It was our lunch break. It was hot and it was humid.

The beach was of white sand, lined with palm trees but sparsely inhabited. I pulled away from the film crew and went to eat my sandwich and drink a cold beer alone. Then I lit up a cigarette and stretched out under a palm tree, dreaming of some cold, rainswept climate...like Paris or Trouville. I finished my smoke and threw the butt behind my shoulder, relaxing, knowing that I still had half an hour before going back to work. When the time came, I decided to check out my cigarette, to see if it was out. Didn't want to start a palm tree forest fire. Much to my surprise, I couldn't find it...but I did see a lot of ants scurrying around. "Wha?" I thought. Then I saw a small pile of sand and the ants very busy around it. With a twig, I broke up the little pile and much to my surprise found...the cigarette butt under it. It was time for a scientific investigation. I relit another cigarette and threw the glowing object next to the ants. They didn't hesitate one instant. Attacking it from the rear, so as not to burn themselves, each ant would grab a grain of sand, climb up the cigarette and throw his tiny grain at the burning end. First one ant, then another and finally hundreds attacked the heat source and within a few minutes had put out the fire. I was amazed. I did it several times and had the same results.

Should we import these ants and spread them out over the dry regions of the earth which are plagued by fires? Could they handle these emergencies, allowing our firefighters the luxury of staying home, drinking beer and watching stupid commercials? Of course, they might also leave them without jobs, thus increasing human misery. Or maybe, they would enter an ecological niche and eat baby lambs, along with putting out fires. I let them be. Don't fool around with nature.

4) **Puerto Ayacucho, Venezuela:** Our film crew was staying in the best hotel in town, which means we had hot running water (No cold water available — the outside temperature hovered

around 45 degrees Centigrade and 98% humidity) and air conditioning from machines that made more noise than World War II jeeps...but we were thankful for little goodies and did not complain.

One night I was awakened by something biting me on the shoulder, and then on the back, and then the legs and feet. I turned on the lights and ran from the room in my underwear. The floors, ceilings and walls were covered by millions of tiny little black ants which bit like a mothafu. The management kindly gave me a new room and went after the little devils with DDT, soap and brooms...but I did not go back to live there.

NICHOLAS RAY, SAMUEL BECKETT

1961 continued

April: My mother arrives back in Paris for the first time since the war and Tante Georgette dies of a cancer three days later. At the funeral, my mother very angry at chef *"croque-mort"* who is very stiff and insists on everyone standing around and formally shaking hands.

> Editor's Note: *croque-mort* is a term used for the mortician's assistant. This slang expression comes from the archaic term *croquer*–to eat or to make disappear.

∞ ∞ ∞

One day, in Madrid, my father asked me to accompany him to have lunch with director Nicholas Ray (*Johnny Guitar, Rebel Without a Cause*). Since my father was a little deaf and Ray only spoke English, I could translate if necessary.

It was an interesting lunch, in which both men spoke of films, books and people. At one moment, Nicolas Ray leaned over and said, "Listen, Buñuel, of all the directors I know, you are the only one who seems to be truly free, does what he wants. What's your secret?" My father drank his wine down. "It's easy," he replied, "I ask for less than $50,000 dollars per film." Ray coughed loudly and changed the subject.

∞ ∞ ∞

I knew a girl in Paris by the name of Constance Abernathy. She was an American architect and had worked with Buckminster

Fuller, but she had been living in Paris for several years. We went out together for a while.

One evening we were sitting in a café, having our evening aperitif when an older man, handsome, with a thick mop of white hair crowding the top of his head, walked up. He was very angry. I did not really catch the conversation, something about her not being somewhere, of not coming to a date they had made. I tried to stay out of it; it was none of my business. He acted like a spiffed lover. Then, with a huff, he walked away. Constance looked sad. She said, "Sammy's very angry. We've broken up and he can't stand it." I found out that "Sammy" was Samuel Becket.

Later she gave me an unsigned print of Rembrandt, an engraving of a sea shell.

1962

February – March: Paris to New York, I take old "France" *paquebot* (mailboat). Stay at Charles'.

April: Mexico, then back to New York.

May: France. Take my father's THE EXTERMINATING ANGEL to Cannes Film Festival.

1963 Summer in Formentera

Death by drowning of Wolfgang (we were sharing a small house with him) while skin diving. Charles finds body of Wolfgang two days later on sea bottom.

September -October-November: Assistant on my father's DIARY OF A CHAMBERMAID (JOURNAL D'UNE FEMME

DE CHAMBRE). Shot in Paris. Meet Jeanne Moreau and Michel Piccoli.

December: Zaragoza. Family fight. Pedro Christián fights husband of Alicita. Everyone cries. Rafael sick from overeating of light Spanish food (*Huevos al salmorejo*). My father thought Rafael was having a heart attack. Wanted to send him back to Mexico. Was very relieved when he found out it was only an upset stomach.

Huevos al Salmorejo: Two eggs, fried with *chorizos* and another type of sausage in one liter of olive oil.

VIVA MARÍA

1965

Director Louis Malle, and Brigitte Bardot.

During the filming of VIVA MARÍA (co-written and directed by Louis Malle), the whole crew lived in a rather bad hotel near Papantla, the vanilla center of Mexico. Since the food was so bad, we would go to a little *palapa* restaurant on the banks of the Tecolutla River. The señora would prepare us fried *mojaritas* (small white fish like tilapia) and fresh hand-made tortillas, and the Dos Equis was cold. She also made great guacamole. One evening, after supper, we were sitting around drinking beer. Under the table the usual pigs and chickens were snuffling around. The sun had set and a light breeze was blowing in from the Gulf of Mexico through the coconut trees. We were slightly high. So we started arm wrestling. I went at it with Brigitte Bardot's boyfriend at that time, Bob Zagury. Nobody was paying much attention when suddenly a heavy hand grasped my shoulder. I turned around. A drunken Mexican General was trying to focus his bloodshot eyes on my face. Next to him, a delicate man in a clean *guayabera* introduced himself.

Editor's Note: A *guayabera* is a white linen men's shirt with close pleats and stripes, worn in Cuba, Mexico, the Phillipines, etc.

"I am Alfredo R..., the mayor of Papantla." A slight odor of vanilla emanated from him.

"*Much gusto,*" (How'dya do?), I mumbled.

He turned to the staggering General. "The is el General Onofrio Millepistolas and he would like to have the honor of doing *el brazo fuerte* with you." The General wanted to arm wrestle me and his bloodshot lidless eyes looked mean.

I stood up. "The honor would be mine."

He hitched his belt up, which contained a holster with a cocked .45 Colt automatic, and sat down. The gun accompanied him. I did not like the idea that he had a piece on him.

We started to arm wrestle. He was smaller than me, hefty and very drunk. It would have been very easy to beat him. BUT, he was a general, a drunk general and carried a .45...so I let him beat me. He then tried to smash my hand against the table. I gently resisted him and he knew that I could control him. He was furious and his face kept getting redder and redder. I was getting more and more frightened.

Then my savior appeared. His chauffeur. A little Private with a meek smile. "*Vénganse, mi general, ya es hora de irnos al*

250

quartel" (Come, sir, it's time to go back to the base). At first the general resisted, but with the help of the Mayor of Papantla, who also was scared of the deteriorating situation, the private got the general into the jeep and away into the tropical night. I felt very relieved...That put a stop to my arm-wrestling career in the state of Veracruz.

∞ ∞ ∞

I travelled around Mexico hunting locations with Volker Schlöndorff, the other assistant on VIVA.[37]

---

[37] Volker Schlöndorff (b. 1939) became a German filmmaker of *The Tin Drum* (1979) and *The Handmaid's Tale* (1990), among other films.

Jeanne Moreau and Brigitte Bardot learning how to shoot.

I taught Brigitte Bardot and Jeanne Moreau to use rifles, pistols and other weapons.

While preparing VIVA MARÍA, Louis Malle, Jeanne Moreau and Brigitte Bardot had taken houses in Cuernavaca. On Sundays we would all go to one of their houses for lunch. Each house had a swimming pool, and we would lounge around, drink Cuba Libres and relax.

One Sunday, we were all at Louis Malle's house. My father and mother had been invited. For a few moments, my father left the bar and walked out by the swimming pool. Brigitte came tripping up to him from her pool-side lair. She was in a very skimpy bikini and her long blond hair was flowing and rippling around her shoulders. A world-famous look. She said to my father, "*Bonjour* (pout) *Monsieur Buñuel.*" My father very courteously shook her hand, and then turned to me, "*Y ésta, quién es?*" (And this one, who is she?). Everybody broke out in laughter but poor Brigitte was taken aback. Finally he recognized her.

The miracle of Bardot. She was not a very good actress, had an awful voice and her first films were not that good. But all she had to do was pout and the world flipped. Strange phenomenon...

∞ ∞ ∞

D.F.:

At home in Mexico, my parents would have friends over about once a month. My mother would make a paella, or a *cocido madrileño* (Madrid stew) or a saurkraut. One day, a large group of older Spaniards came over: the Mantecones, Ernesto García, the Alcorizas...for a *cocido*. My father decided to segregate the sexes. He cut the dining room table in half by using the curtains which separated the living room from the dining room.

Of course all the women complained but the older Spaniards thought that this was perfect. In this way they could argue about the Spanish Civil War without being interrupted by the women's local gossip.

The meal was almost perfect but there was one event which destroyed the harmony of that afternoon. Several of the men defected near the end of the meal. They crossed the barrier to visit the women. Loud cries from behind the curtains insinuated that they were "*Maricones!*" Strange...because the men who went with the women were considered *Maricones*...or homosexuals. The ultimate in "Machismo" was told to me by a Peruvian friend, Estella. She had met a man who was so macho, that going with women indicated that the person was queer! "*Soy macho, y eso de ir con mujeres es cosa de maricones!*" (I'm macho, and being with the women is the stuff of homosexuals!)

SHOOTING AND GUNS

Juan Luis, Club de Tiro Moctezuma, Mexico, ca. 1960.

My father and I belonged to the Club de Tiro Cuautemoc. It was on the old Toluca highway, just a few minutes from the Lomas. We used to get up early and, without having breakfast or drinking coffee or smoking, would drive through the chilly early morning D.F. sun to the Club de Tiro.

It was important to shoot without having had coffee or other stimuli. When you shoot big guns (30.06 Mannlicher) at targets that are two hundred yards away, your arms and eyes have to be rock-steady. No trembling possible. Your heartbeat might deviate your trigger finger, making you miss the target. And coffee or cigarettes make your ticker beat faster

The club was situated on the edge of a *barranca,* a dry valley, which started out relatively narrow...30 meters and opened up to over 200 meters. Targets were situated at different points and you could choose your distances. Some of the targets were metal *guajolotes* (turkeys), inch-thick cast iron bird silhouettes which gave off a loud CLANG when the bullet hit them. Others were mounted on a small motor-driven rail car. The assistant on the other side of the valley would start up the tiny engine and launch the full-sized metal sheep silhouette...and you would bang away until the little *"carito"* got to the end of its run...or until you knocked it over.

On special days, *días de fiesta,* the targets were live turkeys tied to a stake. You paid a certain sum and were allowed five shots at it. If you missed, the club kept the turkey. If you hit it, you could take the bird home to make a *mole.*

Juan Luis, Club de Tiro Moctezuma, ca. 1959

One morning an old man, a little ga-ga...his hands trembling, started shooting while the turkey handler was tying the fowl to the stake. The older man fired, and from a hundred meters away, we saw the bird handler drop out of sight. An official of the club came up and calmly stated, "If you killed that man, you'll have to pay...maybe as much as 3000 pesos..." (at that time about 300 dollars). Luckily, the bullet had killed the turkey in the man's hands and our handler was unhurt.

When we arrived early in the morning, we would use the big guns. After about half an hour of intensive shooting, we would go up to the clubhouse, where a big breakfast of *huevos rancheros*, tortillas and *café con leche* was waiting for us. Then we'd smoke a couple of cigarettes and go on to the second part of our shooting exercises: rapid draw and fire at human silhouettes. The targets, human forms printed on large paper sheets, were stretched out on frames and were set up against a high dirt embankment. We'd stand, with our backs to the enemy and, on command, start to walk away. On a given signal, a stopwatch was punched. You then would draw the .45 automatic, slam a bullet into the chamber as you turned, then quick-fire eight rounds at the vital parts of the paper man. My best was Draw, Turn, Load and Fire eight shots in 3.5 seconds. And all the shots were either in the head or chest area. Mortal wounds. Just a little brag. I've never shot anyone, or been in a gunfight...but deep down inside...it might be interesting.

Back at the house we would strip the guns down and clean them carefully.

ST. MARK'S PLACE

Manhattan

Back in New York, I rented a place at 11 St. Mark's Place, 8th street between 2nd and 3rd Avenues in the East Village. It was a "railroad" apartment. The entrance was through the kitchen which contained a stove, frig, bathtub, and cockroaches. Usually the bathtub was covered by a heavy piece of plywood and would double as a work surface for the kitchen. On the left, and overlooking the back alley, was the bedroom and a small toilet. On the right, overlooking St. Mark's Place was the living room. All the furniture was taken from the streets on Wednesday nights when the heavy garbage was thrown out. Chairs, tables, bedframes, racks, drawers...what you needed could be found easily on the sidewalks and some of the material was of good quality. Rafael, who lived downstairs, picked up a Tiffany bronze antique lamp and a new Hi-Fi record player with 50 new classical discs. Your only purchase would be the mattress, naturally.

Eventually I bought a secondhand air conditioner for the horribly moist 40 degrees (104 degrees farenheit) nights of July and August.

Tenants of 11 St. Marks Place included: Charles Fitzgerald, the two Buñuel brothers, and 30 Puerto Ricans. We were living in a regular WEST SIDE STORY "*ambiente*" (atmosphere). When I first moved in, the Latinos were a little unfriendly, thinking we were Anglos...so I waited, didn't say anything...and one night four of them cornered me in the grim, gray, one-bulb lit garbage-strewn corridor. They had been drinking. They started pushing me around, speaking poor English, picking a fight. I waited and when things looked a little unhealthy for me, I

259

let them have it in Spanish. I claimed that their great grandmothers were whores on the waterfront, that their *puta madres* went to bed with all the policemen in New York and the Bronx, their sisters etc., etc. The more I insulted them in Spanish, the wider they grinned...soon we were all laughing and we went off and had a couple of beers. No more trouble in 11 St. Marks.

There were also some interesting characters. Ángelo was our short-order thief. He'd come around asking, "What can I get you?" Charles would say, "A rug of about 20 by 30 feet..." "What color?" Charles would think..."Dark red."

Three days later he'd have the rug. Where did it come from? Ángelo would smile, "An uptown hotel."

Then one day he walked in and offered us some brand-new classical records...at 50 cents apiece. "How many do you have?" "About 50,000." Ángelo had ripped off a truck from some big record company.

Once he disappeared for a year. Finally he appeared, very thin, very pale...weak. "What happened?" we asked. He had been walking with some black chic near Washington Square and a jealous boyfriend had walked up behind him and stuck a knife **through** him. He had been in the hospital for a long time. And then he disappeared forever.

∞ ∞ ∞

There was Red. He was a pimp but also took care of Charles' garbage. He called Charles "Teach" because he respected Charles and knew that once he had been a teacher in a language school.

260

He would let himself into Charles' apartment in the middle of the night while he was asleep and announce that the garbage cans in the street had been kicked over. Charles would yell at him, "Not at three in the morning!" "Don't worry, Teach, I'll clean it all up." We all had a hard time getting back to sleep after that.

Red would also offer us first choice on the new and untrained prostitutes who came in from the provinces. "Hey, Teach, got some new girls in...brand new...you can try them out for free..they're fresh...."We would thank him but decline the offer. He never understood why we didn't accept.

Red's brother, on the other hand, was a very straight bookkeeper and took care of Charles' income tax forms for many years.

∞ ∞ ∞

Charles had his store across the street. It had been an old Hungarian Restaurant. At first, since he had bought the whole building, he kept it intact for parties. We would either cook ourselves or bring in a guest cook who would prepare dinner for six to forty people, depending on the occasion. If we had a large crowd, we would make a large circle with all the tables, like covered wagons stationing themselves in a wide circle to protect themselves against an Indian attack. Usually, everyone would come dressed up and for a while we would be very formal. But the wine and pot would take hold and then strange things would happen. Once we had forgotten to buy paper napkins. The meal was to be spaghetti with Bolognese sauce. We needed some form of napkins. So we went to the stock room of the restaurant and found a huge roll towel used in automatic distributors in public toilets. It was clean, wide, and the cloth was white and impeccable. So we sat in our large circle, about 40 guests, and passed the cloth around...a huge circular napkin which was on everyone's lap. We started to eat. At first nothing happened. Then one person lifted up his part of the hand towel to wipe his mouth, thus pulling the cloth towards him. Someone on the other side of the room felt the cloth being pulled away, so he pulled back. Another guest, ten chairs away, felt the cloth being pulled away, so he pulled. Within seconds a huge Tug o' War was in progress, twenty persons to each side, tables turned over, spaghetti and sauce spilling over the antagonists. The room was destroyed in a matter of minutes.

Another time, there were about 25 guests. For a while everything went well. The meal was almost over and we were starting dessert. Charles put on a record...The drums of Calanda. Pretty soon everyone started to keep time with the rhythm by beating on the table. Charles turned up the volume of his powerful hi-fi. Then someone grabbed an orange and used it as a drumstick, beating the table. Another person grabbed a melon, and then a cauliflower, and apples and fruits and vegetables. The rhythm got louder and more powerful. By the time the record was over the room was in shambles.

Note: How to spot a boiled egg from a raw one. Spin them. The boiled one spins with ease. The raw one starts to spin and then slows down and stops.

Around the corner, on 7th Street, was MacSorley's Tavern. Built in the 1880's, it was the typical old New York, sawdust on the floor, beer tavern. It was a man's world. In other words, women were never allowed to come into the place. You'd go in there to drink beer and have onion and mustard sandwiches. During the Sixties, when the Women's Liberation movement was in full swing, a group of women decided to invade the tavern, to break into the most holy of men's sanctuaries. They announced the date of the invasion. It was to be on a Saturday night.

The barkeepers were not fazed. They announced that the girls could have all the beer they could drink...free. Dozens of women showed up and many gallons of beer went down their thirsty throats. But all that goes up must come down...and they found that the sit-down toilets were out of order...only the stand-up ones worked. It was many years before women came back to McSorley's Tavern. But now it is fully integrated and the toilets work properly.

1964

January: New York

February to August: Mexico City- Start working with wires. Tamayo sees them, gives suggestions, says they should be exposed. In June, first exposition of sculptures at the Galería Diana. Trip to Acapulco.

1965

April: Film CALANDA with Jacques Renoir[38] as cameraman. Jean Louis Bertucceli as sound engineer.

October:

Assistant to Louis Malle on LE VOLEUR*(The Thief of Paris)* with Jean-Paul Belmondo as a professional thief, and Geneviève Bujold as his cousin Charlotte.

1967

January to October: Mexico. Assistant to Henri Verneuil on THE GUNS OF SAN SEBASTIAN with Anthony Quinn and Charles Bronson.

---

[38] Jacques Renoir is the son of Claude Renoir (director of photography), who was himself the son of Pierre Renoir (director Jean Renoir's brother). He is the great-grandson of the painter Auguste Renoir.

Calanda, 1967

Juan Luis at charity bullfight during filming of
The Guns of San Sebastian.

Editor's Note: Juan Luis told me that the viewers laughed and encouraged him, shouting "*Él es más grande que el toro*" (He's bigger than the bull!). Although Anthony Quinn did the promenade in the bullring, he didn't even try to face a small bull.

5 October: Juliette Clothilde is born in Mexico City. I wasn't present when she was born because I had gone home to get a camera. She came quickly. IT WOULD CHANGE MY LIFE.

MALRAUX IN MEXICO

1967

General Charles de Gaulle came to Mexico on a state visit. The 14th of July, Bastille Day, was celebrated by an invitation to all French citizens who lived in the D.F. We were invited to meet the General and have free access to the champagne cellar at the Embassy. Meet De Gaulle and all the champagne you could drink...this was an interesting situation...especially since the General had just given his "*Mano en la mano*" (hand in hand) speech in Spanish from the Presidential balcony situated in the Palace on the Zócalo. No American head of state had ever had that honor. Tens of thousands of Mexicans had cheered him. Mexico had always liked France, especially since it was the only foreign country that it had beaten and driven away from its shores (Maximilian fiasco). And France liked Mexico.

Anyway, the American embassy was seething over the General's success. Usually, the American manner was to speak in a condescending manner to the poor dumb Indians (Big Brother will give you cookies if you're good, etc. ad infinitum ad absurdum ad nauseum). De Gaulle had treated them like equals.

So I arrived at the embassy a little early to get a good place at the bar (though that wasn't necessary, because there was enough champagne to float a *chinampa* from Xochimilco [a flat-bottomed boat pulled by a pole]). De Gaulle and his entourage arrived. He had visited the Pyramids of Teotihuacán that morning and his face, large nose and bald head were a bright red. He had refused (pride) to wear a hat and the high altitude Mexican sun had taken its toll.

Everyone shook hands and I started to talk to a very powerful but pleasant Frenchman. He was as wide as he was tall. Mr. Five by Five. His name was Monsieur Puissant. He was in charge of the General's bodyguards and safety. He informed me that the big problem on this trip had been to get a bed long enough for De Gaulle's (well over 1 meter 90) stay at the Embassy residence. We were quietly getting the champagne bubbles into our bloodstream when a friend from the Cultural Office ran up and pulled me away. "Quick, come with me. Malraux is alone and everyone is scared to speak with him." And suddenly I was placed in front of the Minister of Culture...and abandoned.

What does one say to André Malraux? I signaled a waiter to bring over a couple of glasses of bubbly and asked, "Monsieur Malraux, isn't it boring to go to all these cocktails and ceremonies?" He sighed and downed his champagne. "If only you knew..." I waved for two more glasses. We moved out of the sun into an open room which overlooked the Embassy gardens. My second question, "What do you think of Mexico?" And those were the last words I spoke for the next hour and a half. "Well, young man, Mexico is..." And he gave me a course in Mexican history, the Spanish conquest, the Aztec and Mayan cultures, the Spanish Civil War, the Incas, French cooking, Medieval paintings, Chinese calligraphy and why the U.S. did not like France...different subjects, but all were skillfully intertwined as he flowed from one to another. I just stood there and listened. What else.

Then we had to leave.

MAY 1968 PARIS – MEXICO

1968

    May '68. One event. The French Army was going to enter Paris to quell the student uprising, or so the rumor said. Everyone at the **États Généraux du Cinéma** got very excited. Louis Malle and Doniol-Valcroze, knowing that I had a .22 caliber pistol in my house, ordered me to set up a barricade near the Parc Montsouris. I raised an obvious question: I alone, with a .22 pistol, was to hold off the French Army? Would Louis Malle and Doniol-Valcroze be with me? No, they answered, they had to take care of political affairs.

May '68 protests: Directors Alain Resnais, Louis Malle (with beard).
(From documentary footage by Juan Luis.)

I did not set up a barricade at the Parc Montsouris. I still wonder what effect a .22 caliber pistol would have on a French Army tank. And what the French Army would have thought of this idiot shooting at them and yelling *"Vive la Révolution!"* (Long Live the Revolution!). I would have been the only person killed by a tank in 1968.

There were groups of students running through the streets, little red books in their hands, chanting, "Mao! Mao! Mao!"

États Généraux du Cinéma (The general meeting of people involved with the cinema): All the technicians of the cinema industry had organized to film the events, but also to put in question the way films were made and produced. The meetings were boring and longwinded. As you stood up to speak, you'd have to give your profession. "Dupont, cameraman!" or "Sánchez, *maquillage!*" (makeup). Well, during these meetings, everyone was suddenly a *"metteur en scène"* or *"réalisateur"* (film director).

Not being able to keep my eyes open during the interminable discussions, I chose to be on the Defense Squad. In other words, we were to patrol the streets around the meeting hall to protect our assembly against an attack from the Fascists.

We were never that lucky. They never attacked.

We had all the virgin film (which was very little) available plus few cameras. I was in charge of giving out film. One day a group of pseudo-Maoists came in and demanded that I give some film to a butcher so he could make his revolutionary film. I asked if he had any training with a camera. He did not but was sure that he could do his film. I then asked him, if I gave him film and a camera, would he let me go to his butcher shop and let me cut up his meat? He refused...so I refused to give him the equipment. They all accused me of being a tool of the Capitalists.

But there were some great moments, especially in the Odéon Theater where everyone could speak. The sessions lasted 24 hours and it was fascinating to hear a baker airing his views, and then arguing with a banker.

At one moment, the banker asked the assembly why they thought they could win this battle. There was a silence. A young man in the third balcony stood up, long blond hair waving as he pointed to the banker, his face deformed with hate. "We're going to win," he shouted, "because we are pure!"

Police retaliation

The last big "*manif*" (protest) was at the Gare de Lyon. The Etats Genereaux du Cinema met at the Gare and before us, all the way to Bastille, were 100,000 people. We were at the end of the tail. Everybody chanted, cheered, gave speeches and then the "*mot d'ordre*" (instructions of the day) went out, "Everyone go home! Keep calm!" So we turned around, marching back. With a group of film technicians, I headed for the Left Bank. But as we reached the bridge, our way was barred by hundreds of CRS (French riot control police). They would not let us by. I asked politely if we could please go home. Their answer, "*Ta gueule!*" (Shut up!). I had my little 8mm camera and started filming the triple row of CRS guarding the access to the bridge. And then they charged behind me. Since my eye was blocked by the camera, I did not see them and was the first person hit by a riot that went on for three days and nights. Even the Bourse de Paris was set alight. I have some of this on film.

∞ ∞ ∞

That summer, when we got to Mexico after Paris' May '68, the student movement was in full swing. The Universidad campus was aflame with banners and graffiti. I took Juliette there for her first political meeting. The next day I went to a big meeting in the Zócalo. Tens of thousands of people, bearing torches and candles, demanding the PRI get out, demanding a political liberalization. The next manifestation was to be held in the Plaza de Tres Culturas, a site in the D.F. which, around a certain plaza, had Aztec ruins, colonial churches and modern architecture...hence,

Tres Culturas. I was going to go with Luis Alcoriza.[39] We were going to take cameras and film the event. Then, the night before, Luis got a phone call. "We understand that you and Juan Buñuel are going to film the manifestation at the Plaza. It would be a good idea that you do not go." The voice was official and menacing. They had us marked. We did not go. Ángel Bilbatúa,[40] who was the official presidential cameraman, went...and almost lost his life. He was filming from the sixth floor of a modern building when the shooting began. The army and police opened fire on the crowded demonstrators point blank. Thousands were killed. Bilbatúa immediately threw himself down and hid his camera. Another cameraman kept filming and called him a coward and then a bullet slammed into him and he fell, spraying blood and calling to Bilbatúa to save his life but the firing was so heavy that Ángel could not move and pretty soon the other cameraman was quiet. Then some Red Cross workers came to pull him away.

∞ ∞ ∞

The Secretaria de Cultura tried to organize an official *Salón de Pintura y Escultura* (Salon of Painting and Sculpture). We all refused and decided to create the Salón de los Independientes, a way to show our discord with the Mexican government and what it stood for. Our Salón lasted for three years.

---

[39] Luis Alcoriza (1918-1992) was a Mexican screenwriter, film director and actor. With Luis Buñel, he wrote the screenplays for El gran calatrava, Los olvidados, El Bruto (1953), and ÉL (This Strange Passion, 1953).

[40] Ángel Bilbatúa was also the cameraman of the documentary Buñuel (1984), directed by Rafael Cortés, and of Tiempo de lobos (1985), among other films.

> **NOTE: Always carry a Swiss Army knife.**

Camping trip to Grutas de Cacahuamilpa, Estado de Morelos. Trip organized by Manuel Felguérez[41] About thirty painters, sculptors and filmmakers, all belonging to the Salón de Independientes, went on an overnight camping trip into the interior of the *grutas* (grottos). When we got to the entrance (itself big enough to fit Notre Dame), we stripped down to bathing suits. All our food was stashed in waterproof bags, as were our sleeping bags and dry clothes. We went about five kilometers into the interior of the earth, crossing the underground river about five times. At one moment there was no more light, so we had to use flashlights. Some of the children were scared.

We finally reached an immense cavern where a large white sand beach was located. There we set up camp. Lilia Carillo, wife of Manuel Felguérez, disappeared to re-emerge almost instantly in a silk lounging suit and a long cigarette holder. She lay back on a rock, smoking and sipping tequila. A bar and a kitchen were set up, fires built and soon we had a magnificent and varied supper. At one moment I shined my flashlight to the roof of the cavern, several hundred feet above us and noticed that there were tree trunks jammed into outjutting crags. This meant that during the

---

[41] Manuel Felguérez (b. 1928) is a Mexican abstract artist (painting and sculpture), and a noted teacher.

rainy season, this chamber would be full of murderous and swirling waters. Luckily this was not the rainy season.

The next day after breakfast, we wended our way out into, as one of the children said, the "real world." There, by the banks of the river we set up another camp for lunch, swimming and sunning ourselves. After many tequilas and cold beers, we decided to have our own Olympics: the 3-Meter Dash, the 40-Centimeter Broad Jump and the 6-Meter Marathon. Nobody made it.

Los Novios – The Lovers (Juan Luis Buñuel)
in Salón de los Independientes.

PANAMA

Ángel Bilbatúa asked me to help him on a documentary he was doing for General Omar Torrijos in Panama. We flew down on Air Panama and spent a few days in Panama City with Torrijos. Then we flew in his private Guardia Nacional helicopter down into the jungle to film some tribal people.

As we flew over the densely packed forest, Ángel said that he suddenly needed a woman. He asked the helicopter pilot if he knew of a nearby village where he could satisfy his animal cravings. The pilot jammed the aircraft into a tight curve and in a few minutes we landed on the square of a small town. There, besides a bar, was a house of ill repute. Ángel went in and the rest of us went to have a cold beer, which was a welcomed event. It was very hot and humid.

Relaxed, Ángel came out a few minutes later and we took off, the *putas* (whores) of the region laughing and waving us on.

About half an hour later we flew over a tiny village which was half hidden in the jungle of the Darien region. Upon seeing us the Indians ran into their thatched huts. They probably thought, "White man comes in bird of iron and we must hide!" All to the contrary. When we landed they all rushed out, painted from head to foot...they had put on their makeup and were now ready to give us a party, The drums were brought out and soon we were all dancing about. Then the bugs started biting. The so-called savages had their painted bodies...the paint was a powerful insect repellent...and we, the "men in the bird of steel," were bitten to pieces.

We got back to Panama City and played dominos in some sleezy bar for a couple of days. The next three nights were spent with Torrijos, talking and drinking scotch. This was his only luxury (it may have included a couple of women on the side). His house was a small one-storied bungalow with a primary air conditioning system. He had organized his country as well as could be expected, given the lack of money in their treasury, and had the Guardia Nacional (Army) out working, building schools (this I saw from our helicopter trip over different regions) and hospitals. A lot of other countries could take example instead of having their armies practicing ways of slaughtering people.

One night I heard Bilbatúa warning Torrijos about one of his officers, el "Cacarizo" (one whose face had been marked by smallpox) Noriega who was very corrupt and power-hungry. Torrijos said that he was aware of this fact and that he kept him under control. Not quite. Several months later, Torrijos' airplane was blown apart, killing him and his officers. Noriega took over Panama. At that time Noriega was working for the C.I.A. and the head of that sinister organization was George Bush...who later became President of the United States. As head of the C.I.A, he had organized the transport and sale of drugs, the money being used to maintain Right-wing guerrilla actions against governments who were against United States policies in Latin America...like Nicaragua.

Talking about Bush, a friend of mine was doing a documentary on the Mexican petroleum industry. He came upon two very clean and protected oil wells near Poza Rica, Veracruz. He asked why the wells were so neat and in good shape. At first nobody wanted to answer...so he greased a few palms. The answer: They belonged to the George Bush family. Mexican petroleum was nationalized in 1938. What was the Bush family doing owning something that belonged to the Mexican people?

Gulf War...started by Bush. His friend and second -in-chief when George had been head of the C.I.A was "President Directeur Generale" of a large oil company in Kuwait. Also his son was president of another company in Kuwait.

And the Silverado Saving Bank scandal where billions of dollars mysteriously disappeared. The money was never found. The American taxpayer is going to have to foot the bill for many years to come. The president of that bank was one of Bush's sons.

Hmmmm...interesting family.

(written in **1999**): Bush's sons are now governors of Texas and Florida. One might be a candidate for the next presidential elections of the United States. Interesting.

Panama with General Torrijo's helicopter (Juan Luis on right)

BLACK PANTHERS

BLACK POWER Documentary on the Black Power movement in New York. At first I could not make contact with the Black Panthers because they thought I might be from the police or a white racist organization. They just didn't trust me. Finally I met a French girl who was married to a black guy...and through her, I convinced them that I wasn't a cop. I managed to get into the Black Panther organization, went to their political meetings in Long Island and Manhattan, heard speeches by Eldridge Cleaver.

Eldridge Cleaver

Filmed Sun Ra (Musician) in Charles' building. I toured Harlem with two Black Panther body guards. Some places were so rough that they were scared to be seen with me. We'd stop for lunch and the Panthers would tell me to stay in the car while they went to get our daily hot dog or hamburger.

Two members of Black Panthers

The documentary started on Wall Street with a close-up of the huge George Washington statue and the following text: "George Washington, father of a country which preached liberty and equality for all...he himself had several hundred black slaves." The film was never seen. De Gaulle, who was anti-American, was voted out in France. In the U.S., Nixon was voted in ...the two new governments kissed and made up. Since my film was slightly anti-American, no one ever saw it. The film was never shown in France either.

April: In Buenos Aires for UNESCO reunion of documentary filmmakers from Latin America, France, Canada, Czechoslavakia, and England.

WILLARD, CALDER AND MIRÓ

1969 New York

I had a sculpture exposition that year at the Willard Gallery and several blocks up, on Madison (Willard was on 82nd and Madison Avenue), Man Ray was also showing. When things were slow in my gallery, I would rush up to sit and talk with Man. Once he sat back and smiled. "When we first exhibited, back in the late twenties, and even into the thirties, we were sure of one thing...we would **never** sell anything!"

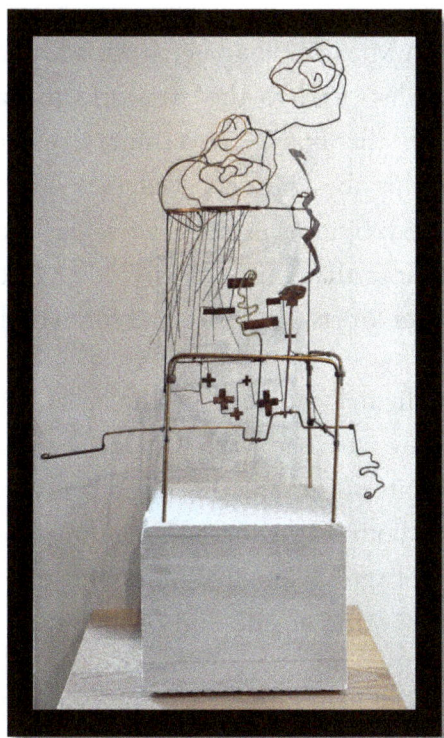

"Thunderstorm" bronze sculpture (Juan Luis Buñuel)

Usually, when one had an expo at the Willard Gallery, for lunch Marion Willard would toss a fresh salad, put some nice cheeses on a board and open a bottle of wine. Friends would drop in and we had many pleasant meals in this manner. One day Sandy Calder was there and we were waiting for Joan Miró to join us. Finally Joan arrived and he told us the following story:

> He had been crossing Central Park on foot on the way to the gallery. Suddenly he heard a loud Catalan voice call out, 'Joan!' He turned. Dalí was stepping out of a black limousine and waving his hands, his moustache upright. Miró stared at him for an instant, and then, without a word, turned and left him standing there.

It had been Miró who had befriended Dalí and introduced him to the Surrealists and to the art world in Paris...but Dalí's comportment with the Franco government, especially after the assassination of his best friend Federico García Lorca, his publicity-hungry exhibitionism, his *"payasadas"* (clowning), had destroyed any feelings that Miró, or any other of the Republican Spaniards and other artists, had once had for Salvador Dalí.

During a lighter moment of the meal, Miró told us of another lunch they had had with Calder several weeks before. Sandy had a habit of settling in his chair, after we all had consumed several bottles of wine and gently falling asleep...or so we thought. There were about five of us and the meal was over. Sandy was gently snoring at one end of the table. The friends all looked at each other, and in a very low whisper, decided to leave the establishment, telling the waiter that the sleeping Calder would pay the entire bill. As they carefully pulled away from the table, Sandy, without opening his eyes, rumbled out, "My part of the bill was $4.95! "

SACHÉ

Louisa and Sandy Calder always invited us to their house in Saché, Indre-et-Loire. At first he had a house down by the river which was called La Maison de François Premier...because, so the legend goes, François I stayed there. The front of the house was of stone, brick and plaster. It was built against the hill. When you walked inside, the back wall was made of living rock. There was a huge chimney in the one big room which served as living room, dining room and kitchen. Most of the implements in the large counter had been made by Sandy. Many times, as I sat watching him work in the studio next to the house, Louisa would call out,"Sandy, please make a grill that will hold 14 lamb chops." He would drop the sculpture he was doing and make a beautiful and functional grill.

Next to the house, and dug into the cliff, was a deep *cave a vin* (wine cellar). It had three chambers, a little like a three-leafed clover. Every year he would order hundreds of bottles of the good wine from the Touraine, have them put down in these cellars, and then forget about them. There were thousands of bottles. Well, it wasn't really forgotten. I would go in, pick five or six bottles at random, and that would be our day's supply. Once we drank so much that at supper we tried to pour small tops into the empty wine bottles. We'd start them spinning, pick them up with a large soup spoon and then try to fit them into the bottle as they spun.

Once we made a big *mole poblano* (meat or turkey fricasee with a sauce of chili and bitter chocolate) with Miguel and Carola Condé doing the cooking.[42] It was a nice feast.

Sandy had a big studio next to the house where he made his smaller mobiles. Across the road, he had a very small stone hut where he made his gouaches...it was called the Gouache Room.

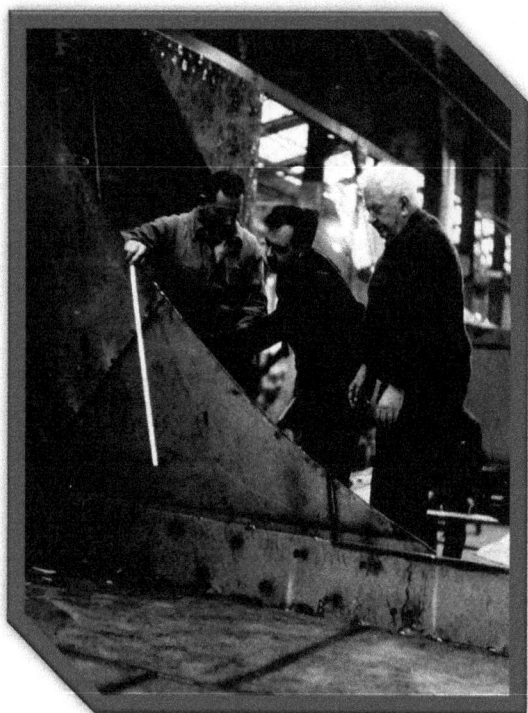

Calder at foundry.

At times I would drive him to the Etablisements Biémont in Tours where he had his big stabiles built. Usually we would go

---

[42] Miguel Condé (b. 1939) is a Mexican figurative painter and engraver. Exhibitions of his work have been held in Barcelona, Bilbao, and the Cleveland Museum of Art, among other sites.

in after lunch, after having finished off a couple of bottles of red wine. I would drive in the general direction of Tours and Sandy would immediately fall asleep...or so I thought. I would come to a fork in the road and have no idea where to go. "Take the right road," he would rumble. How he did it, I swear I don't know. He never opened his eyes.

His Stabiles were made in this fashion: first he would make a small model, maybe a foot high. Then they would make a larger model, six to ten feet high and try it out in a wind tunnel. This was of utmost importance. Imagine one of his big 20-meter Stabiles being brought down by a high wind in, for example, Canada. The engineers who did these tests told me that Sandy was never wrong and his sculptures were conceived to withstand the highest winds.

Because of the humidity, the Calders built a larger house up on the rim of the valley and the François Premier was used for friends. Once I decided to do a little sweeping up, Usually there were large spider nests around the windows, and I supposed, under the bed. So I pushed a broom under the bed and pulled out a dusty painting...a small Mondrian of the first period.

Sandy said, "Oh yeah, I put that under there a few years ago." I also found a Max Ernst.

LEONOR

PARIS

I presented the script of my feature film LEONOR to United Artists France. One producer, Sol Cooper, liked it but said it had to get the o.k. from the top man in Paris, Sandy Whitelaw. A date was set for a meeting. I walked into a fairly large office in the Paris United Artists building. Sandy Whitelaw, tall, elegant, cold, looked me up and down. He said, and these were his words, "If you want to make this film you have to fuck your mother." I did not quite understand what he meant. He repeated himself, "You have to fuck your mother!" I stood up, excused myself and walked out of the room. LEONOR was not going to be made by United Artists.

A year later, Oscar Dansigers, who had gotten me my original job with Orson Welles, liked my script and said that he might be able to get it through at the annual United Artists meeting in Rome. I was quite happy. He came back from Rome crestfallen. "What did you do to Sandy Whitelaw? He hates you!" Nothing...I had never even seen the man before my first meeting. Again the LEONOR project fell to earth.

The years passed. Sandy Whitelaw left United Artists as a producer and established himself as an independent film director. He had artistic pretensions.

In the meantime, the new producer at United Artists, Sol Cooper, liked my first feature film AU RENDEZ-VOUS DE LA MORT JOYEUSE (At the Meeting with Joyous Death) and produced it. It won several international prizes.

Actress Yasmine Dahm, *At the Meeting With Joyous Death,* 1973.

Bronze snail sculpture (Juan Luis Buñuel)

When you win international prizes, you are usually asked, at different times, to become a member of different film festival juries.

I was asked to become the member of a jury on a small international film festival. What joy, when I arrived at the festival hall, to see the list of the films in competition, and to find Sandy Whitelaw's celluloid masterpiece inscribed. And even greater was my joy when I met Sandy on the sidewalk in front of the festival palace. Just the look on his face as he recognized me made up for all the years I had lost because of him. Revenge is a delicious dish and it must be eaten **cold**. When the time came for the voting, I did not even have to open my mouth. Sandy's film was stupid and pretentious. The rest of the jury did not want to spend one minute discussing it. Neither did I.

I should have walked up to Sandy and said, "Now **you** go fuck your mother!"...but I didn't. A gentleman does not do such things. But I knew damned well that is what he thought I was thinking.

∞ ∞ ∞

Madrid—New Year's party at Torre de Madrid with Father, Tías Conchita and Margarita, and with Pedro Christián. Aunts were going to cook a meal in my father's apartment but everyone was very nervous. They got together a wonderful meal. We sat down to eat at 9 p.m. By 9:20 we had finished, and the two aunts had washed the dishes and pots and cleaned up by 9:35. Big problem. What were we to do until midnight? Finally sat around and drank and told stories.

BILBAO FILM FESTIVAL

1970 Paris:

One day, Mary Meerson of the Cinémathèque Française called me. "Jean Louis," she barked into the phone. "You leave in one hour. You'll be representing La Cinémathèque Française and form part of the jury at the Bilbao Short Film Festival!" "Oui, Marie!" I answered. One obeyed Mary Meerson. Three hours later I was in Bilbao. The other members of the jury were a little man from Poland, a Spanish director, Emma Cohen[43], a Spanish actress (who later had a role in LA FEMME AUX BOTTES ROUGES/ *The Woman with Red Boots*), and Richard Lester, an American director who lived in England and had done the Beatles' first film, A HARD DAY'S NIGHT.

All went along without incident, we saw many films and had many great meals, official and in *tascas* (popular low-priced restaurants in Spain).

And suddenly the news came out. Several men were to be executed by the Franco government. They were to be put to death by the *garrote vil* (execution by strangulation using a metal ring around the neck). International opinion demanded leniency. We on the jury had a special meeting. Richard Lester and I wrote up a strong statement which we wanted the jury of the festival to sign as a form of protest. The Spanish director said, "Emma and I agree to sign, but remember. Tomorrow you'll both be out of Spain...and

---

[43] Emma Cohen (b. 1946) is the stage name of Emmanuela Beltrán Rahola. She was married to the Spanish actor Fernando Fernán Gómez until his death in 2007.

we'll still be here,.with all the consequences due." Richard and I toned down the statement, made it a bit more abstract...about freedom and justice. But it clearly aimed at the upcoming executions. The Polish delegate did not sign the declaration.

That evening the winners were announced and the prizes given out. The city auditorium was packed with officials and their guests. After giving out the trophies, Richard Lester stepped forward and read out our document. It was received with polite applause. Then we were taken back to the hotel to dress for the gala ball given that night in honor of the members of the jury and the attending "festivaliers." We were supposed to be picked up at 10 p.m. Richard and I came down from our rooms at the appointed hour. We sat in the bar, drinking and chatting until 12:30 a.m. and then bid each other goodnight. The next morning we had breakfast and then went to the airport by taxis which we had to procure. The Festival had completely dropped us. Luckily no reprisal was taken against the Spanish delegates.

YUGOSLAVIA

1971

Yugoslavia: Zagreb, mid-winter, hunting for locations for LEONOR. Went to look for castles in the area around Zagreb. It was so cold that when I got out of the heated Land Rover to take pictures of a castle, the camera would freeze up.

One late afternoon we entered a lonely valley surrounded by a forest made up of mixed hardwood and pine trees. All these trees were covered by a thick coat of transparent ice. The wind passed through the branches, producing a tinkling and crackling sound...it went through the forest like a frozen breath.

In the middle of this valley was a small hill where a restored medieval castle stood. During the summer, it was used as a youth hostel. But now, in the middle of winter, with the sun setting, it had an unusually sinister look about it. The rays of light were barely passing over the rim of the valley, lighting up the castle parapets. We drove up to the monumental door. I pushed it, not expecting anything to happen, but it slowly swung open, creaking and grinding as it slammed against the opposite wall. We had to hurry. There was very little light left. The inner courtyard was perfect, surrounded by high galleries, all with gothic arches. But I needed a perfect cellar, or catacombs. We found an old wooden door which also gave way to our curiosity. There were stone steps leading into the lightless entrails of the chateau. Luckily the assistant had brought one flashlight, which gave off a weak yellow ray. As we started down, the sun finally disappeared behind the mountains. We thrust our way into the darkness of the cave...and the night. At the bottom of the steps, a huge arched room held a granite coffin. We approached it, our sickly lamp barely making out the dimensions of the sarcophagus. On one side, chiseled in the black stone was the head of a werewolf, fangs bared. Beneath, the words, "Conte Graetz." I could imagine, at that moment, the flashlight starting to die out and, in the last flickering of the light, the cover of the coffin starting to open...and a long-clawed finger poking out.

Of course this didn't happen and we left a few minutes later, half frozen to death. Within an hour we were in the bar of our hotel in Zagreb around a bottle of Postub red wine. Sadly enough, LEONOR was not to be shot that year.

WOMAN WITH RED BOOTS, 1974

To do LA FEMME AUX BOTTES ROUGES, I needed a star. I went to see Catherine Deneuve at her house. She had read the script but was not completely convinced...yet not unfriendly. We talked for a while. She still wasn't sure. Then she brought out a bottle of wine but could not find a corkscrew. My Swiss Army knife came to the rescue. The bottle was opened, the atmosphere became more friendly...and she finally agreed to do the film. I always carry a Swiss Army knife with me.

Catherine Deneuve and young actress, *Woman With Red Boots*.

1972: Summer in Greece. Spetsai with Clem Wood and Jesse Vilmorin. Skin diving with James Jones. Our prey—sea urchins, to be washed down with Retsina.

December: Madrid, Zaragoza and Calanda with Father and Tío Leonardo. New Year's Eve alone in Alcañiz. Tío Leonardo and father went to bed early.

1974

I had just finished filming LA FEMME AU BOTTES ROUGES when I went to a friend's house for dinner in Paris. Joan Miró would be present. In BOTTES ROUGES, I had a sequence in which Fernando Rey burns and rips a Miró painting. Naturally, it was a Miró which a studio painter had imitated. I told Joan about my film and what we had done to one of his paintings. Miró laughed. At that time, there was a huge Miró retrospective at the Gran Palais. He told me to go to the exposition and to keep my eyes open.

The next day, I was there at opening time. And on one wall were several Miró paintings which he had burned and ripped to achieve a desired effect. He had beat me to it.

MASTROIANNI - BERGMAN

During the filming of LA FEMME AUX BOTTES ROUGES, Catherine Deneuve's gentleman friend was Marcello Mastroianni. He would fly in from Rome every weekend with his suitcase loaded with fresh spaghetti his mother had specially prepared. The airport customs officials would always embarrass him by saying, "What do you have to declare?" and then laugh at the pasta-filled suitcase. Saturday nights, at Lucia Bosé's[44] home he would put on a white apron and make magnificent Italian dishes.

One night, after dinner, we went to a Flamenco club in downtown Madrid. We settled down and, as the dancers were dancing about the stage, Marcello leaned over and whispered to Catherine and me, "I came here several years ago and I was forced to dance flamenco." Catherine was indignant, "How ridiculous you must have been...no sense of dignity, etc. etc.!" She insulted him up and down.

Suddenly the music stopped and the leader of the "*quadrao*" stood up. He faced the audience. "Tonight, ladies and gentlemen, we have the very famous Catherine Deneuve with us!" The audience started to applaud. He pointed to Catherine. "Please come up and take a bow!" The clapping got louder, more insistent. Catherine, with a worried look on her face, headed for the stage. Marcello started to smile. There were cheers and whistles...the

---

[44] Lucia Bosé (b. 1931, former Miss Italia) was an Italian actress who appeared in films by Antonioni, Juan Antonio Bardem, Luis Buñuel (*Cela s'appelle l'aurore/That is the Dawn*, 1956), and by the Taviani brothers, Fellini, and Marguerite Duras, among others. She was married to the bullfighter Luis Dominguín.

minute she arrived and faced the audience, everyone started to yell, "*Que bailé, que bailé!!*" (Dance! Dance!)

The guitarists broke into a wild rhythm...and Catherine danced...**she had to**...Marcello just sat back and smiled. Catherine came back to the table furious, refusing to speak to anyone for the next hour.

∞ ∞ ∞

LEONOR was shot in November and December with Liv Ullmann, Michel Piccoli and Ornela Muti. It was a sheer delight to work with Michel and Liv. As for Ornela, I won't say anything.

Swedish actress Liv Ullman and French actor Michel Piccoli.

1974

Maine—House of Charles in Dover-Foxcroft. A tractor passed by the house pulling a heavily loaded hay trailer. On top a young man was sitting, legs dangling over the bales of hay. He did not see the branch from a roadside tree which slammed into his head and knocked him ten meters to the pavement. We rushed out from the house. Charles called an ambulance. The kid was writhing on the ground, his neck and back broken...he most likely suffered a skull fracture...his eye sockets were filling with blood. We tried to hold him from moving, to limit the destruction. The ambulance finally arrived and they strapped him to a stretcher. They took him away and he died.

1975

January: Santiago de Compostela. I awoke at two in the morning and could not sleep. So I put on my Spanish cape and went for a walk in the light drizzle. Santiago was beautiful at that hour. No one in the streets, only the sound of the rain. Then I heard footsteps resounding against the granite stone sidewalk. In the distance a figure appeared and came my way. It was a priest. He also was wearing a cape. We both bowed, rewrapped ourselves in our capes, and went on our way. For several moments, I wasn't in the 20th century.

20 JULY: Diego Luis born. As he is handed to me in the hospital, his hair neatly combed, a large rat crosses the hall, several meters from us. I was going to call him Rat but changed my mind later. I WAS HAPPY TO MEET HIM.

Bergman:

I went up to Stockholm to show Liv Ullmann LEONOR. She, at that time, was shooting a television series with Ingmar Bergman. She asked me if Ingmar could come to the private projection. Of course he could come.

After the showing, he **kissed** me. He said he loved the film. But there was one scene which he insisted must be taken out. A group of peasants are sitting around a fire discussing the manner in which they could destroy Leonor (who was killing their children). They are grilling *chorizos* (Spanish sausage). There is a big close-up of the *chorizos* bubbling in their own grease. This is the shot Bergman wanted me to cut out. We had a little argument. He probably would rather have liked a scene of boiling cod...with no salt or spices. Two civilizations clashed at that moment: Mediterranean and Nordic.

Later we went to Liv's apartment. It was dark outside and as we walked in, the phone rang. She picked it up and sat by the window looking out. Bertyl, her gentleman friend at that time, took me aside. "Look!" He pointed to an edifice across the wide tree-lined avenue. On the top floor of that building a single window was illuminated...and in that window, speaking on the phone, was a dark sihouette: Bergman. Bertyl smiled. "That's Ingmar's apartment. Every evening they speak like this for hours. About the film, I suppose." It is interesting to note that Liv and Ingmar had been lovers for many years and had had a daughter together.

∞ ∞ ∞

Hot summer at journalist Michèle Manceaux's house. The Ayatolah Chomeni was our neighbor.

Madrid—Shoot for Gaumont, MORT DE FRANCO. As I was interviewing Fernando Rey, I noticed that he was not smoking. I asked him what had happened. He said, "God touched me. I won't tell you where he touched me, but he did, and I stopped smoking." I then and there stopped smoking.

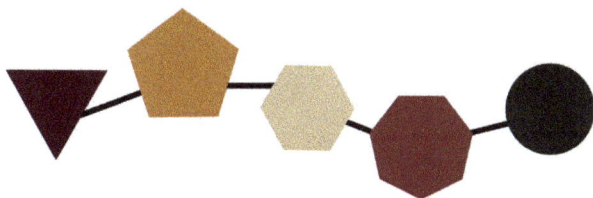

Synopses Of Feature Films

Au rendez-vous de la mort joyeuse (At the Meeting with Joyous Death):

A family moves into a strange house in the country. They try to fix it up but the girl, a 16-year-old, does not like what they are doing to the house. In the meantime the house falls in love with the girl. Strange things happen. All the windows break; a small garden table destroys the living room furniture, and a friend is attacked by the kitchen.

A television crew comes to try to film the incredible events. Then a priest and his charge of 15 girls (who used to camp out in the house before the family moved in) also arrive. The young girl is very bothered by all these people. A series of happenings kills two of the television crew. Everyone is driven from the house. The young girl stays to live there alone...and the house covers itself with wild ivy.

La femme aux bottes rouges (The Woman with Red Boots):

Fernando Rey plays an immensely rich man who dislikes artists, people who can create. With his great fortune, he could have the artists killed. But that is too simple. His object in life is to stop them from creating. If he finds a great sculptor who has a soft spot for alcohol, he sends him cases of fabulous wines. The artist puts all his creative effort into the alcohol and thus ceases to make his fantastic sculptures.

In this manner Fernando Rey has destroyed the creative process in many lives.

Then he runs into Françoise (Deneuve) who is a talented writer with a great future in front of her. Not only can she create with her writing but she can also invent and turn her thoughts into a physical reality.

Rey and Françoise clash in a ferocious battle in which, naturally, the creative person wins. Part of their battle is played out on a multi-level transparent chess set.

Leonor:

Leonor recreates a medieval atmosphere with its castles, drafty halls, great banquets, scenes of bubonic plague, swords, and bows and arrows. Filmed over eight weeks in an area north of Madrid (an authentic castle), *Leonor* presents a compelling story of obsessive love that develops in an unexpected direction.

> Editor's Note: At Oberlin, Juan Luis was enthralled by the Gothic novel (in English), and *Leonor* reflects this fascination. The film is based on a story by Ludwig Tieck entitled "Wake Not the Dead." Also in the Buñuelian tradition are scenes of a snake, a priest who commands no respect, worldly-wise maids and gardeners, and "*sueños horribles*" (terrible dreams). As Juan Luis explained to me: "I show that the Middle Ages had a sophisticated, but brutal, atmosphere." He did his research carefully, down to details of a children's ball game of the period.

Leonor took more than five years to make, from conception to realization. It opened the Festival de Cine du Môyen Age at Conques to favorable reviews.

HOUSE IBIZA (1977)

That summer I rented a place on the island of Ibiza. It was a white and lonely sprawling peasant house overlooking the rugged coast. The house was surrounded by fig and almond trees. Charles came over with Khatadhin and Beth Anne. Kuki and Toni came, with Daniel, Eva and Alicita. In the mornings breakfast consisted of going out into the fields with two rocks. The fig trees were bent to the ground under the weight of their fruit. The rocks were used to crack the almonds. Later the adults had *café au lait*.

One day I noticed that Juliette's friend, Agnes, was scratching her head. I investigated. Lifting up her dark red mane, much to my horror, I discovered thousands of tiny lice eggs attached to each individual hair. Then I started scratching. Kuki came over and almost fainted. We checked everyone. Tragedy. We all had lice. At that time, the known remedy was to shave the heads of the infected carriers and burn the hair...Kuki, Eva, Alicia, Juliette...all these beautiful curls and twirls. I started to hone my razor. But a friendly pharmacist saved our scalps. We could get rid of the invaders by smearing a certain product on our heads...and then covering our hair with a bathing cap. This would kill the lice and their eggs .but the caps had to remain on our heads day and night...for three days.

We arrived the next day on the seashore...there were about 12 of us, all wearing our multicolored bathing caps. We were immediately put into quarantine by the other families. They understood the reason for our odd *"chapeaux."* We had half the beach to ourselves. We could have been dressed in yellow garments with bells around our necks. We were humiliated...but we got rid of the beasties.

Every morning, Charles and I would go spear fishing. We would spend about four or five hours in the water, usually catching some form or other of fish: rougets, ray, or grouper. Upon reaching the house, we were obsessed with visions of juicy tomatoes, cool wine, lettuce, cucumbers, olives...after all that sun and salt water, our bodies demanded liquid freshness.

One morning, as we were preparing to go spear fishing, Juliette, who was 10 years old, and her little friend, Agnes, suggested that they would prepare lunch. They wouldn't go to the beach that morning; they would stay at the house, set the table, and get everything ready for when we would all come back, sunburned and thirsty from the beach. We thought this was a grand idea and left the girls proudly fussing about in the kitchen.

It was a hot day and we spent about four hours in the water. We rushed back to the house, anxious to get out of the sun, looking forward to water, coolness...and a satisfying meal.

The table was elegantly prepared and here is the menu that the two girls set before us:

Appetizer: Chocolate cake.

Main course: Crepes with peach jam.

Dessert: Strawberry jam with sugar and candies.

Drinks: Hot chocolate.

They didn't understand and were very sad when we threw them out of the kitchen and went after the tomatoes.

ONCE I WENT SPEAR FISHING OFF THE COAST. I SHOT AN OCTOPUS. THE SPEAR WENT THROUGH HIM AND HE WRAPPED HIS TENTACLES AROUND THE SHAFT OF THE SPEAR...AND THEN HE LOOKED UP AT ME. IT IS VERY DIFFICULT TO KILL AN OCTOPUS. I HAD TO RIP THE SPEAR FROM HIS BODY AND THEN BEAT HIM ON SOME ROCKS UNTIL HE EXPIRED. WE HAD HIM FOR DINNER THAT NIGHT...*A LA GALLEGA*. BOILED, WITH STEAMED POTATOES AND A LTTLE DASH OF OLIVE OIL AND PIMIENTO AND A SPRINKLE OF ROCK SALT. AND A GLASS OF WHITE CATALAN WINE. DELICIOUS...BUT I DID HAVE SOME *REMORDIMIENTO* (remorse) AND NEVER SHOT AN OCTOPUS AGAIN. THOSE EYES...

Painting (Juan Luis Buñuel)

1981

January: Mexico

February: Filming of L'HOMME DE LA NUIT. Alsace-Paris. George Wilson, Bulle Ogier, Pierre Clementi, and with Pedro Christián as an extra.

Portugal to Cinémathèque Lisboa.

November Hommage Buñuel at Beaubourg: Conchita and Margarita arrive. Wax figure of Luis Buñuel. Drums of Calanda at the Tour St. Jacques and Pompidou Center. Inside Pompidou drums and vibrations are so loud that plaster starts to fall. We are asked to stop.

1983

January: Mexico- Meet with Rafael. Father has problems with diabetes. Everyone worried.

February: Bristol YOU'll NEVER SEE ME AGAIN. Stonehenge and Bath with Helene.

March: Belgium, Liege. INPUT FILM FESTIVAL with Fernando Rey and Pierre Kast.

May-June: Mexico: Poppa very sick.

July-August: Filming of AVEUGLE, QUE VEUX-TU?

29 July 16:05 p.m. Father dies in D.F. in hospital.

August: Mexico to see Mother.

DEATH OF MY FATHER

1983: I was sitting in my father's room, reading, keeping him company. He was sick. He looked up and said. "How strange, Tristana (our dog) used to come in here and keep me company but now that I'm dead, she hasn't stepped into the room." He went back to his book.

My father told me to gather all the physicians who were taking care of him for a meeting at the house. There was a doctor for his diabetes, a doctor for his blood, another general practitioner...a total of four doctors. They all came one afternoon. Behind his desk, my father had the Larousse Medical Dictionary.

He knew exactly what he had. He stood the doctors up in front of him and said, "*Basta!* (Enough). No more medication. We stop everything." They were all shocked. "But, Don Luis, we must..." He cut them off. This was it. He knew and did not want to prolong. Four months later he was dead.

My mother told me about his last moments and words in the hospital. He had been delirious for some days. His body chemistry was off. He thought he was in the bar at the house. Or putting a table cloth on the long dining room table at our house. Friends were coming over for a paella. Then suddenly he called out to my mother. She went over and took his hand. He looked at her. "Jeanne, *me muero*" (I am dying). And he died. My brother was there. He called me in Paris.

When my father died, I cried.

THOUGHTS OF LORCA

I was just thinking back about what my father told me about Federico García Lorca. They had met at the Residencia de Estudiantes in Madrid. Both were very young men, very excited about the new world that was opening up to them. He said that Federico's real art was not his poetry or his music...but himself. He had never met someone who was so warm-hearted, outgoing and intelligent. His *being* was his art. He had laughter and humor.

Salvador Dalí, José Moreno Villa, Luis Buñuel, Federico García Lorca, and José Rubio Sacristán, May 1926, near Manzanares.

Last known photograph of Dalí, Buñuel, and Lorca together.

One night, during the early 60's, I was walking with my father through the narrow streets of Toledo. We arrived at a small square. One side overlooked a cliff which dropped several hundred feet into the Tajo River. I leaned on the stone parapet and looked down. The moonlight made the river look like a slithering snake. Then I noticed that my father had tears in his eyes. I asked him what was the matter, if he felt all right. He also leaned on the stone railing and said, "This is where Federico and Salvador and I came to vomit when we were drunk." Then he turned away. "We laughed so much!"

As we walked slowly back to our hotel, he said, "I can only imagine the horror that Federico must have felt as he was being led away to his execution. He was such an exquisite being, so conscious of everything around him, of life. He knew what was going to happen to him."

∞ ∞ ∞

Years later I went to the spot where García Lorca had been murdered. When I saw where it had happened, I could only stare, shocked. Fifty meters from some ugly modern building, several feet from a small motor road, on a poorly wooded and dry hillside rested a small nondescript cement monument. Nearby stood an old splintered tree where, it seems, Lorca received his ultimate present. A few feet away, a pile of garbage which had not been picked up: ripped blue garbage bags, banana peels, rusty cans, a few letters, disintegrating cardboard boxes, sanitary napkin containers...it looked like this *stuff* had been lying around for quite awhile.

One hundred years after my father's birth I can only think of this event.

1984

January: Paris. Lunch with French Prime Minister Laurent Fabius and Mexico's President Miguel de la Madrid. Dinner at Elysées with Mitterand and de la Madrid. Sat at table with nuclear submarine captain. Both intimate reunions with only 300 people at each gathering. The bread was better at Fabius' lunch. Mitterand's bread mediocre but the wine excellent.

1 May to 15 May: Operation vesicula.

July: Calaciete, Zaragoza, Cuenca (visit with Antonio Saura), Sitges.

August: Mexico

September: Exposition in PALMA DE MALLORCA . GALERIA PRIVAT.

November to December: Argentina-(Buenos Aires and Patagonia) for filming of TROPIQUE DU CRABE.

December: Mexico to visit Mother.

1985

December: Mexico, then New York with Juliette and Diego. Go to Maine. Lost in the snow with Charles. Kids take small plane, land on frozen lake. When Charles' car breaks down, we have to cross-country ski in minus 20 degree (minus 4 degrees Fahrenheit) weather.

Carmen

1990

Pablo born 30 January at 1:30 a.m.

Madrid — Meet Pablo. Has very round head.

GUANAJUATO

January to April: Mexico GUANAJUATO documentary for UNESCO. Carmen comes to Mexico.

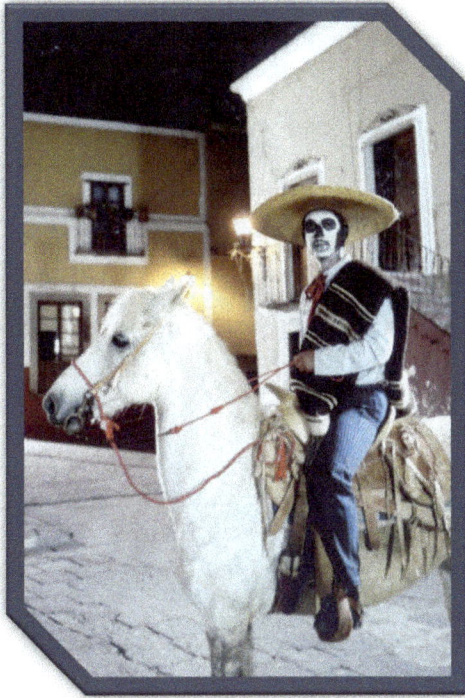

Guanajuato, una leyenda (1990)

I did a documentary film for UNESCO on Guanajuato, a strange beautiful city located in central Mexico whose mines once produced a third of the world's silver. It is also known for its mummies. The air and soil of Guanajuato are so dry that the skin of the dearly departed, instead of decomposing, takes on the quality of dark brown parchment. One can visit a great aunt who died several decades ago. There is a very disturbing museum near the cemetery where some of the more famous cases are exposed: El Ateo Francés, El Niño Marinero, La Enterrada Viva, etc.

Guanajuato, una leyenda (1990)

At the cemetery's parking lot were postcard and curio stands where you could get a postcard of your favorite mummy. One "*puesto*" (stall) had a large box upon which were inscribed the words "*Momias Francesas*" (French mummies). They turned out to be little plastic movable keychain figures who, when activated, went through pornographic motions. *Momias Francesas*.

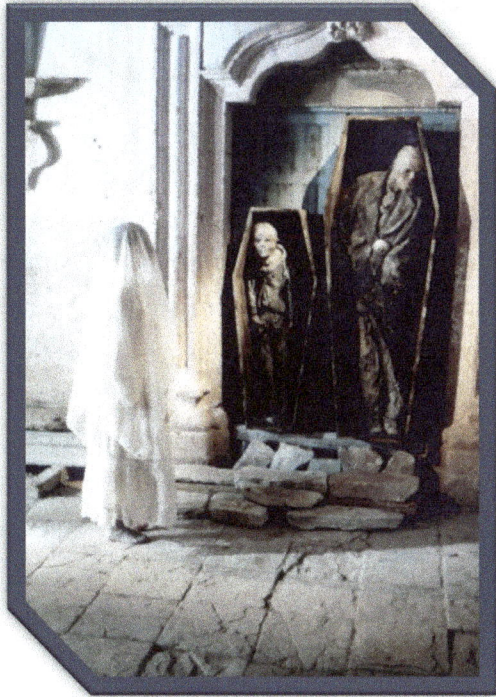

Guanajuato, una leyenda (1990)

Having finished the filming of GUANAJUATO, Carmen and I decided to visit some of the colonial villages in the region, namely San Miguel Allende, where my friend from American High School lives and works, the painter Peter Friedberg. One morning, leaving Pedro to his paints, Carmen and I decided to take a short trip to Atotonilco, some thirty kilometers away, to see the naïve paintings and "*milagros*" (paintings of miracles) hung in the entrance of the church. Atotonilco is a very small village in the middle of the desert which, at different times of the year, is visited by as many as 30,000 pilgrims...one day all the women of the different villages arrive, a few days later, the men. The atmosphere is very religious and calm although the wares that can be bought in the streets are crude stools, whips and lashes, and crowns of thorns.

After having spent several hours midst the dust, horses, dogs, *carnita* stands (a Mexican pork dish), and highly motivated Indian peasants, we headed back to San Miguel. At one moment, we decided to take a detour along a rough stone-littered secondary road which turned into the desert, to study the cacti and insects. We parked my mother's blue Volkswagen Beetle near a giant nopal cactus and started to walk across the cactus-covered plain to a large colonial structure which, upon inspection, had been abandoned since the 18th century, give or take a century. We saw a few scorpions, two black widows and we were heading back towards the car when I saw a train making its way along the horizon. Carmen was walking several feet behind me. I started to explain that the trains were not very efficient in Mexico because the government policy had been to build roads and speedways. Carmen mumbled something, "AK-47!"

I did not pay attention and kept talking about trains. Again she muttered, "AK-47!" I turned to ask her what she meant and saw that she was pointing to her right, looking very scared. About thirty meters away stood a man in a short leather jacket, pointing a Russian AK-47 directly at as and making motions as if he were going to shoot us. I raised my hands, "*Hola! Que paso? Buenos dias!*" (Hello! What's up? Good day!). We walked directly towards him, smiling. What was going on? Then we noticed that a large brand-new black American sedan, tinted windows flashing in the afternoon sun, was parked by our little bug. Two other men stood there trying to look into the interior. Our friend with the AK backed off and joined his cronies. We did too. I noticed that they all wore heavy waist-length leather jackets, all had .45 automatics in holsters at their belts. Two carried AK's, the other a riot gun. They seemed very nervous.

We started speaking with them. They asked us who we were. I mentioned that we had done a documentary on Guanajuato, showed them my official papers from the *Gobernador del Estado de Guanajuato* (governor of the state of Guanajuato). Where was I from? I showed him my passport. "Ah, la Paris Francia..." said one. He did not seem too happy about this. One man, his lips white with tension, could hardly keep his hand from his pistol. His other hand kept twitching. Finally I asked, as innocently as I could, "Have we entered someone's property? Is it prohibited to come here. We were looking at scorpions. Did we do anything wrong?" Finally one man stuck his hand out and the others relaxed, "*Nada, nada, estamos aquí para servirlos* (Nothing, nothing, we're here to serve you)." I shook his hand, so very thick and hard that I could hardly grasp it. Then they jumped into their car and roared away.

Conclusion: Rurales or Federales usually use 4x4 pick-up trucks or station wagons. This was a brand new car which, on these rough roads, couldn't last too long...therefore money was no object. We had probably blundered on a narcotics drop-off point or property. Luckily nothing happened. But all the man with the AK, or white-lips had to do was twitch a finger twice, and two more "*desaparecidos*" (disappeared) would have joined the statistics. The *zopilotes* (buzzards) and coyotes would have taken care of the rest.

1991: November: Paris. Edited Chile documentary.

French artist and poet Guy Roussille meets Pablo: Guy goes over to Pablo who is sitting in a high chair, drinking his bottle of milk. Guy says, "*Salud!*" Pablo holds out his bottle and they clink glasses. Guy is very happy and gives Pablo several paintings.

1992

May: Portugal for film directed by my ex-assistant, Juan Estelerich. Co-acting with Mickey Rooney.

LATER YEARS & FAMILY HISTORIES

CAN'T SLEEP

I have a hard time sleeping at night. Suddenly I wake up at 3:00 in the morning, wide awake, thinking, racing ahead about tomorrow's events. The only way to get back down into the world of dreams is to plug myself into my small short-wave transistor radio which turns off automatically in 15 minutes. In the old days of Communism, Radio Tirana would be the best. They would announce, "The People's Tractor Factory has produced last month 300 tractors, each tractor has four wheels of which the rubber has been, etc. etc...." Interminable statistics and soon I would be back asleep again. Or else I listen to the BBC...always interesting ...except for the shipping forecasts. But then, as the wavelengths vary or solar flares disrupt the audible quality of the programs, I hunt around for a clearer reception. I invariably fall upon the idiotic radio preachers who always have a perfect sound for their nameless drivel. How can anyone believe for one single moment the truth of the nonsense they blabber?

There was one I would listen to in Ohio: Prophet Jones, a black preacher. He had earrings on his left ear and none on his right ear: God spoke to him in that one. When the Mighty Creator whispered to him, Prophet Jones would whistle...and then give instructions to the faithful for collecting more money. They finally caught him on a morals charge. His Vestal Virgins were all minors.

I don't really blame him. At least he *tries*. It's the idiots who believe in his blather and send him money...Hmm, same for those who give money to the Catholic Church or the Synagogue. Same garbage. There was another one out of Los Angeles who received instructions from His Lord. Buy cars: two Rolls Royces, three Cadillacs, and a couple of Lincoln sedans. But they belonged, he insisted, to all his listeners who had sent him the money for these purchases. When asked if his fans could ride in these very cars, he said "No!" "Why not?" "Because God had ordered it so."

Now the very idea of gods bores me.

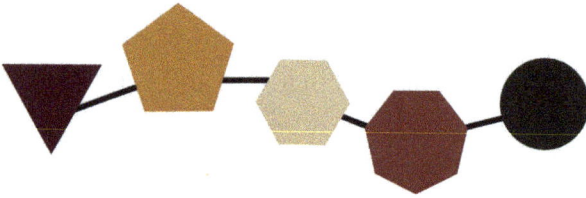

DREAMS

DREAM #1

1995- I was in a strange house but I knew it well. It was the house of Cerrada de Félix Cuevas, but strangely lit...a bright intense light, artificial. My mother was very sick and we were all worried because we felt there was no solution. Then she decided, calmly, to commit suicide. We (I don't know who the "we" were) looked to my father to see if it was all right. But there was one problem. He was already dead—a fact that no one wanted to tell him. It was almost embarrassing. He said, "Well, if that's what she wants, give her the pill." We gave her a pill, snuggled in a sandwich. She ate it, knowing full well what she was doing. I quickly left the room. There were many people there, friends, but I could not recognize them. She died. Then my father said, "Now she has to be cremated...and her ashes thrown into the sea. That was her wish." And then the people were all gone.

DREAM #2

We were Eskimos on a march across the frozen tundra. My mother was very sick and very tired. Then, as we were whipping the dogs across the barren landscape, she suddenly stopped, wrapped a blanket around her shoulders and said, "I've had enough, go on without me." She didn't seem scared or sad. She said it in a matter-of-fact manner. We tried to convince her to come with us but she gently refused. So we left. I wanted to stay but we had to leave. I felt terrible. We waved good-bye. I had this dream many years before her death.

DREAM 3

I was working in the White House in Washington D.C. and was the official private butler of Ronald Reagan. I would set out his dark blue suit, tie and stockings. Then I would shine his shoes. I did a very good job and he complimented me on it. Then I woke up and could not go back to sleep because I couldn't figure out where such a ridiculous dream had come from...Oh Freud, where are you, etc. etc...

DREAM #4

And then there was the dream of the huge spider, larger than my hand, which I chased on the terrace of my home in Mexico. Finally I manage to kill the beast and then proceed, with scientific curiosity, to perform an autopsy on it. This dead arachnid had a huge abdomen, and in my dream I gently cut it open. The cavity was filled with thousands of little baby spiders which, to my horror, spill out onto the floor and begin to run in all directions. I get a hose and start washing them away with a strong jet of water.

DREAM #5

We are having dinner in a fine restaurant. The main dish is a baby in sauce. The body has been cut into small bite-size pieces. I'm a bit repulsed but I'm showing off and pretend to enjoy this dish very much. The meat is very tender and a bit gelatinous. They're so happy that I like the dish, they serve me a an extra large heaping ladle-full. I am forced to eat it.

It reminded me of a crocodile stew I had in the Province of Amazonas, Venezuela. It also reminds me of stewed rabbit.

DREAM #6

Cannibalism. I am being forced to eat human flesh. Young women have been frozen and pieces are cut off, fried and made into tacos. I try not to show it but it is really very unpleasant.

DREAM #7

I keep dreaming of my room on the sixth floor of the 48 Rue Mazarine building. It was a room under the eaves...and the staircase was very ancient. I go back after many years and nothing has changed. It's just very dark and the furniture is covered with dust. It still belongs to me and I'm not sure if I have to move back or not.

DREAM #8

I am a member of the Communist Party and it is my job to infiltrate the kitchens of the Socialist Party. There, I must cook chickens in a special manner, first boiling them, drying them very carefully, then stuffing them in small pans which are to be put into the ovens. In this way I will slowly make all the Socialists become Communists.

DREAM #9

In this dream I am given a recipe on how to make bacon. You take the strips of bacon and arrange them around your forehead, like a wreath on the head of a Roman Emperor. Then you stick your head into a microwave oven and give it full power for three minutes. I was very worried and was not sure if I should do it or not.

CHILE

1994

I went to Chile to do a documentary for UNESCO (EL AÑO DEL CAMBIO) on public education after Pinochet (Dictator of Chile helped by the USA to overthrow the freely elected Allende government).

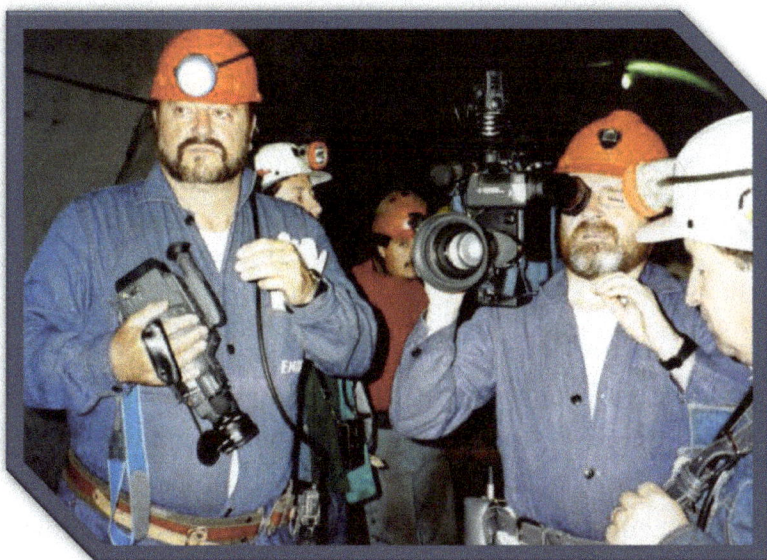

Juan Luis in mine, Chile.

There was a fellow who helped me greatly and who told me his story:

I was arrested for no reason at all and taken to the sports stadium in Santiago. There people were shot or tortured. The smell of fear filled the air. It was impossible to get out. They had us in the stands, and we were surrounded by barbed wire and soldiers. Then I noticed a group of well-dressed young men…"*niños bien*," young adults from the upper economic classes, huddled together. They had been picked up because they had not obeyed the curfew…they were drunk coming out of nightclubs. Since I was wearing a tie, I slipped in with their group and it turned out to be a lucky move. The "*niños bien*" were given a scolding and sent home. I was free!…and I immediately went into hiding.

After a year, I could not stand the pressure of staying in a cellar and so I joined a small group of clowns and mimes. Three men and a woman. We would go around giving plays at children's hospitals, schools and private fiestas. One day we were ordered to give a performance for the children of the military junta. Pinochet himself would be there. I was nervous, but I noticed that my co-actors were even more nervous than I. And then, a few minutes before the performance, I found out that they belonged to a terrorist group that had operated against the Pinochet government…and in a few minutes we would be miming in front of him and his family and cronies. The curtain went up…and our woman comrade fainted. We improvised, pretending that she had fainted on purpose. We laughed and jumped about, then carried her out. The show finished to applause and Pinochet's wife paid us off herself.

I left the country the next day. I went to Nicaragua.

UNFORGETTABLE MEALS

1978 -Spain- Itálica: We had been filming CET OBSCUR OBJET DU DÉSIR (*That Obscure Object of Desire*) in Sevilla and one Sunday, our day off, Pierre Lary, the other assistant director, Suzanne Durrenberger, the script girl, and I decided to visit Italica, some 40 kilometers outside of Sevilla. Since we did not have a car, we took a bus which dropped us off at Itálica itself.

Luis Buñuel and the two actresses (Ángela Molina and Carole Bouquet) while filming *That Obscure Object of Desire (*1977)

Imagine the Colosseum of Rome, perhaps bigger, totally ruined, situated in the middle of olive groves, trees which barely survive in the sun-burnt fields. The heat was terrific...or terrorific. We were the only ones there as we wandered about in awe in the desolation that was once the grandeur of the Roman Empire (an entirely original phrase never heard before). Anyway, all this grandeur and heat was very tiring and our thirst rose with the thermometer's mercury. We headed for the bus stop. To our dismay, a bus would only come by in another hour and a half. We almost panicked. Across the road we noticed a rather large humble clapboard structure whose roof was made of twisted wheat stalks and palm leaves. Compared to our sun-blasted bus stop, the interior seemed cool and inviting. A sign hung over the wide entrance, inviting: *La Alegría de Itálica* (The Joy of Italica). We crossed over the highway and made out way into the shade. The first obstacle we came to was a large barrel full of huge Sevillian olives swimming in their salty water. They were about the size of small apples. The owner stepped out from behind a well-furnished bar and offered us a table which he quickly covered with cold beers and a large plate of the previously mentioned olives. They were bitter and salty. Then he asked us if we wanted to lunch there. "What did he have?" we asked.

First a large platter of red tomatoes, with great chunks of sweet white onions and crisp lettuce leaves, coated in green olive oil, a dash of wine vinegar and salt. Then he took the hind leg of a freshly slaughtered baby lamb and cut it end-wise into small flat chunks which he tossed on a grill. Hot wood coals seared the flesh. A handful of thyme was sprinkled over the meat. Crisp Arab bread to sop up the juices of the olive oil and tomatoes. Interminable jugs of very cool Valdepeñas.

We missed three buses back to Sevilla.

We went back the following Sunday, this time in a car with my father. He was moved by the ruined Itálica but seemed sceptical about the restaurant Alegría. We gently forced him to a table. The first jug arrived.

If we had gone back by bus, we would have missed four trips. Luckily we had a chauffeur who limited his intake of the Valdepeñas. It was a good afternoon.

334

When we were location hunting with my father, it was normal for us (and his other assistants) to classify the restaurants as if we had been judges for the Guide Michelin.

We voted and declared La Alegría de Itálica the best restaurant in the world. We felt very sorry for Maxim's.

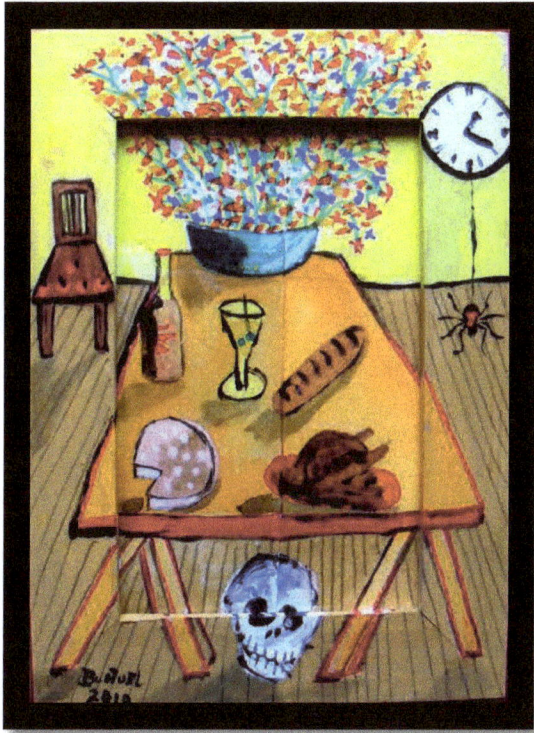

Dinner table with flowers and skull (Juan Luis Buñuel)

LA COUPOLE

La Coupole: Not the best restaurant in the world but the place was "*simpático*" (pleasant, friendly) and you could get a meal until 2 a.m. Great gathering place for everyone from the arts: students, painters, filmmakers, writers, etc. In fact, it was my "office" for many years. My father had gone to the opening of La Coupole in 1927 and was still a faithful client until the end. We would go at 12 noon, while the place was relatively empty. There was an old waiter, Joséph, feet flattened from 50 years of service, who served us. If we asked for something that wasn't too fresh, he would smile, wink and insist we try something else. Across the aisle, Sartre and Simone de Beauvoir would have their lunch. In the evening Giacometti, sitting alone near the door, had his late night "*demi.*"

La Coupole was divided into two parts by an invisible wall. As you walked in, the tables to the right were all covered by impeccably white tablecloths. This was the "restaurant" side. The tables on the left-hand side of the room were covered by humble paper tablecloths. This was the "*brasserie*"...where all decent and non-pretentious customers went and where you could draw, or take notes or doodle on the paper table cloths. We were very formal. Since we were decent and unpretentious, we laid down the law. **No one should sit on the right side i.e., the restaurant side!**

But the magic moments were in the morning, for breakfast. The huge room, which can hold several hundred patrons, was almost empty...three or four persons at the most. There was a rack with all the morning papers, English and French. My breakfasts would last an hour or more...croissants made on the premise, *café au lait* and the newspapers...and silence

During the summer of 1999 we went to Martha's Vineyard, at Charles' house. That first afternoon we went to Paradise Point and dug up a couple of kilos of "*navajas*," razor clams. That night we grilled them up with a little garlic, olive oil, parsley and salt. These were accompanied by Charles' tiny roasted pea-sized potatoes and a bottle of red wine. A great meal.

TRIP TO NORMANDY:
LETTER TO JERRY LINDNER

Dear Jerry, (I've put stars **** on the good restaurants):

So, we left one morning, early (10 a.m.) from Paris, took Rue de l'Ouest, direction Le Havre-Rouen-Caen, and within a few hours we picnicked on the French invasion Juno Beach where the English landed. Then we made out way up the coast towards Grandcamp-Maisy. On the way we stopped at the American Cemetery...10,000 soldiers buried there...and that is only 35% of those killed. The others were shipped back to the US.

The coast road is very nice. Luckily the sun was shining, which in Normandy is rare at this time of the year. Just take rain clothing (hats, hiking boots good for the beaches) etc. With a bit of luck in May the weather might be better.

Anyway, we got to Grandcamp around 3 p.m., checked in and then walked around. It is a fishing port, and in the early mornings (depending on the tides) the fishing boats come in and unload...clams, crabs, fish, *coquilles Saint-Jacques* (scallops in their shell), etc. Nice place to walk around.

The hotel showed me your letter and they say they will answer you soon. You have two double rooms in the main hotel with a view to the sea and the single room is in the annex (just a few feet away from the main building) but no view of the sea. Life is tough.

That night we ate in the dining room*** (make reservations the evening you want to eat there because they are usually filled by 8:30 p.m.). The food is good, the menus are of different prices and "à la carte" is fine...try the oysters. Delicious.

There is one restaurant to avoid in Grandcamp...Restaurant de la Mer. I've marked it on the brochure map. It ain't good...crabs have been in the icebox too long, etc etc.

What is amazing is the coming and going of the tides...every six hours they come in and out...you'll have the water lapping at the hotel entrance...you have lunch and suddenly you can't even see the ocean it's so far away.

Down the coast from Grandcamp, just several kilometres is Pointe du Hoc. Must not miss this...it was a group of very large and well-armed bunkers, on top of a cliff. Commandos were told to take the place. You'll understand why this was a tough job when you see the place. Shell holes all over the place and the poor commandos had to climb up 90-degree cliffs with the Germans firing down and dropping grenades on them. There you can visit the insides of a bunker. It must have been awful and the deaths on the American side were over 50%.

The next day we went to Sainte-Mère-Église where the American parachute hung from the church steeple...then we went back on the coast to Utah Beach and worked our way up. There are several museums and sites that are interesting.

Farther up the coast is Barfleur (which we immediately nicknamed "BarFly") and a good little restaurant Café de France**...fish, meat, right on the port. Try the Moules à la Normande (mussels).

Muy simpático. There are also several land points, lighthouses etc. Behind the restaurant is a pottery store with very nice objects. I bought a couple of mugs and a serving platter.

Then we went back to Grandcamp.

Next day we motored to Cherbourg (not very interesting. It was destroyed by shelling) but the coast is nice and then you go on up in the direction of Cap de la Hague along the coast road...very nice...hedges, small granite houses...but this ain't a poor country. Lots of money there, cheeses, fish, beef...

There is a little port by the name of Anse St.-Martin..Almost at the point of the peninsula (it's not even a village and is not marked on the map) which has a nice small restaurant for lunch...*muy simpático*...and very good.*** Then you can go for a pleasant walk (after a meal of wine, cheese, fish, meat, and mussels, it is necessary) down the coast. The remains of huge castle walls hover above the bay...looks like Ireland.

You should also visit the German Cemetery, which is only eight or nine kilometers from Grandcamp. Very impressive and sinister. Thousands of young German men buried there. But, when you are there, you'll see signs announcing Calvados and Cider for sale. Follow them. They'll lead you to a huge Normandy farmhouse and yard where they press their own cider and distill their own Calvados (this part of Normandy is called the Calvados). We naturally bought a couple of bottles.

That's about all we did...you'll find plenty of other places to go...stick to the coasts. You can also cut across the peninsula and go to Mont St.-Michel...a little touristy but very interesting and imposing and even go to Saint-Malo...a large walled city-port. It all depends on how much time you have.

Enuf for now, BUN

BUÑUEL FAMILY HISTORY AND STORIES:

BUÑUEL

The Great Grandfather was Joaquin Buñuel, a well-to-do landowner. He owned several farms. He had two sons, Joaquin Jr. and Leonardo.

Juan Luis' grandparents in staged photo nicknamed "The Exodus From Egypt."

Joaquin Buñuel Jr.: Studied medicine but fell in love with the daughter of a pharmacist. He then changed his studies and got a degree in pharmacy, married the young woman, and they opened up their own pharmacy in Calanda. They had a son called:

Leonardo Manuel Buñuel: 1855-1923 (He was to father Luis, María, Alicia, Leonardo, Conchita, Margarita and Alfonso.

All in that order.) He was supposed to be called Manuel Leonardo but the priest made a mistake because he was baptized on St. Leonardo's day.

Leonardo studied in Calanda with El Maestro Soler. He was a very good teacher and taught him to write with a perfect hand which later saved, as we will see, our Grandfather's life.

At fourteen he joined the army and was Trompeta-Coroneta of his battalion. At first he was stationed in Jaca but then was sent to Cuba. Because of his perfect handwriting, he stayed in Havana at army headquarters, while the rest of his battalion went off into the jungles where they all died of Yellow Fever. That in itself is a very good reason to learn perfect penmanship...though today with computers...

When Leonardo's military service terminated, he stayed in Cuba, moved to Matanzas and opened a hardware store.

Later he moved to Havana and joined two other men to open a large and successful hardware and general goods store called CASTELIERO Y VIZOSO. There he made a fortune. Finally, his partners did incorrect business with him. He did not want to stay with them anyway because of their unclear business practices during the Spanish-American War. He sold his part of the business and moved back to Spain, a retired man at forty-three.

He went to Calanda and fell in love with the Portolés girl, María, whose father had a pharmacy in town. She was 14 years old. He then made a deal with her father. Send her to a finishing school. She was to get an education, learn manners and how to handle a home. He went back to Cuba for several years to finish up his business. Then he came back to marry María. When Luis was born she was 17 years old and he was 45.

He was a *señorito*. It was unheard of for a man of his social stature to carry a package in the street. A maid or man servant would do that, walking several feet behind the master. There was one exception. At times he would stop by a gourmet shop and buy a can of caviar which he allowed himself to carry home.

In 1923 he died of pneumonia. Luis arrived home just after his father's death. He was 23 at the time. He helped the family dress his father for the burial. That night, as his father's body was lying on the big family bed, Luis, alone, smoked a cigarette on the balcony of the building. It must have been 2 a.m. when he heard a noise in the room behind him. He turned and saw his father, eyes fierce and a stern expression on his face, coming towards him. Luis stepped back in fear and the image disappeared. That night he went to sleep between two servants who were keeping vigil on a mattress on the floor set up near the entrance to the main room. The next evening, after the burial, he slept in his father's bed (where his father had died) but he kept a loaded pistol close to him...under the pillow. One of the first things Luis did after Don Leonardo's death was to wear his father's shoes.

Don Leonardo was 68 when he died. He was known to have been a kindly and just man with a sense of humor.

PORTOLÉS:

The Portolés family had a coat of arms. A shield with two arcades...or Portales...Medieval entrances built into a stone wall.

A grandfather of the Portolés had been a *guerrillero* (guerrilla fighter) for the Carlistas (who sought to establish the Bourbon family on the Spanish throne). He fathered 24 children by several wives. He had the title of *Nobleza de la Bragueta* (Nobility of the Fly of the Pants). One of these boys was Tomás Portolés, the future father of María Portolés, our grandmother. He died of pneumonia at the age of 68 and his wife died of cholera.

María (La Madrina) was born in 1883 and died in 1965. During her youth she spent some time at an uncle's house in Logroño. He was an archbishop. Her Tio Santos taught her to play the piano. He kept over a hundred canaries. During the day he would sit by their immense cage and play the flute for them.

María was brought up by her half-brother Eloy who was very severe with her.

∞ ∞ ∞

Leonardo Buñuel and María Portolés were married in Calanda and went to Algeciras for their honeymoon. In the evenings, María would sit in the lobby of the hotel and play *La Caballería Rusticana* and *La Boheme* on the piano. They say she interpreted the music with much feeling. Once, when she stopped playing, a very distinguished English gentleman came up and urged her to continue playing. It was the Prince of Wales.

In 1899, Leonardo and María came to Paris for the Universal Exposition. Luis was engendered in a hotel in the passage of the Musée Grévin (a wax museum). The couple bought a great amount of furniture and decorations for their house in Calanda. It was shipped back to Spain by train.

Leonardo was known for never having spoken in anger to his wife...except for once. They were having a picnic on the Cabezo, a small pine-covered hill next to the Torre (outside of Calanda). María was very young and at times waxed poetic. She was admiring butterflies in flight and suddenly sung out, "Oh, Leonardo, where do you think butterflies sleep at night?" "*En sus camas, tonta!*" (In their beds, silly!) responded the older man, probably fed up with all this poetry.

My father's godfather was a Cuban sponge merchant. This well-traveled man had one of the most beautiful sponge collections in the world, and the house in Calanda was decorated by many of his most interesting specimens, presents to our grandfather.

STORIES from TÍA MARGARITA

A rich priest was to leave Leonardo a relatively large fortune. But the holy man's maid accused Leonardo of having killed her husband in Cuba. So the priest left everything to the maid. Leonardo came back from Cuba with the maid's husband to prove that he had not killed him. But it was too late. The maid had spent everything.

That maid had a daughter who, in her later years, was called *La Tía Pedora* (The Farting Aunt). She would offer candy to the children of the village and, as they stretched out their hand to receive the sweets, she would fart at them. Then all the children of the village would run after her, shouting insults.

Working in the Buñuel household was Campos, chauffeur and *homme a tout faire* (man of all trades). He would sweep up the courtyard where the horses were kept and would put the droppings and fecal matter in boxes, tie and wrap them in delicate papers and fancy bows. He then would leave the presents early in the morning in front of the church (which was right across the square from the Buñuel house). Twice the Tía Pedora fell for the trap, greedily taking the beautiful packages home to unwrap them in her parlor.

∞ ∞ ∞

There were two brothers who lived on either side of a narrow street in Calanda. They were poor farmers and the land was harsh and sterile in that region. When a horse or a mule dropped dung in front of their houses, both brothers would rush out and fight over who would get the droppings. Finally they came to an agreement. Each one would take his turn. Then one day, one of the brothers cheated and they never spoke to each other again for the rest of their lives.

Then there was Tío Baldomero who would nervously walk around saying, "*Carajo, carajo*"(a swear word for penis). He then would go out to the patio where the animals were kept, urinate, and would walk back into the house. He would not say "*Carajo*" until the next time he felt the urge.

∞ ∞ ∞

During the summers, before supper, a *tertulia* (gathering) was always organized in the cool interior patio. Family and guests would sit around, sip wine and talk.

After dinner, in the cool of the evening, eight or nine of Leonardo's friends, all very cultivated and liberal men, would take chairs and sit around in the street, in front of the entrance to the house, talking and commenting on world events. The mayor was an atheist and it seemed he influenced Leonardo in his ways of thought.

Leonardo Buñuel, who was a very cultivated man, made his children read good books and go to the opera or to concerts.

At supper time, the women, his wife and daughters, would sit on one side of the table, the invited male guests and the boys on the other side. A great cutting board was brought in with several *chorizo* (sausages) on it. He would cut paper-thin pieces for the male members of the family. Never for the womenfolk.

Note: My father also cut the *chorizo* and ham in paper-thin slices. He said it was better that way. When I left home, my first act of rebellion was to buy a *chorizo* and cut great thick slices to munch on. My father (and his father) were right. Ham and *chorizo* tastes better when the slices are cut thin.

A couple of kilometers from Calanda, Leonardo built, on the high banks of the Guadalope River, a Roman-type chalet, with running water, a small waterfall, a waterwheel and a small pond. Many trees, broad leaf, pine and fruit, were planted. It was to be their summer vacation home. It was called Villa María but everyone called it "La Torre." Later Tío Alfonso brought in a few more exotic trees: Cedars of Lebanon and a Sequoia which grew to enormous heights. The pond also had a metal rowboat in which the children could paddle around.

When the summer heat started, the whole family was moved out to the cool tree-lined Torre by mule-pulled coaches. A series of maids and coachmen attended them from June to September.

On the first floor there was a toilet designed by Sir John Crapper.

STORIES FROM TÍA CONCHITA

Once, in Aragón, while under the fascist regime of Franco, a young girl had an illicit affair with a young man. She became pregnant. Alone, she decided to get an abortion and went to a doctor in a poorer neighborhood of Zaragoza near the Río Ebro. Feeling sorry for these ignorant women, the physician would help them out. But it was up to them to get rid of the fetus.

So this girl had her operation and after an hour of recuperation, the doctor handed her a tightly sealed jam jar which contained the two-month-old fetus. She wrapped the glass jar in her battered raincoat and staggered towards the river. Walking across the large bridge which spans the Ebro, she threw the jar into the water. Much to her terror, the jar, tightly sealed, floated. She quickly picked up some stones and tried to sink the incriminating evidence. But she was weak and her aim bad. Suddenly two Guardia Civils stepped up. They were friendly. She almost fainted. They laughed. What a bad shot she was. Throwing stones was not a thing girls knew how to do. One Guardia put his machine gun down on the edge of the bridge, picked up a stone and, with perfect aim, broke and sank the jam jar...along with the fetus.

∞ ∞ ∞

During the Spanish Civil War, Conchita was condemned to be shot. The night before, she sneaked into the woman's prison chapel, set up some boards between two chairs, placed candles at all four corners and took up a corpse-like position just before the women prisoners came in for morning mass. Conchita was well liked by her co-prisoners and when they saw her body stretched out, they all began to cry and wail. *"Pobre Conchita!!!"*(Poor Conchita) "They shot her!!!" Then Conchita jumped up and made faces. It was all a joke. Finally her mother, La Madrina, who had influential friends, got her off with a light prison sentence.

Luis Buñuel (left) and Juan Luis (right) in Calanda
during the annual 24 hours of non-stop drumming.

Mamá, mi hermana Georgette y yo

Mi padre

Lille, 1920 Tenía doce años

Mi hermano Gastón

Mi hermano Maurice

Juan Luis' mother's family photos.

Top:Jeanne (left), Sister Georgette (center), and Mother (right)
Middle: Father (left), Jeanne - 12 years old (right)
Bottom: Brother Gastón (left), Brother Maurice (right)

LEMPEREUR-SÉNÉCHAL-RUCAR (mother's side)

During the last part of the 19th century, there was a young orphan by the name of Hacquet who was born in Douchy, in Northern France. She inherited a great amount of land. Once she came to Escaudain au Moulin Menard for her vacations. Escaudain was a small spread-out village, as many were in the north, where the tallest structure was the three-story Hôtel de Ville. There she met a young groom by the name of Sénéchal with whom she fell in love. She was a natural-born business woman and he was a quiet sort of chap. In other words, from the very beginning she handled all business matters.

They married. They had many children. She built a huge factory which produced a great variety of soaps. It was a large red brick building filled with gleaming copper and brass machinery, tubs and vats. (I went there once with Juliette; now it's a mosque.)

They had a servant girl who came from the orphan asylum. She had been "found" on the steps of the local church. Therefore they gave her the name of Marie Trouvée (Marie Found).

She installed her uneducated husband in a milk distribution business.He would go around to the farmers of the region in a horse and buggy. He bought all their milk and sold it to the "cooperative" of the village where it was transformed into white cheese. He also cultivated the land around the soap factory. But he had one flaw. Alcohol. Genever (juniper-flavored alcoholic drink). One freezing winter night, he went out on horseback for a ride. He was quite drunk. The horse came back but not Sénéchal. They found his frozen body the next day. The word went out. He died because he had not drunk enough alcohol.

The Hacqet-Sénéchal union produced, among others, Séraphin who begot Constance who in turn begot Jeanne and Georgette.

And then there was Jeanne Augustine Marie Lahure who had a big nose. That's what she was know for. She married the rich son Haquet Sénéchal. They lived in a "*chateau*" in Nice.

LEMPEREUR

The original Lempereur came from Waterloo and was a shoe-repair man, a cobbler and his first name was Victorien. His son Léon, who was also a cobbler, married Laure. They had six sons who all grew to be over one meter ninety in height (over 6 feet 2 inches). Hence the height of Rafael and Diego.

Laure was famous for her nasty temper. Once, she had invited all her grandchildren for lunch. When they demanded a dessert, she went out to the barnyard and brought back a cow-pie on a plate. Slamming it down in front of the wide-eyed children, she shouted, "There, I hope that satisfies you!"

Legend goes that her grown daughter baked her a birthday cake with the points of a hundred pins cooked into the dough.

Victorien Lempereur bought the original Hacquet-Sénéchal house and continued with the soap factory.

Origin of the family name Lempereur

Legend has it that, in a small town in northern France, there lived a beautiful but quite dumb girl. On his way to Waterloo (where he got his behind kicked), Napoleon Bonaparte stopped to rest in this above-mentioned town while his troops were gathering. One dusky night, he seduced our beautiful young girl...it was a one-night stand. But, since he was such an important man, she immediately became pregnant and gave birth to a son. People would ask, "Who's the father of that little boy?" And the answer was, "*C'est le fils de l'Empereur*" (It's the Emperor's son). There's a pro and a con as to the truth of this story. The fact that it is mentioned in our family legend that she was of sub-normal intelligence gives this romantic tale a tinge of truth. What might disprove the story is that all the Lempereurs were over one meter ninety; Napoleon was half their size. There's a problem of genetics there.

RUCAR

Bourgeois family from La Madeleine near Lille. Georges Rucar, a public accountant, married Constance Lempereur and they begot Jeanne and Georgette and Georges Jr. and Maurice.

Constance was a kind but tough woman who spent most of her time in the kitchen, cooking, washing clothing (by hand, with water heated on the coal-burning stove. There were no washing machines at that time). She had four children and ran the house with an iron hand. My mother told me this story:

> When I was little, whenever I did a "*bêtise*," something foolish, this wet hand would appear over me, give me a resounding slap and then disappear. As a little girl I never figured out how this hand would appear and disappear...and always wet (my mother was always doing laundry).

Once a week she would go to the market for her supply of butter, return home and salt it herself. Since there were no refrigerators, salt was the only way to keep butter fresh.

She also used to make her own beer.

They were still in Northern France when World War I was declared and the Germans invaded France and my mother's village. They were forced to board two ordinary soldiers. Both were nice men who had been forced into the Army. They hated politics and, whenever free, would play with my mother. They kept saying, "If the politicians want to make war, why don't they come out and fight? And leave us alone."

To escape the battles which started to rage across northern France, the Red Cross gathered up the civilians and shipped them out. Georges Sr., Constance, Jeanne and Georgette Rucar were moved to Paris and remained there. The two boys, Georges Jr. and Maurice, were drafted into the French army.

Maurice got mustard gas in his lungs during the war and died in 1921 of a horrible death, choking on his own spittle. His mother (my grandmother) Constance took all the Bibles and crucifixes in the house and said, "If there is a God who allows this to happen to young men and to my son, I want no part of him!" And she burned all the absurd crosses and Bibles in the family fireplace.

∞ ∞ ∞

Interesting detail: It seems that when Vlad Dracul, the historical figure who inspired Bram Stroker for his DRACULA, needed loyal fighting men, he would go to a small village which is situated in Transylvania. The name of this village is Rucar. There is absolutely no proof that it has anything to do with our grandfather's family but one likes to believe it did.

Jeanne, Juan Luis, Rafael, Luis Buñuel, Mexico (1981).

DEATH OF MY MOTHER (1994)

I was supposed to go to Mexico on the 3rd of November but all the flights were full. I wanted to see my mother before starting a long film project in Venezuela. She was very sick and very sad. Her eyesight had been failing for the past seven years and she was bitter and bored with the existence around her. She had always been optimistic and gay and now she was neither.

Then, on the fifth of November, Juanita, the Mexican woman who had been actually running the house since my father died in 1983, called me. Her voice was sad on the phone. "*Ya pasó...*" My mother had died. "*Nada más se acostó después de comer para tomar su siesta y allí se quedó*" (She just went to sleep after eating to take her nap, and there she stayed).

The Venezuelan production company got me a ticket through a special travel agency and I got to Mexico City on the evening of the 6th. The body had been taken to a "*funeraria*" (funeral parlor) out near Tlalnepantla. My brother also arrived an hour later. Nestor, who had been my father's driver during many films and who had helped my mother when we weren't there, drove us out. The children of some of my mother's friends came out...we had all known each other since childhood. We stood around, and I made some stupid jokes. I refuse to be serious during situations such as this.

The next day the body was taken out to a crematorium near Xochimilco, a simple white structure surrounded by thousands of flowers. There were bees and butterflies everywhere and a few birds busily eating them.

An official said one of us had to recognize the body. I refused to go...too sad. Nestor went to recognize the body. The cremation in itself lasts four to five hours. I asked everyone to go back home. A small vase was picked to hold the ashes. I tipped a worker to do the work. Then we left. I've never gone back. Juanita went to pick a niche and we paid the rent for five years. It all really doesn't matter.

My mother was a good person and I loved her very much.

How difficult it is to write all this down. Sounds so phony.

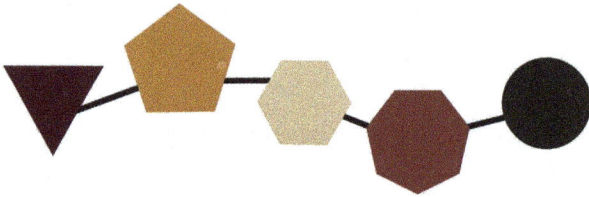

Stories My
Father Told Me

PARIS

It was the night of the first showing of UN CHIEN ANDALOU. He was very nervous and thought the audience might react in a violent manner. The film was, at that time, silent and he stood behind the screen, feeding records to an old windup record player. He had filled his pockets with rocks so, if the audience came after him, he could stone them. The guests turned out to be people like Picasso, Cocteau, Man Ray, Max Ernst, etc. They liked the film very much, so he threw the stones discreetly behind a potted plant.

CALIFORNIA

When my father lived in Hollywood in 1930, he was invited by Charlie Chaplin to a Christmas party at his home. Chaplin liked to have visiting Europeans over. They were more fun than the Americans.

One of Chaplin's favorite films was the CHIEN ANDALOU. He had acquired a copy and would at times screen it for his friends. He had a Chinese projectionist. Invariably, when the cutting-of-the-eye-with-a-razor scene appeared, they would hear a loud "thump" from the projection room. The projectionest had fainted again.

One Sunday, during the filming of LA MORT EN CE JARDIN (*Death in the Garden*, 1956), my father invited actors Michel Piccoli, Simone Signoret and Charles Vanel to our house. My mother was to make a paella. The Alcorizas were also invited. The meal went on without a problem, the paella was very good. Everyone was in good spirits. Then Luis Alcoriza stood up and made the typical Spanish black humor joke. "This meal was horrible, made by a French woman. If you really want to taste what a Spanish paella is like, you're all invited to my house next week!" Neither my father nor my mother reacted. It was a typical joke. But the others did not understand.

Next Sunday, Luis and Janet Alcoriza made a fantastic paella. In the meantime, Piccoli, Signoret and Vanel had stopped by a grocery store and had bought cans of sardines and baked beans which they had hidden in their pockets. After the aperitifs, everyone sat at the long table and the magnificent paella was brought in by a proud Luis Alcoriza. It was then that the French delegation acted. They pulled the cans from their pockets and proceeded to eat the sardines and beans. They never **touched** the paella.

Even twenty years later, when Luis Alcoriza was reminded of the incident, he could not force himself to smile. The blow had been deadly, inflicted by French people who did not understand Spanish humor.

∞ ∞ ∞

A good example of this humor is, upon the knowledge of Luis Alcoriza's father's death, Domingo Dominguín sent a telegram to Luis. His father had been dead less than 24 hours. "I have just gotten the news of your father's death. I would like to have the stuffed and be-horned head of your father to hang in my living room. Signed: Domingo."

Luis' father had been one of Domingo's dearest friends. Luis Alcoriza did not get angry.

NEW YORK 1943

My father and some friends devised a revolutionary scheme. They were going to open up a restaurant called AU COUP DE CANON (a cannon shot). In France, when you get overcharged in a restaurant, it's *au coup de bambou* (because it feels like a blow to the head). Therefore they were going to open up the world's costliest restaurant. Oysters from northern Finland, Sveruga Caviar, the best 18th-century French cognacs, etc. etc. The prices would be exorbitant...and, when your bill reached $1000 dollars, a small brass cannon situated in front of the establishment would be fired. Today a thousand dollars is not that great of a sum. But in the 1940s, it was a lot of money.

And thus, some factory mechanic who had just been fired, in Brooklyn, would be awakened at two in the morning by the explosion of the cannon. He would sit up in bed, cursing. "I have no job, my children have nothing to eat, and some sonofabitch has just spent a thousand dollars on luxury food and drinks." Furious, he and other workers would rise from their beds and start a revolution.

(Nowadays they would probably be jealous of the people who are able to spend that amount...and never think that they are being exploited.)

MEXICO

Once my father invited some Cuban filmmakers to the house for lunch. They consumed martinis and bottles of wine. We were sitting around the table having coffee, cognac and the great Cuban cigars the guests had brought with them. My father had just finished telling them the history of his family, how Leonardo, his father, had settled in Cuba and made his fortune there. Then he leaned over and said, "Once, my father was sitting in a bar in Matanzas and he overheard a bearded man saying stupid things about liberty and freedom. He stood up, went to the table and knocked the man down. It was José Martí (the Liberator of Cuba)." The Cubans were disconcerted.

He continued. "My father (Leonardo Buñuel) was in the Spanish army. That's how he got to Cuba. Once he was in charge of a firing squad. They were about to execute Maceo, a Cuban revolutionary hero. He blindfolded Maceo, tied him to a post and gave the order, 'Ready! Aim!...' The soldiers were about to fire. At that moment, an officer galloped up on a sweating horse. He handed my father an official paper. The Governor of Cuba had pardoned Maceo. My father studied the paper, then turned to the firing squad and barked out, '*Fuego!*' (Fire!)."

My father then leaned over again, "My son, Juan Luis, was in a *cantina* in Mexico City. There was a big bearded man haranguing a group of young men in impassioned tones. He had many political theories. They started to argue. Juan Luis knocked him down." The eyes of the Cubans were about to pop out. "It was Fidel Castro when he was in exiled in Mexico!" They all looked at me, shocked. I started to laugh, so did my father...They had almost believed the three stories.

∞ ∞ ∞

One of my father's favorite stories was that of his own death.

(1) As he was lying on his dying bed, he would call in his friends. When they were all present, a priest would come in and he would confess, accepting the Catholic faith. Afterwards all his atheist friends would then go spit on his grave.

(2) After his death, my mother, my brother, and I would go to the lawyer's office for the reading of the will. The lawyer would announce that he couldn't start the reading until David Rockefeller arrived. "David Rockefeller?" we would all exclaim. "One of the world's richest men?! Why in the world was he invited to this reading?"

Finally Rockefeller arrives and the lawyer rips open the testament..."I, Luis Buñuel, sound of mind etc., etc...leave everything I own to David Rockefeller...." In this manner he leaves his wife and children without a cent. We would then go and spit on his tomb.

Aunt Margarita, Luis Buñuel, Uncle Leonardo, Aunt Conchita.

TRISTANA was based on a Galdós novel, but the true inspiration was that of my father's sister Margarita. When they were little, Margarita used to play this game: She would put two identical objects in front of someone and asked them to choose. "But they're both the same," the other person would point out. "It doesn't matter," Margarita would argue. "You have to choose one." The person would then choose one of the beans, or pebbles, or identical pencil, and Margarita would ask "Why did you choose that one and not the other?" In the film, Tristana is walking down the narrow streets of Toledo and comes to a crossing with two different but identical streets in front of her. She chooses one and that choice changes her life. If she had chosen the other street, nothing would have happened.

> Editor's Note: Juan Luis told me that Spanish audiences would laugh at the line in Tristana when the Guardia Civil said it took two shots to kill the mad dog. Why was this funny? Because the Guardia Civil were usually shown in films as so heroic it would only take one shot for them to kill anything!

MORCILLO

From this Spanish painter's name comes our expression 'Morcillismo'...a trait shared by many, many people. Morcillo once met my father on a street in Madrid. "Come up to my studio and see my latest works." My father agreed but said that he wasn't a very good judge of paintings. They reached the studio, Morcillo served some wine, then started to show the new paintings. "Please, I beg of you, in all honesty, tell me what you think of my work." The paintings were quite good and my father said so. "No, no, Buñuel, be honest. I don't mind." He kept bringing out the canvases...and at one moment, one of the paintings did not please my father, The work was shabby, quickly done and uninteresting. "Look, Morcillo, you asked for my opinion...well, I don't think this one is as good as the others." Morcillo became furious. "Al contrario (On the contrary), '" he shouted, "that one is the best of them all!"

Hence the expression, 'Morcillismo.'

DREAM

My father had a recurring dream. He was on a train, a voyage to some destination that was not very clear, but it was an important trip. The train had pulled into a small station. The conductor had announced that they would stop there for half an hour. The passengers could get off for refreshments. But my father was very worried. If he got off his carriage, the train would leave without him. Yet the station was full of people, some stretching their legs, another having a smoke, a few drinking beers by a small bar.

Nervously he decided to get a bottle of mineral water. He was very thirsty. He checked the platform again. Everything seemed normal. But as soon as he had both feet on the ground, the station was totally empty and the train was pulling rapidly away from him with all his suitcases aboard. And there he was, in an empty train station, the bar closed, without his suitcases...alone.

MUSIC

Apart from the drums of Calanda, my father liked music but, because of his early deafness, never listened to it in his later years.

1) Stories he told me about going to a concert in Zaragoza. The importance of music at a time where even radios were rare. He remembered when the Berlin Symphony orchestra was destined to come to Zaragoza. They would talk about the symphony (Wagner), get the music, dream about it. And the great day arrived. Everyone was spellbound...and then they would talk about it for the next few weeks. Nowadays, with a flip of a switch, you can get any kind of music and it seems a little less important.

2) We would listen to Wagnerian operas on the classical music station Sunday mornings in New York during the war. He would tell me all the legends and stories that these operas illustrated.

3) He had left his wind-up gramophone and 1930's jazz record collection in Paris in my Tante Georgette's apartment on Rue Mazarine. This collection also contained some of Gustavo Pittaluga's adaptations of Spanish Civil War songs and music.[45] In 1958 I would go under the Pont Neuf with friends and bottles of cheap red wine to listen to this music on the wind-up gramophone. Why under the Pont Neuf? It was always raining and my aunt had to get up early to go to work. At times the police

---

[45] Gustavo Pittaluga (1906-1975) was a composer for *Los Olvidados*, *Mexican Bus Ride*, and *Viridiana*. He exiled himself from Spain during the Civil War, lived in Mexico from 1948, and returned to Madrid in 1962.

would stop by to see this ragged bunch listening to old jazz records (sometimes a *clochard* would join our group). Usually they stood around for a while listening to the music, and then they would leave us.

4) We had a record player in Mexico City. I had this machine to myself but my father had several records of his own which he never listened to. O CANGACIERO, TRISTAN AND ISOLDE. There was one record which he did listen to once in a while, SPECIAL EFFECTS: TRAIN SOUNDS. Since he and his friends liked to travel on trains, he would mix some drinks, put the Special Effects Train Sounds on the record player, and they would pretend they were in the restaurant or bar carriage going from Zaragoza to Madrid.

Trumpet player (Juan Luis Buñuel)

SAN JOSÉ PURUA, MEXICO

In the state of Michoacán, some 400 kilometers north of the capital, Mexico City, there can be found an interesting geological phenomenon: deep from inside the earth, hot waters gush to the surface, rich in sulfur and other minerals, gathering into pools and eventually forming a small river.

The topography, for kilometers around, is flat desert. The plants are spiny cacti and yucca. Rains come only during the months of May, June and July. The rest of the time it is hot and dry.

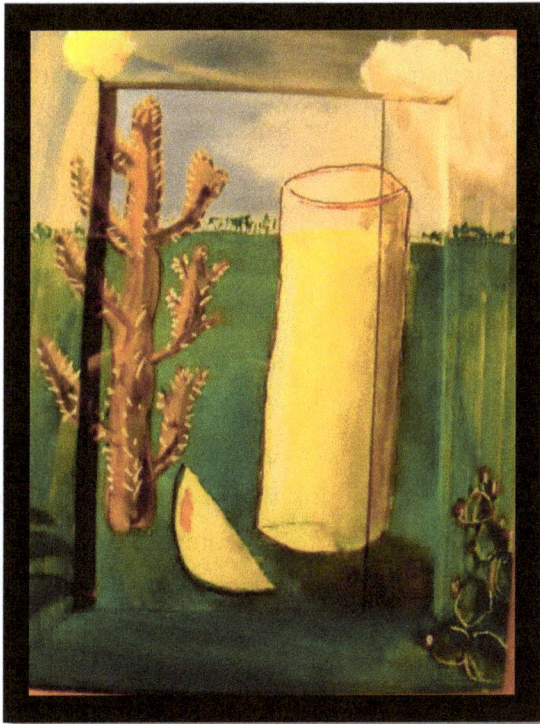

Mexican cactus and tequila (Juan Luis Buñuel)

Then suddenly, the ground opens up. An immense canyon, over a thousand meters deep, falls away before you. Aztec emperors had their vacation residences there, to take hot baths in the sulphur waters which spew from the center of our planet. They would cover themselves with the ill-smelling healing mud created by those waters. Centuries later, a hotel complex was founded on the edge of those cliffs. There, my father, mother, brother, and I went several times for short two-day vacations. We could never afford longer stays. On other occasions, my father would go with Jean Claude Carrière, and other writers, to work on his scripts. The tab was, naturally, picked up by the producer. This establishment was called the Balnearios de San José Purua.

Constructed of stone and whitewashed walls, terraces, gardens and swimming pools, bars and restaurants, the hotel could, and can, lodge up to 700 guests.

Usually, during the week, the hotel is empty.

A perfect place to work.

Breakfast is served at 7:30 a.m. in the large dining room overlooking the canyon. After several hours of working on the script, the writers take a break by dipping into the hot sulphur baths in private bathing cabins which line one side of the large swimming pool: one person to a room. It is prohibited to lock your door. The waters are very warm and bubbly...like taking a bath in mineral water. The gases and heat given off might make the bather loose consciousness. The Bath Master passes by every few minutes and raps on the door. "*Perdón, están bien?*" he asks (Excuse me, are you ok?).

If you answer, he continues on to the next cabin. If you do not answer, he rushes in to pull you from the boiling waters.

Then you wrap yourself in large white towels and lie on a cot, in the same little cabin, for a 20-minute nap.

Now it is time for the pre-lunch aperitif. This is considered a work session, which goes well into the actual meal and coffee afterwards.

After a one-hour siesta, another work session is started. The writers sit in comfortable rattan and leather sofas which line the interminable corridors. These lonely passageways also look out onto the canyon.

Below the *zopilotes* (vultures) wheel about looking for carrion.

During the late afternoon, once the sun has weakened, exercise is taken in the form of a hike down into the canyon. The path is lined with paving stones...the walk down is easy...Coming back up is another sweaty story.

There is an interesting aspect to this *paseo* (stroll). You go from a desert region (cacti, snakes, *zopilotes*, black widow spiders), and drop down into a lush tropical setting. Upon approaching the bottom, the flora and the fauna change. Hibiscus, palm trees, tropical ferns, hummingbirds, parrots, orchids, banana groves...and at the very bottom, a clear sparkling stream.

Since usually there is no one present, we use this opportunity to pull out our .22 or .38 pistols and ease off a few shots against disgustingly designed and gaudy flowers that are much too obvious. Somehow they remind us of some Walt Disney creature. We never shoot animals, no matter how cute...though the desire is there...shooting the cute ones, that is.

Back at the Balneario, sweaty and a little tired after the long climb, we change into our bathing suits and go to the pool, where an obliging attendant covers us with the magical foul-smelling sulfurous mud. We roast in the sun for an hour. The mud dries and we take on the aspect of well-cured mummies. Then, jumping into the pool, we wash off this rough coating. Our skin has now the softness of a baby's bottom.

At that moment, a 20-minute visit to the hotel Podologiste (podiatrist or chiropodist) is a possibility.

Before dinner, our feet freshly pedicured and caressed, we take a pre-dinner nap in our respective rooms. At 19:30h precisely, we meet in the bar for the nightly dry martini. The bartender, who has been strictly trained over the years, knows the exact proportions of Noilly Pratt, English gin, Angustura bitters, and ice. The makings of a perfect cocktail. We have two Dry Martinis, never more.

Again, this seemingly alcoholic meeting is in reality a very intense work session extending well into dinner and lasting over two hours.

Then to bed at 22:30h.

The only day that this schedule cannot be kept is Sunday when carloads of overfed and underdressed American tourists invade the pools, restaurants and bars. Then, all work is done in the rooms where scenes can be acted out without being bothered by the screaming of children.

Nearby is a small village. Many of the Indians there are blonde, a strange phenomenon...When Maximillian was declared Emperor of Mexico, a small group of his French troops were stationed in this village. Some never went home.

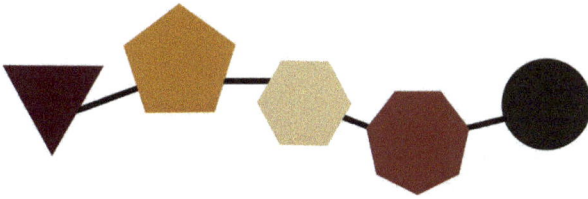

1996 - 2010

1996

January: Went to Madrid to sell Legado Buñuel to Minister of Culture. Went back to Madrid to inaugurate the Sala Buñuel in the Reina Sofia Museum. Meet Felipe González, Prime Minister of Spain.

April: Director of Reina Sofia Museum tries to keep objects of mine for the Museum. Big fight with Minister of Culture, Director de la Cinematografía. We win. They give me back the objects they had borrowed. **Big Expo Buñuel in July at Reina Sofia in Madrid.**

Expo in Cadaqués. Then trip to Zaragoza, Huesca to see cousin Leonardo, then to the Vendée to see Christian Garnier, then on to Saché to see Sandra Calder. Learn of death of Louisa Calder a few weeks before.

Paris. Diego in San Francisco. L'EAU D'ARGENTIERE cancelled.

December: Mexico for Expo Buñuel at Palacio Bellas Artes. Carmen and I very sick with *"gripe"*(flu). Mexico very dirty and very sad. People are scared. New York: See Charles and Brian, St. Mark's Place. N.Y. has changed, everything cleaner and people friendlier.

1997

May: Chicago to see Diego's school, Northwestern U. in Evanston. Lucky Diego: Great school, and living in a nice pad, Russian girlfriend and a car. Nouveau riche...One Sunday went to their house. He introduced me to a new drink. He called it "Sex On The Beach": Vodka, rum, gin, orange juice, grenadine syrup, and many more things. Deadly.

Christmas in Paris with Carmen, Juliette, Pablo, Diego, Alfonsito...we ate fresh *foie gras*...Alfonsito sent to hospital with possible appendicitis attack.

1998

Famous phrases from Pablo: He made up a phrase for school using the sounds "a" and "ha." "*Nous avons abattu les Haricots!*"(We have assassinated the green beans!) True surrealist statement.

JULY-AUGUST: Bilbao to see Guggenheim Museum, then Bueu, Madrid and Aragón to see Leonardo. Then voyage to Paris via Aix and Arles.

Dijon: President of Jury at Dijon Film Festival.

Huelva: Trip to Huelva to talk with Edward James Olmos to convince him to be in LA RECONQUISTA.

1999

New Year's dinner with Alfonsito and Juliette. This time it's Juliette's turn to go to emergency hospital...but it turned out to be all right. Nothing serious...so she says.

Vacations Feb and March: Go to Côte d'Azur with Carmen and Pablo and Nico. We want to go to Picasso Ceramic Museum in Vallauris. Not sure where to go. Ask old Spaniard directions. Turns out to be Picasso's barber. Very pleasant, took us to museum. We questioned him about his job as Picasso's barber. It seems the painter was almost completely bald at that time. "Those are the most difficult to give a haircut to..." he answered.

Then we went to visit the Noailles' house in Hyères. Then on to Italy, Genoa, Turino and back to Paris. Nice trip. Lots of driving.

> Editor's Note: The Noailles financed Luis Buñuel's film *L'âge d'or* (1930).

Death of Tía María 7th of March in Zaragoza. 98 years old.

Pablo gets hit by a car on Rue Didot. Ran out between two parked cars. We were very scared. Nothing bad happened. I didn't know if I should hug him or yell at him. Poor thing.

Trip to Montana. Strange place. Went to Ellen's house with Rafael. Met the ranchers there, went to a Fourth of July Rodeo. I asked the cowboys and ranchers who they fought against during the American Revolution. They didn't know. The children were very surprised. These Montana people were like residents living on another planet...and not of this galaxy.

2000

Cannes with Rafael. Up the red-carpeted steps at the Palais du Festival with Catherine Deneuve and Rafael who had two black stockings around his neck in the guise of a *foulard* (tie). Dinner afterwards with Almodóvar, Deneuve, Piccoli etc. Laughed a lot

2001

Twin Towers in New York. We immediately thought that it was a set-up by Bush.

2003

August meeting with Pedro, Alfonso, Leonardo, Alicia in Aragón (Huesca).

2004

Murcia for symposium on Dalí

Speaking trip to Oberlin, Wooster and Case Western (Tech). Going back after 50 years to Ohio. Interesting to go back after so long. Shock at remembering a class from that period.

Morelia, Mexico: Break shoulder. Cast put on, then in Paris, two operations to put slab of steel in upper arm.

2005

Aragón with Pablo. Write CURE CHABOT in Calaciete. Visit Kuki and Toni in Sitges, then Alicia and Xavier near Huesca, then Leonardo in Sta. Clara de Sores.

Trip to Ecuador to show *Calanda* in Quito and Baranquilla.

2006

Returned to Calanda and was surprised at how the village had changed. When I filmed my first film, a documentary on the village and the drums, it was a medieval town existing on olives, grapes and peaches. Now, 40 years later, it had factories, industries and workers from Eastern Europe, Transylvania, Romania, Hungary and Morocco. It had become a bourgeois society.

I went to the seat of Government in Zaragoza and proposed to make CALANDA: 40 YEARS LATER (aka CALANDA REVISTED or CALANDA 2). Using the old black and white film and the new material to be filmed in colour. The project was O.K.'d.

2007

Returned to Calanda for the filming. Had Christian Garnier and Diego as cameramen and edited the film in Calanda with Anita Fernández.

Calanda: 40 Years Later

In my *Calanda Revisited*, there's a whole section on the making of sheepskin drums...but now the younger people prefer plastic drum heads because they are louder and you can really roll the drumsticks.

Calanda: 40 Years Later

Filmed ÚLTIMO GUIÓN (*The Last Script*) in Paris, Madrid, Zaragoza, Toledo.

2008

Trips to D.F., Los Angeles and New York to film ÚLTIMO GUIÓN.

Trip to Nantes Film Festival as member of jury.

Visit to Amsterdam to show both CALANDAS.

Trip to Berlin Internatinal Film Festival to show CALANDA 2. Visit museum, see Gates of Babylon and Nefertiti.

Trip to Zaragoza to Water Festival to show *Calanda 2*

2009

Pedro Christián dies.

Expo little paintings, Calanda with Rafael.

Voyages to San Sebastián, Málaga, Valencia, Zaragoza and Madrid for ÚLTIMO GUIÓN.

Trip to Calaciete for meeting with Leonardo, Alfonso, Marisa and Ian Gibson. Discuss what to do with books and photos left by Pedro Cristián.

Met with Chema Prado of Filmoteca in San Sebastián to offer books and photos.

Trip to Czech Republic.Zlín

2010

Heart electric shock...before rhythm at 80 per minute...now at 62.

Expo BOURGES (June and July) of sculptures and little paintings.

Expo Paris Artligre art gallery.

Trip to Mallorca for four days. Talk about films.

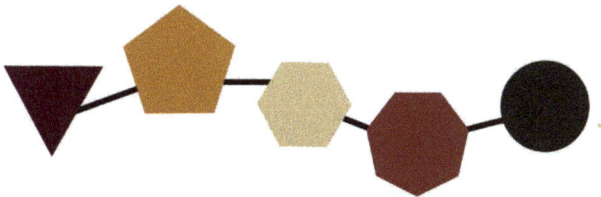

Things I Like
& Dislike

Likes:

1) Guns and knives.

2) Clean virgin sheets of paper.

3) Good wines and alcohols.

4) A good meal with friends.

5) Silence.

6) Classical music. But not too much.

7) The mountains around Mexico City before 1953.

Dislikes:

1) Drugs.

2) Unwashed persons.

3) Perfume.

4) Walt Disney and everything connected to that company.

5) People who keep walking under their umbrellas after it has stopped raining.

6) Above all: crowds and discotheques.

7) Restaurants where the *maitre d'hote* recognizes you and takes you to a table. The pretension. Above all things: Pretension.

8) Things that are cute.

9) Watered-down *Agua de colonia* (eau de Cologne).

10) High-heeled shoes for women.

Favorite Foods:

1) Alsacian Sauerkraut with Beer

2) Gazpacho

3) Caviar with finely chopped boiled potatoes and onions...with a tiny drop of lemon...and iced vodka or aquavit

4) Oysters with a little lemon

5) Tacos and different salsas...and not the kind sold in the U.S.

6) *Jamón Serrano* (Serrano ham). *Pata negra* of Jabugo (the black legs of pigs from Jabugo. Those pigs have been allowed to roam freely).

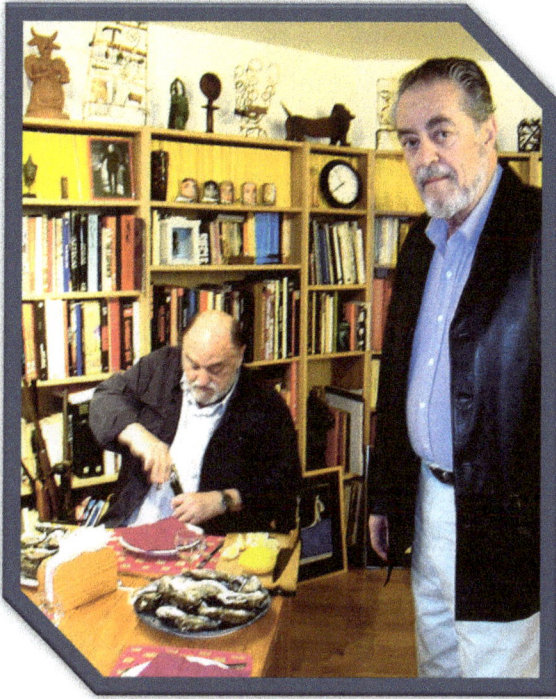

Juan Luis and Rafael preparing oysters, Paris.

PEOPLE I HAVE MET

ANDERSON, BIBI (Swedish actress-Bergman films) Very attractive and intelligent. Spent one night in Stockholm walking the streets with her and Liv Ullmann as she cursed Bergman..."He's taken advantage of us, pays us very badly...but we have to work with him...nobody else gives us jobs!" Very bitter.

ANTONIONI, MICHELANGELO (film director) Met him on top of the Pedrera (Casa Milà) in Barcelona while he was filming THE PASSENGER. Had met him before in Cannes when he presented his film L'AVVENTURA. The public had laughed, booed and left the Palais du festival. I spotted him in an upstairs hallway, with his wife, Monica Vitti. Both were crying. It was a disaster...so they thought. They won the Palm d'Or that year.

ASTURIAS, MIGUEL ÁNGEL (writer) Tours Film Festival-1968.

AUB, MAX (writer) Gruff, friendly, curious, always asking aggressive questions.

BACALL, LAUREN Balboa Beach, California 1945. I was on a small outboard motor boat with two older friends. We went away very happy to have seen a star.

BARBARA (singer) would come to the Contrescarpe to sing. Extraordinary voice. Nice, friendly...strange. She'd sing, get paid 20 francs, and then go on to another bar, L'ÉCLUSE.

BARDOT, BRIGITTE During filming of VIVA MARÍA. Funny, more beautiful off-screen than on. Lazy. In Paris organized trips to take her to the cinema. Impossible for her to go alone. Crowds would rip her apart. We'd leave her apartment (5 of us). She would put on a black wig and dark glasses...Two friends would go in and save the seats. As soon as the film started, the other three would sneak her in. Before film finished, we had to hustle her out into a waiting car.

A little tight-fisted. Every time I went to her house for lunch, the same menu: endives and *jambon en sauce béchamel*.

Fan mail very interesting. From all over the world. Two secretaries quit on her. They couldn't stand to open her mail because of disgusting things sent. One letter from Catholic school class in the U.S. The students wanted her to send money so they could buy a Cadillac for their teacher, Sister Beatrice, who was forced to take the bus every day.

I used to accompany her as she walked her dog. One day we were strolling along, talking quietly when a very well dressed, middle-aged woman, typical of the 16th arrondissement, started calling Brigitte a whore, a no good bitch etc. etc. Brigitte said, "*Mais, madame, qu'est-ce que je vous ai fait??*" (But, madam, what have I done to you?) And the lady got angrier and angrier. Finally we had to retreat. Bri told me this happened quite regularly.

BASIE, COUNT Concert at Oberlin College. 1955.

BECKETT, SAMUEL Paris- I was going out with a girl, an American architect. One evening, sitting in a café, this white-haired man came up and, without looking at me, started yelling at her. I didn't know what to do but was ready to protect her honour. Then he walked away. It was Samuel Beckett.

BELMONDO, JEAN-PAUL (actor)-Nice. With age he lost his charm, but he used to be funny.

BERGER, HELMUT (actor) Strange person, neither Man, nor Woman but a Thing.. A chair, a tree, a left-handed frog, nice person. Once while preparing a scene during the filming of FANTOMAS, he sent me a note, "I'm in love with you, I want your body." I sent a note back, "All right, but I want your salary!" His answer was short and precise, "No!" Drank a lot, took drugs. Bisexual. Not a bad person. His make-up man said that Visconti had used him as a perverted pet...fed him drugs, used him.

BERGMAN, INGMAR Met him in Stockholm while he was filming with **LIV ULLMANN**. Strange look, intelligent...could be very cold...or very nice.

BERLANGA, LUÍS GARCÍA (Spanish film director) Anti-Franquista.Made some very good films despite censors. Story he told me:

> When he was very young, because of his social class, he had joined the Division Azul, a crack military group that Franco had organized to thank Hitler for the aid he had given the Spanish Fascists during the Civil War. The Division Azul was sent to the Russian front. Berlanga, being very young, was given night-guard duty the first day. It was very dark. His officers positioned him and told the young soldier to keep a keen watch. The Russians could sneak up on them and cut their throats. Luis stared into the pitch-black night, trembling. As the dawn light slowly rose...he could not make out a horizon or any features in the landscape. Everything seemed flat. It was. He had been standing about a foot's distance from, and facing, a blank wall all night, his back to where the enemy action was supposed to be.

BREL, JACQUES On the island of Antigua during the filming of Lelouch's L'AVENTURE, C'EST L'AVENTURE. Quiet, retired, would sing songs as he drove the jeep that would take us to the location.

BRUBECK, DAVE Oberlin College. 1953.

BONDARCHUK, SERGEI Important Russian film director of the 40's and 50's. Acapulco Film Festival. Could not hold his tequila. Put him to bed several times.

BRONSON, CHARLES Brutish animal. Worked as assistant director with him on THE BATTLE OF ST. SEBASTIAN. Once, Uli Piccardt (Silberman's *chef de production*) called me. "Charlie is in Paris and lonely, go to the George V Hotel and see if you can do something to cheer him up. He likes you." I went over and saw Charlie in his apartment. Since he wasn't the King of Conversation, I started, "Let's go have a drink in the Champs Élysées..." His answer, "Fucking Champs Élysées!" So I said, "How about going to St. Germain, nice little bistros there..." His answer again was "Fucking St. Germain!" "Charlie, do you like Paris?" "Fucking Paris!" I left him to his own fucking self.

CALDER, ALEXANDER A French farmer once was asked to define Calder. "It's easy," he said, "When you meet Sandy on the path, he's the first one to say hello."

Once while watching him work in his studio (he was making small mobiles) he looked up. "Now what do I do?" I shrugged. "Let's go have some wine," he chuckled. I helped him put together and repaint some old fly-specked sculptures...

Just before dinner we would play billiards in a cellar game room he had in the new house. Funny thing, his hands would tremble, but when he picked up the pool cue, or the pliers, they would be rock-steady.

One night, in the old house we drank too much wine. He had a huge treble-shaped cave embedded in the side of the mountain where he had thousands of bottles of good country wine. The labels had fallen off so he had forgotten which was which. He'd just say, "Go get a couple of bottles from the far pile." They were always cool and delicious.

In the garden of his house we would always make paellas or grilled lamb chops. He would arrive loaded down with wine bottles and would be the last to leave. Louisa would play the accordion.

During the Vietnam War, Calder would give prints and paintings to organizations that were against the war. His son-in-law, Jean Davidson, Sandra's husband, would help get deserters out of France and into Switzerland or over to Sweden. Of course they were on Nixon's "blacklist." Sandy even protested against the War in front of the American Embassy.

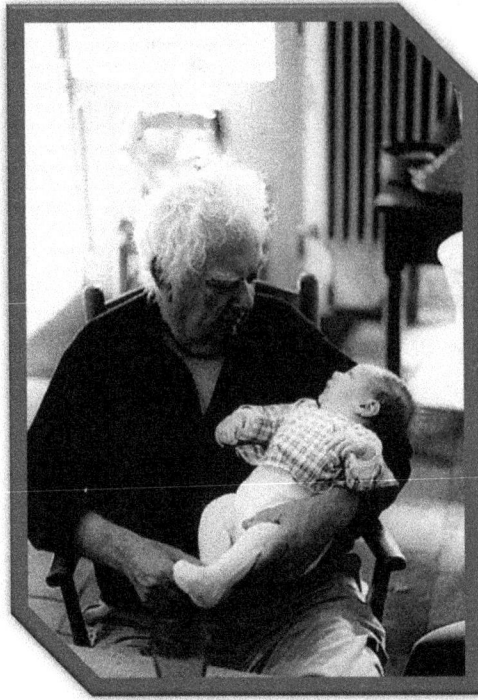

Sandy Calder with Juan Luis' baby, Diego.

CARRINGTON, ELEONORA (painter) In Mexico City. Used to go to her house for "seances"...try to raise the dead by making a table move. The only trouble was that the table that she had for this experiment was so heavy that I could hardly lift it. I told her that we would need a very strong ghost to make the table move but that did not dampen her enthusiasm. The table never moved

CEDILLO, ERNESTO President of Mexico-1996-Palacio de Bellas Artes-Expo Buñuel.

CLEAVER, ELDRIDGE New York 1968-While making documentary on the Black Panthers and the Black Power movement. Great speaker. His book SOUL ON ICE and his speeches were criticized because of the street language he used. But when he started a speech, he would explain street talk. This is the way we do it in the streets. He would use perfect English to prepare his audience. Then, with a warning, would slip into the MOTHAFUCK gears. He would talk for three or fours hours. Of course, *Time* and *Newsweek* magazines would never mention the fact that he did explain why he used this language. He was guarded by six-feet-tall Black Panthers. Once, at one of his speeches in Harlem, his personal bodyguards let everyone rush up for autographs and to shake his hand. I yelled at them to keep the people back, to not let what had happened to Malcolm X happen here. (Malcolm X was assassinated right after one of his speeches.)

Last saw him sitting sadly alone at an outdoor café on the Place Denfert Rochereau during the '80's.

Finally made it back to the U.S. where he became a clothes designer and developed men's pants, bringing back the codpiece.

CLINTON, BILL Martha's Vineyard. As they were boarding the Kennedy yacht.

Finally I did meet Clinton when he was signing his book in a Martha's Vineyard bookstore. This was just before the Bush-Gore elections. I told him, "You know, Mr. Clinton, in Europe we are very worried about the United States." He took me aside and whispered, "So am I."

DE GAULLE, CHARLES French Embassy Mexico D.F. He was all red. Sunburned because he had refused to wear a hat while visiting the Pyramids.

DELON, ALAIN Met him several times in studio restaurants or around Paris. Talked about guns. Not very smart, good actor.

DENEUVE, CATHERINE Good actress.. Liked to take chances with different scripts. She told me once that you have to treat people with "*mépris*" (contempt) for them to respect you.

Juan Luis with Catherine Deneuve at a showing of *Tristana,* 2008.

DEL RIO, DOLORES Sweet, not too smart. Kept talking about how the *rebozo* should be the Mexican woman's national dress.

> Editor's note: A rebozo is a long rectangular flat woven garment, like a shawl with fringes, used by Mexican women for warmth, to carry babies, etc.

ELLINGTON, DUKE Played at Oberlin College 1956.

FELLINI, FEDERICO Cannes Film Festival...after projection of LA DOLCE VITA.

FELIPE, LEÓN (Writer) Very kind man. Went to a Shakespeare-in-Spanish play with him in Mexico City at Palacio de Bellas Artes.

FELIPE, Rey de España (King of Spain)-Met him at inauguration of Spanish *liceo* (high school) in Paris. Very *simpatico*, felt like having a beer with him.

FÉLIX, MARÍA Tough but funny. Once, on SONATAS, Bardem's film, she asked me to play poker at night after the shoot. We were in a small hotel near Tajin, Veracruz. I was third assistant director with a salary of .003 pesos a week. The game started and I found myself with three aces. I bet all I had. About $20 pesos. María looked at me coldly and raised me $10,000 pesos. I protested, "María, you're the star of this film and make a thousand times more money than me!" "Juan Luis," she murmured, "If you don't know how to play..." I folded and then quit the game. She took my $20 pesos. But she was funny...

FERNÁNDEZ, EMILIO (*El Indio*) Film director. Dangerous man when drinking. Killed four persons. Last one was an extra in one of his films. He had dared criticize one of Indio's cinematographic works. Shot him in the back. Once in Cannes he made me smoke three Delicados cigarettes to prove that Mexican tobacco was better than French tobacco. I agreed. Did not want to be shot down on the Croisette. Also I was not carrying a gun. My opinion is that Indio's "art" was more the creation of Gabriel Figueroa's cinematography.

FINNEY, ALBERT (Actor) Met him around 1972 at Deauville Film Festival. In Paris, he came to house, played the guitar and sang Shakespeare sonnets he had put to music. Very warm, funny, friendly.

FUENTES, CARLOS Parties in Mexico during early '60s. Showing off with girls. Going into bedroom with tall blonde American chick during festivities...coming out hair and clothes wrinkled, girl coming out after. Straightening her dress Did it to let everyone know what had happened. Very nice, great talker. Parties at the Mexican Embassy in Paris while he was ambassador.

DE FUNÈS, LOUIS (Actor) At bar of Studios de Billancourt. Sat next to him; started chatting in Spanish. He was born in Valencia. Came to France when very young.

GABOR, ZAZA Jean-Claude Carrière once called me up. "Quick, come to diner tonight. ZaZa Gabor is coming over and I don't know what to say to her!" Nobody knew what to say to her. We weren't of her glittering show-biz world, didn't know any gossip. She had on a very elaborate dress and was heavily made up...we weren't. Just didn't have anything to say to her. Poor thing, she was bored. So were we. The dinner broke up very early.

GAGARIN, YURI In Saint-Germain-des-Prés, on Rue de Buci at a Communist bookstore. Shook his hand. He was the first man to circle the globe in a spacecraft. Was in Paris to promote his book...sponsored by the Soviet government.

GARBO, GRETA One night at a party in the Dakota in Zachary Scott's apartment, I was sitting on a pile of coats on the bed, talking with someone. An elderly lady was trying to extricate a coat upon which I had settled. I excused myself and chatted with the lady: Greta Garbo. Very discreet, nice.

The Willard Gallery was on 72nd Street East and Madison Ave. I had two shows there. In the mornings I would watch, from the second floor window, Garbo, dark glasses, short fur coat, scarf around her head, going to the market carrying her canvas shopping bags. I could not help but notice her very large feet. She was quite tall and did not wear high heels.

GARCÍA MÁRQUEZ, GABRIEL Mexico during the early sixties. I had sublet an apartment-studio from Vicente Rojo. Every Saturday night we had parties in this studio or at friends' houses. Everyone was broke...everyone drank a lot (una *cubita-ron y Coca Cola y mucho hielo* [much ice]). One night (1963) Gabo (Garcia Márquez) got fresh with Joyce so I threw him out physically.

One day, as I was driving up Calle Altavista in Mexico City, I saw Gabo hitching a ride. I picked him up and he told me this story:

I had been waiting for a cab for about half an hour. Finally I saw one coming up towards me. Calle Altavista is heavily lined with *pirule* trees and the cab kept passing from shadows to bright sun. He was still far away when I noticed that he had a passenger riding next to him in the shotgun seat. So I turned away and started looking for another cab. Then, as he approached, I faced the oncoming cab and noticed that there was no one riding besides the driver, so I flagged him down. Either I had made a mistake or the passenger had gotten off when I had turned away. I also got into the right front seat, gave him my address and added, "You know, I could have sworn that someone was riding next to you when you were down the block." The cab driver looked at me in a frightened manner. I noticed that his face was white and strained. "You know," he said, "You're the fifth person that's told me that today." I sat frozen for a while. Was I then sitting on someone who was occupying the seat? I was glad to get out of the cab and wished the driver a good day. He drove off without answering, a worried look on his face.

GODARD, JEAN-LUC Cold, condescending. Big graffiti at the Sorbonne during May '68: "*Godard est le plus con des Suisses pro-Chinois*" (Godard is the worst Swiss jerk of the supporters of Mao's China).

GOYTISOLO, JUAN (Spanish poet and novelist) Paris-Friendly, quiet, warm...

GONZÁLEZ, FELIPE (Prime Minister of Spain)-1996-Reina Sofia Museum during small expo dedicated to L.B. Charismatic. Tried to show him small print in a book, Felipe pretends to read, looks at me, smiles, embarrassed, "I haven't put on my glasses." Too many reporters. I was forced to read the passage to him in a low voice.

HAN SUYIN-(Writer)-Met her in Angkor Wat, Cambodia in 1962. I was assistant to André Michel on a film she had written CAST THE SAME SHADOW (based on her novel of the same name). A very impressive woman. I called her, behind her back, the Dragon Lady. The film was pretty bad and never distributed.

HOPPER, DENNIS (Actor) *Chez les Grenier*. Very turned on, funny.

HOUSTON, JOHN- D.F. House of Alice Rahon, painter, and Ed Fitzgerald, set designer of L.B.'s films in Mexico. L.B. makes loud comment about how Houston has sold out many times. Houston himself pleasant enough. Nobody said much.

JONES, JAMES (Writer) Lived on the Île St.-Louis. Wanted to name his son Charles Orson Jones...in this manner he would have the initials of C.O. Jones. This should be read in Spanish.

His wife, Gloria, tough New Yorker, had been Marilyn Monroe's stand-in. When he sold the rights to FROM HERE TO ETERNITY for one million dollars, Gloria walked into La Coupole flashing the check to everyone.

Gloria hated nature and Jim always told this story: "On the so and so golf course, there is a bar situated near the 10th hole. Once Gloria was sitting at the bar having some champagne. She turned around and **looked** at the green of the 10th hole, shuddered, and turned back to her drink. That's the closest Gloria ever got to Nature."

Spent two summers on the island of Spetsai (Greece) at Clem Wood's house. Did a lot of skin diving with Jones. We were expert urchin fishermen. He rented a large fishing boat...all the families would clamber aboard and we'd drop anchor in a small quiet bay on the far side of the island. Jones and I would dive down to get the sea urchins while the ones who remained on board would cool the Retsina wine, open the urchins, and cut the bread. Thousands of urchins and as many bottles of Retsina were consumed.

He'd written a novel on the social life, the gossip and the intrigues of the foreign colony of Spetsai. Everyone recognized themselves and some people were not very flattered by the naked manner in which he described them.

One night we were invited to an English Lord's (Beaverbrook?) home for drinks and dinner. Gloria told him not to start a scandal. But we had a few drinks before going and a few more in the horse-drawn carriages (cars were not allowed on the island) on the way out. Jim called Beaverbrook "Lord Beaverfuck" and we got thrown out...so we went home and had a couple more drinks.

Jim died of massive heart attacks and he tape-recorded himself as he died. One could hear the cries of pain and his commentary on this final event. He was cremated. As friends and family headed back to New York City in a limousine, Gloria, his wife, looked at the small urn in which Jim's ashes were kept and said, "Jesus, Jim's pecker was bigger than this."

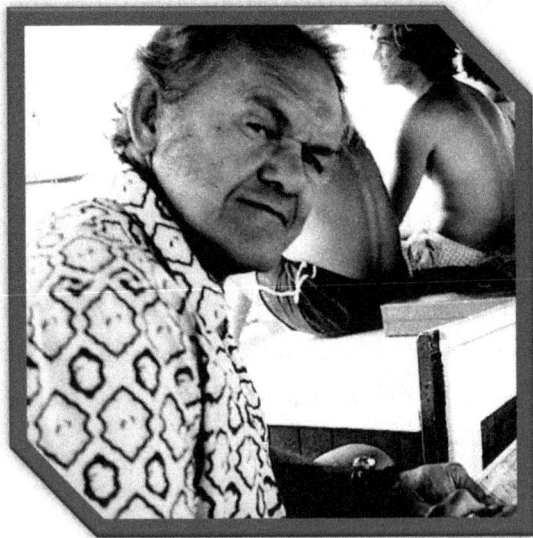

KELLY, GENE At the Cinémathèque in Paris. A not very tall, smiling man. Nice.

KEROUAC, JACK Cannes Film Festival 1959 or 60.

LELOUCH, CLAUDE (Film Director) Did L'AVENTURE, C'EST L'AVENTURE as an actor with him. He always worried about how much public each different camera angle would bring in. "This shot, with the mountains in the background, will bring in 50, 000 viewers." He wanted me because I reminded him of Fidel Castro. I warned him, "I'm a director also and I know that I'm a bad actor." "It doesn't matter, you'll see!" he replied. When the filming was over I asked him, "Well?" "You were right," he acknowledged.

KAUFMAN, PHILIP (American film director) Acted in his film HENRY AND JUNE. Did two scenes, seduced María de Medeiros (both María and I had horrible colds.Our kleenexes covered the set's floor) and tried to pick up Uma Thurman (this scene was cut from the final montage).

LAFON, MONSIEUR (Founder and owner of La Coupole) Very tight-fisted. Owned an empty lot next to Coupole on the Boulevard Montparnasse and his brasserie was a two-storied structure. Opened in 1927, my father went to opening. Lafon's sons wanted to sell the empty lot and build above the restaurant. The old man would say, "While I'm alive, there'll be nobody above me." One of his son told me, as I was doing the documentary on the Coupole, "We're waiting for our father to die so that we can sell."

LANGLOIS, HENRI Director of the Cinémathèque Française.

LEE, CHRISTOPHER "Dracula." Interviewed him for a film in Paris. very frustrated man. Was an opera singer but was typecast as The Vampire and couldn't get out of that role. Bit of a bore. Kept talking about himself. "I did over 120 films but I'm known only as Dracula!"

LEMMON, JACK Acapulco Film Festival 1961. Went fishing with him Very pleasant person. Not pretentious.

Actor Jack Lemmon

LEONE, SERGIO In Rome while preparing LEONOR. Had lunch several times with him at Morricone's home. Very friendly, funny and warm.

MACKENDRICK, ALEXANDER (American-born Scottish film director) THE MAN IN THE WHITE SUIT, SWEET SMELL OF SUCCESS. Acapulco film Festival. Had long talks with him in the bar of the Hotel Presidente. He said:

> In the final analysis, the only countries where one can live decently are Catholic countries: Mexico, Spain, Italy, France...The worst are the Anglo-Saxon or Protestant

countries: England, U.S.A., Germany, Sweden...There Man is responsible for himself to his God. In the Catholic countries, things are cooler. You sin, womanize, eat, drink too much, kill a couple of children...just go to a nice priest, confess and for the right prayers or sum of money, you're morally free again. What peace!

MADRID, MIGUEL DE LA (President of Mexico) At a reception for him given by Mitterand in the Élysée Palace.

MALLE, LOUIS Assistant on two films: VIVA MARÍA and LE VOLEUR. Born into a very rich northern France sugar family, les Sucres Béghin. There were four brothers; When each one reached the age of 21, their father gave them one million dollars to start their lives. Louis used his money to produce LE MONDE DU SILENCE with Cousteau.

One day, during the filming of LE VOLEUR, Louis' mother came on the set. Louis had warned me that she was a little eccentric. I was standing next to Jean-Paul Belmondo discussing the next scene. Louis came up and said, "Mama, let me introduce you to J.-P. Belmondo." And then he pointed to me. Mrs. Malle grabbed my hand, pumping it enthusiastically, telling me how she'd seen all my films, that she was my biggest fan. Jean-Paul stood besides Louis' mother, laughing. At last she left, convinced that she had met the famous actor.

Louis died from an infectious disease he had caught in a hospital during an operation and the services were held in St.-Sulpice. He was an atheist but his family decided to put on the show.

MALRAUX, ANDRÉ Mexico D.F. French Embassy

MAN RAY 1965 in New York at his Gallery. There he told me, "You know, during the thirties when you had an exposition, you were sure of one thing...you *never* sold anything!" Later saw him in Paris when he was very old and sick. His mind was still sharp but his body had ceased to function.

MARAIS, JEAN (Actor and friend of Jean Cocteau) Acapulco Film Festival. One night I heard loud shouts and footsteps running towards my room at the Revolcadero Hotel. Suddenly Breno Mello, the handsome black star of ORFEU NEGRO, rushed into my room."Lock the door," he pleaded. "Jean Marais is after me!" He was scared. I locked the door just in time. Marais was outside, in the corridor, banging on the door..."Breno, come out! I want to speak to you!!" He had fallen in love with the young man, had drunk a little too much and now was hot on his tracks. Breno pleaded with his eyes. Jean at that time was quite strong and Mello was an innocent Brazilian soccer player turned actor. So I didn't open the door and saved Mello's virginity.

MARCH, FREDERICK (American actor) I went to the same school as his son in New York...1943.

MASTROIANNI, MARCELLO 1974 During filming of LA FEMME AUX BOTTES ROUGES.

McCARTHY, MARY (Author) During the 60's. Met her at Clem Wood's house, along with James Jones. Distant, not much to say to each other. Handsome woman.

MEERSON, MARY One of the directors of the Cinémathèque Française.

MILLER, HENRY Cannes Film Festival. Stayed at same hotel. Had breakfast with him every morning. He was member of the jury. One day he came up to me and said, "Got a hot date tonight but don't have any money, dontcha see.. I don't know what I'm going to do."

Next morning I asked him how it had worked out, "Fine, bought a couple of bottles of *vin rouge* and we went on the beach with a blanket, dontcha see...." He must have been 70 years old.

MIRÓ, JOAN New York during the 40's, then at my expo at the Willard Gallery, New York, then in Paris. Last time at the Maeght Gallery. Later we had lunch with Calder and Maeght at the gallery owner's apartment. Maeght's wife drops contact lens into soup. Miró and Calder fishing around looking for lost eye. Side note: Maeght had his own "*soubrette*" (maid) to serve him while Mrs. Maeght had a handsome Oriental manservant to serve her.

MITTERAND, FRANÇOIS 1973 Dinner at the Élysée, with Mexico's President de la Madrid. Intimate meal with 300 guests. Small orchestra playing royal music for the entrance of France's president. He was **the King**! Cold, pretentious, intelligent...sneaky. Very small in size.

MONK, THELONIUS At the Five Spot in New York. 1958. You'd buy a beer for 35 cents, stand at the bar and listen to the Monk all night. The Flora and Fauna of the East and West villages would gather there for the sounds.

MONTAND, YVES (actor) Not very interesting and very full of himself.

MOREAU, JEANNE (Actress) Very intelligent. Could do what she wanted with men. Could be deadly with rival female. Once accompanied her on guitar, as she sang, in Cuernavaca during her birthday party.

Luis Buñuel directing Jeanne Moreau, *Diary of a Chambermaid* (1964).

MORENO VILLA, JOSÉ (PEPE) Painter, poet, was part of the Residencia group. Warm, funny...painted on the walls of the garden of our house on Félix Cuevas huge flowers and a sign saying "*Las flores que no planté salieron en la pared*" (The flowers that I didn't plant appeared on the wall). Before leaving for Europe, my father had ordered my mother not to plant any flowers in the new garden.

MORRICONE, ENNIO Did the music for LEONOR. Went to eat several times at his house with Sergio Leone. Asked me what I wanted to eat. "A Rugetta salad." When I arrived he had prepared a huge salad of rugetta (arugula), enough for ten people.

MOYNIHAN, DANIEL PATRICK (Politician, friend and assistant to J.F. Kennedy) In Paris, at a dinner *chez les Greniers*.

NICOLSON, JACK (Actor) In Barcelona, on the roof of Gaudi's Pedrera, he was acting in Antonioni's THE PASSENGER. Very nice, we chatted a while and then I left.

OPPENHEIM, MÉRET (Surrealist painter) In the 60's at María Kahl's house on Rue Campagne Première.

OSBORNE, JOHN (Playwright) Acapulco Film Festival. Picnic at Miguelito Alemán's (his father was Miguel Alemán, president of Mexico) house in Puerto Marquez. Everyone dressed like North American Indians and got very drunk. Conversation not very lucid.

PASOLINI, PIER PAOLO Rome. Went to a private showing of one of his films and to an exterior set where he was shooting.

PAZ, OCTAVIO Mexico. At home and at several expos. Nice, warm.

PHILIPE, GÉRARD (Actor) Paris and on film LA FIÈVRE MONTE à EL PAO.

PICABIA, GABRIELLE Widow of Francis...very old, very frail, at Calder's house in Saché where she was a guest.

POLANSKI, ROMAN First met him in Cannes, then again in London. Friendly.

PRÉVERT, JACQUES Simone Signoret telephoned Prévert and arranged a rendez-vous with him. I went over one morning, early. He lived on top of the Moulin Rouge in Pigalle. From his living room stretched a huge terrace with the sign of the Moulin Rouge sticking up on the street side. He was always smoking, never took the cigarette out of his mouth. Smoke would curl up into his eyes, made them cry but he never spit out the damned butt. Showed me small bistros around Montmartre. Very popular with the inhabitants and denizens of the "*barrio.*" On morning he called me. He had just seen NAZARÍN. He said that I should come over immediately. I took the Metro and rushed to Pigalle. He was very anti-clerical. He sat me down in front of a cup of coffee. He had not liked the film. The priest in the story turned out to be *sympathique.* You must never show a sympathetic priest. No matter what.

RAY, NICOLAS (Film director). Lunch in Madrid with L.B.

RICHARDSON, TONY (film director) Same party I attended with John Osborne in Acapulco.

ROONEY, MICKEY First met him in Mexico at Churubusco Studios where he was shooting a film circa 1948. Then worked with him in Portugal in 1992 as an actor. Interesting and funny and very tiring because of his enormous energy. Never stopped talking. Told many stories.

Walt Disney once asked him if he could borrow his name for a new cartoon character: Mickey Mouse.

While filming in Portugal, an actor's girlfriend came on the set. A beautiful huge blond. Rooney rushed over and spoke with her for several minutes. Then he came back to me and said thoughtfully, "Ya know, someplace in this world, there's a fellow who's very very happy he's not with her!"

He said that the studios screwed them all. They had all been highly underpaid.

He used to go out with Errol Flynn barhopping, getting into fights. Said that everyone wanted to punch little Mickey. He was tough.

He got Marilyn Monroe her first job...a walk-on extra.

Ava Gardner: he said they were both immature, didn't work out. Never badmouthed her.

An anecdote about Samuel Goldwyn:

> On one of the stages, a beautiful set had been built. A whole house, inside and out, with gardens, rooms, furniture, wall paper, paintings, a working kitchen...It was wonderful and had taken several months to build. The proud set designer called in Samuel Goldwyn to show off his baby. Goldwyn took one look at it and, in his heavy Eastern European accent, said, "All right, eliminate it!" and he stalked off.
>
> The technicians were flabbergasted. But the Great Boss had spoken. A wrecking crew went in and, since it is easier to destroy than to build, the set was torn down in a few days. Then Samuel Goldwyn walked into the sound stage. He roared out, "Vat hest heppened to dat beeautiful set, the vonderfull house???"
>
> The set designer was shocked, "But, sir, you told us to eliminate it!"
>
> "Yes," roared Goldwyn, "Eliminate it...illuminate it! Put in de big lights for the shooting of the film!!!" A tragic misunderstanding. The set was rebuilt.

Juan Luis (as actor) with Mickey Rooney.

SAVAL, DANY (Actress)-Acapulco Film Festival: After having ingurgitated a great number of Margaritas, she danced to Latin American rhythms with much fervor. Too much fervor. I held her head as she vomited into a toilet bowl all the delicious tacos and carnitas and guacamole she had eaten earlier that evening.

SIGNORET, SIMONE (Actress) She lived on the Place Dauphine, just a few blocks from Rue Mazarine. I would go over in the afternoons to talk with her and to drink cognac. The downstairs living room was very long, one window looking out onto the Place Dauphine and the other onto the Quai. Montand treated Simone quite badly. If his cigarettes were a foot away, he would snap his fingers and call Signoret over from the other side of the room to have her fetch them.

Once, he was away on a film and I was talking with Simone and drinking cognac. There was a knock at the door. Simone went to answer and a cute, stupid-looking girl asked if Montand was there. Simone asked her name. "Nicole," answered the girl. Then Signoret let her have it. She cussed her up and down with some beautiful words. Then she let the young woman know that, if she wanted to see her lover, she shouldn't do it when his wife was present. She then slammed the door and without a comment, we resumed our conversation and drinking.

She introduced me to Jacques Prévert.

Sometimes she would drop by the house on Rue Roli for a coffee. Once we made up abstract music with an old tape recorder.

Luis Buñuel directing Simone Signoret and Charles Vanel in *Death in the Garden* (1956).

SUN RA Musician and showman-New York-When I did my documentary on Black Power in 1968, he set up a show for the documentary in one of Charles' lofts. Filmed him for two days. He and his group would dress in semi-black African, semi-Egyptian and invented Harlem Village costumes and they would sing and dance. His music was far-out and discordant.

TAMAYO, RUFINO Was my drawing teacher at the Dalton School in New York during World War II. Later pushed me towards having my first expo of wire sculptures in Mexico City at Rosita Gal y Bay's gallery on Reforma near the Cine Chapultepec. Tamayo was always fighting with his wife Olga. She came out with the phrase, "The prettiest green in painting is the shade of green of the U.S. dollar bill."

TAMIROFF, AKIM and his wife **TAMARA** (actors) Played Sancho Panza in Welles' DON QUIXOTE. Both very warm, funny Russian actors. They urged me to continue on in films.

THULIN, INGRID (Swedish actress) One of Bergman's favorites. Very attractive and very very funny. Usually didn't say anything during long-winded conversations but then suddenly she'd drop the "mot juste" and destroy everyone.

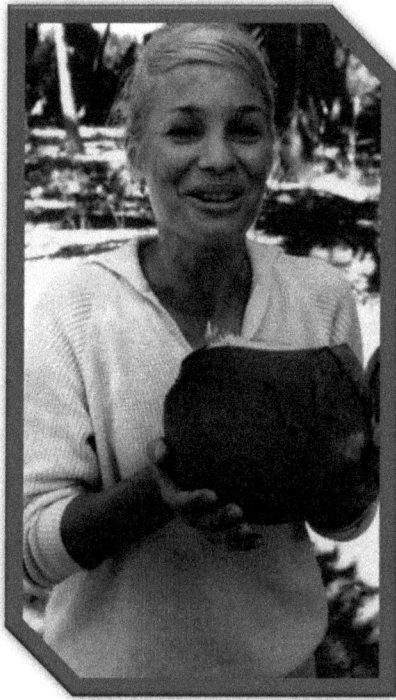

Swedish actress Ingrid Thulin.

TORRIJOS, GENERAL (President of Panama) Hard-working. Hated the Americans. Got up very early to visit his different projects. Ángel Bilbatúa (cameraman and friend who invited me to Panama to do documentary) warned him that he had a rotten apple in his crew...an officer named Noriega. Torrijos said, "Don't worry, I can handle him." Several months later he was blown apart in his plane. Noriega did it...and at that time Noriega's boss was the head of the C.I.A., i.e. George Bush. Later Bush invaded Panama to get rid of Noriega for his part in the drug smuggling... Draw your own conclusions.

TROUILLE, CLOVIS (Painter) Little gallery on Rue Guenegaud...his first expo. Late 1950's. The paintings were relatively cheap but I didn't have any money.

TRUFFAUT, FRANÇOIS Cold, condescending.

B. TRAVEN Met him on set of THE YOUNG ONE. He was a friend of Gabriel Figueroa. Went under the name of Torsvan. Pleasant, smiling, quiet. His wife, Chema, was present. Years later as I did REBELLIÓN DE LOS COLGADOS, Chema came on set. Then I realized that it had been Traven whom I had met years before. We both laughed.

QUINN, ANTHONY Coward. Liked to pick on the underlings. Played FronTennis with him every day in Durango and San Miguel Allende. He was a good player and would usually win, then buy a round of drinks. One day I was lucky and won...it was my turn to buy drinks. Quinn, furious, broke his racket on the ground. Good actor.

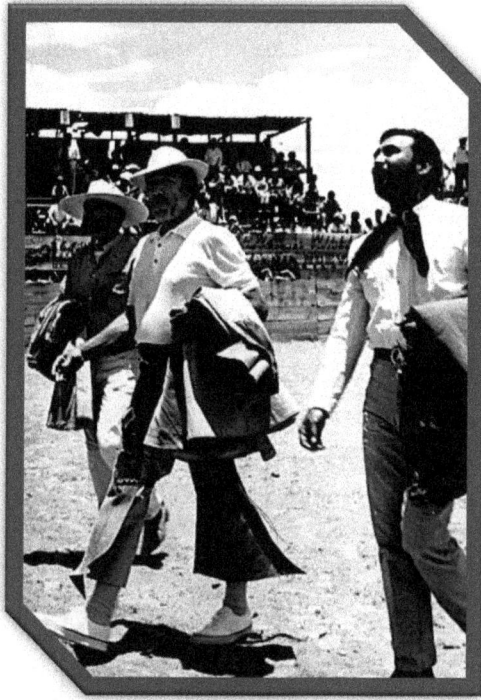

Anthony Quinn at charity bullfight.

VALLI, ALIDA (Italian actress) Very loud and funny. Once in Acapulco she showed me how she was going to kick a hated producer...by kicking me. Later she excused her exuberant action.

VASARELY Met him at a gallery opening in Saint-Germain-des-Prés. Pretentious and cold.

VENTURA, LINO (Actor) I was co-actor with him in L'AVENTURE, C'EST L'AVENTURE, a Claude Lelouch film. Since I have a pretty bad memory, especially for dialogue, I would paste my text on Lino's and Jacques Brel's foreheads. Lino would be furious. Not very sympathetic but a good cook. I wanted to do

AVEUGLE, QUE VEUX-TU? with him but he did not want to play the role of a blind man. Later he told me he liked the film.

VIÑES, HERNANDO and LULU Were present at my birth. Good friends, lived in Montparnasse. Hernando, a marvelous painter, was on the committee who asked Picasso to do GUERNICA.

Hernando Viñes & Guitar (Juan Luis Buñuel)

WARHOL, ANDY 1963 In New York at a party. Boring. Then in Paris at Anne Marie Deschott's house for dinner. Boring...or else we had nothing to say to each other.

WEISMULLER, JOHNNY (TARZAN) Mexico City. Studio Churubusco 1947 during the filming of TARZAN AND THE MERMAIDS. At last I was to see Tarzan. Got to the studio during a publicity photo session. He was supposed to kneel on a stuffed sea turtle. He had a hard time kneeling because of his rheumatism. I was a bit disappointed. The last years of his life he was a swimming pool salesman and lived in Acapulco. Then he got Alzheimer's disease.

When he died, he was buried in the Acapulco cemetery. A large crowd was present. As the coffin was lowered, hidden loudspeakers gave out with his last Tarzan jungle call. Very touching, bordering on the ridiculous.

WELLES, ORSON Mexico-Filming of DON QUIXOTE.

WILDER, BILLY (Film director) Met him at Clem Wood's house. Talked about films...very encouraging.

WINTERS, SHELLEY (Actress) At the Durango, Mexico airport. I was waiting for a plane bringing some actors; she was about to leave. We started talking and immediately she started to complain about her husband, Vittorio Gassman.

Brilliant actress.

A FEW MORE THOUGHTS

Names

Just leaf through a phone book, any phone book. Names...millions of names. Like going into a super American pharmacy and trying to buy aspirins. In Chicago once I went into such an establishment. There were so many brands of aspirins, that I left, my head dizzy, without buying any. Too many, too confusing. And so with personal names. Far too many. Things should be simplified. Just one name, the same name, for everyone. Phone books with only one page. Not having to memorize all your friends' names or business associates, or butchers, bankers, newspaper hawkers. Just one name for everyone. You could never forget a name. No more embarrassment. What peace!

Hola

After having read society magazines like *Hola* and having seen the life of the rich and idle in the television journals, I am always amazed that the jobless workers and poorer segments of the population have not risen up and **slaughtered** those parasites. On the contrary, these deluded people buy the magazines and adulate the highsteppin' and high living.

I've seen *Hola* sold in small Mexican villages. In what manner do these *campesinos* (peasants) associate themselves with the idiotic European so-called "royalty"?

DEATH

When my grandmother, La Madrina, died in Zaragoza, we (my brother, my mother and my father) were in Mexico City. My father got the telegram in the late afternoon. After dinner, my mother came to my room and asked my brother and me to go down and stay a little with my father. She said he was very sad. We went downstairs and he brought out the family albums and spread them out on the dining room table. Then we sat around for an hour or so, looked at the pictures of La Madrina and the early years in Calanda and Zaragoza. My father told stories of his childhood. We had a couple of cognacs and then we all went to bed. He was very sad.

Still haven't figured it out. Neither has Life given me an answer. I've become very obsessed lately with the death of not only human beings, but of tiny creatures. A worm, a beetle...When you squash a mosquito, what is it that exactly happens? That little life ceases to exist. I don't really understand what happens. It is just a series of electrical impulses that suddenly cease? But is this discharge, as death occurs, absorbed into the universe? No, no, I'm not becoming a mystic. No fear of that...but I am curious about an explanation.

What is this "I"? Just a little brain cancer or a small knock on the head and the "I" doesn't exist anymore...or Alzheimers, the old timer's disease. And the Universe? The stars and space ...the Beginning and the End? There is really nothing to understand. But it would be nice to have more details before kicking off. All religions have just been sad attempts by scared men to justify their existence on this planet and especially a ploy to obtain power over other men. We just don't know enough to really explain anything. We can just hint at things. Every science is so complicated. Talk to

429

doctors or physicists and it is almost impossible to understand their jargon. No one yet has put it all together...don't know enough yet. I'm scared too...When the moment comes, I'll really be scared because I'm so sure there is nothing after. And I like it around here, don't want to leave. Maybe it's best to go out with a fizzle, instead of a bang...lose your memory, a little insanity, unconscious, then you slip away gently...not much fun for the family though.

What upsets me the most is the unfairness of it all. Those years of study, of friendships and loves and adventures...and then POOF. So unfair...and sad. It's so unfair...And all the things that I have gathered? All my junk, my collections. My children? Who's going to take care of them, yell at them to go to bed? I worry about them.

Since the age of 16, not one day has passed without Sex and Death slamming their way through my thoughts at least two or three times a day.

Especially Death.

As the joke goes: "I certainly don't believe in eternal life...but I sure as hell don't like the idea of being dead forever."

On The Wrong Track...

It seems that human beings are on the wrong track

For so many thousands of years, poets and singers, writers, musicians, philosophers and religious leaders have all clamored about the goodness of Man, about Love, about Happiness and that we must all strive for those emotions and in that way Man will be happy, will have the perfect philosophy...will finally live above war and hate...

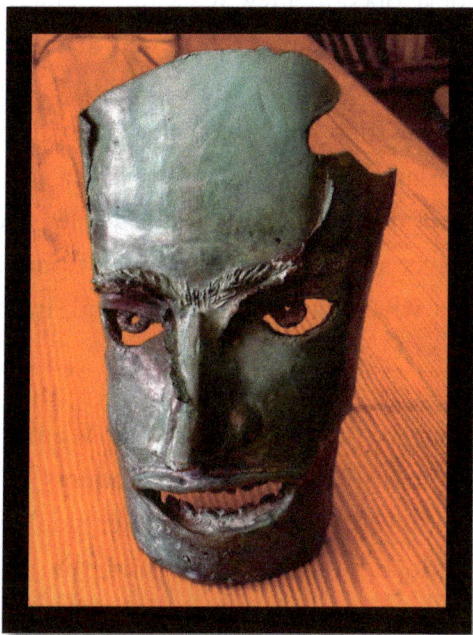

Green Mask Sculpture (Juan Luis Buñuel).

Humans have always fought against themselves. Gangs, tribes, sects...We are the only animals who *train* our young to kill members of our own species. If you kill off enough of your own species, you yourself will disappear. Wolves or rabbits or crocodiles or worms do not organize themselves to kill off their young...or their elders. The creation of religions, especially monotheistic (Jews, Christians, Muslims) with their only **true** god..."My God exists and yours doesn't...."

The joy with which our species goes into battle, the idiotic music and the mind-numbing parades, the cheers...and then after the battle, the rape and the killing...A country like Germany, with an intellectual class which had great philosophers, painters, writers and musicians, developed in a few years an extremely logical way to destroy millions of people. What happened in their minds? What did those people think about when they saw the destruction around them, when they heard the mad and illogical raving of Hitler? And Yugoslavia in the 90's, and Rwanda and the extremist Muslims in Algeria during the late 90's. And let's go back a little farther. The Greeks and the Trojans. Right from the beginning. What is going on, what went on, what goes on, in their minds, in our minds?

I think that we have been all wrong. We need a thinker, a philosopher who will forget about the goodness of Man (it does exist, but overshadowed by his much darker side). Such a person would admit the love that we have of war, the joy of killing, of destruction...and maybe think up a new philosophy that might allow us to live and better understand this viciousness in our being. See us as we are, and not set up goals we **never can achieve.** For the moment we are guided by horribly cynical and hypocritical philosophies, or by stupid and naïve ones. We must realize what we are and then find a manner of life that will protect us from each other.

I am not that philosopher, nor am I capable or interested.

Spanish Civil War (An Introduction)

A friend asked me to write an introduction to a book he was writing about the tortures and humiliations his father (from Calanda) had enduring during and after the Civil War.

Paris, November 27, 1999

Like the majority of the thousands of Spanish Republican families, mine spent all its existence in exile because of the Spanish Civil War. We went from Paris to NY, L.A., Mexico City....etc. From around 1939-1983 (when my father died), I can still remember the heated discussions among his Republican friends until the early hours of dawn. From my bed I could hear the shouting: "Because in the Teruel front...," "The Republican government," "....el POUM, la FAI (Federación Anarquista Ibérica), the communists...the traitors were the British, French, and Americans who didn't even lift a finger." "And why didn't we do...?"

As the night continued, they kept getting angrier and angrier. Until they came to the point of long silences...and a great suffering. So many people had been thrown out of their homes, forced to live in countries that offered them refuge...separated by force from loved ones, finding themselves among customs that were not their own.

"This year Franco will die!"...and so years passed...many of them died with that hope. But finally the day came when the little dictator was no more. It seems his final words during surgery to save him, were "How difficult it is to die!" Poor little thing!

433

The story of Mr. Moliner is a great one—a story of a battle against the fascist elements that reigned in Spain. What courage, what endurance to try over and over again to live a simple life with his family, and to be treated in such an ignoble fashion. Today, thanks to those circumstances, he doesn't live in Spain...while some of his barbaric neighbors sleep comfortably in their beds in Calanda and in other similar towns. This situation continues without the perpetrators having been brought to justice.

We observe the Spain of today and ask ourselves: "All that suffering, all those deaths, what for?"

Power, wealth, and the governing class, hand-in-hand with the corrupt and decadent Church, charged savagely against a segment of Spanish society. There were men like Moliner who confronted them and were punished throughout their life. This must never happen again. We must not forget.

(translation from Spanish by L. Ehrlich and Elena Fernández)

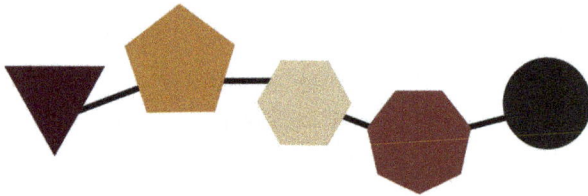

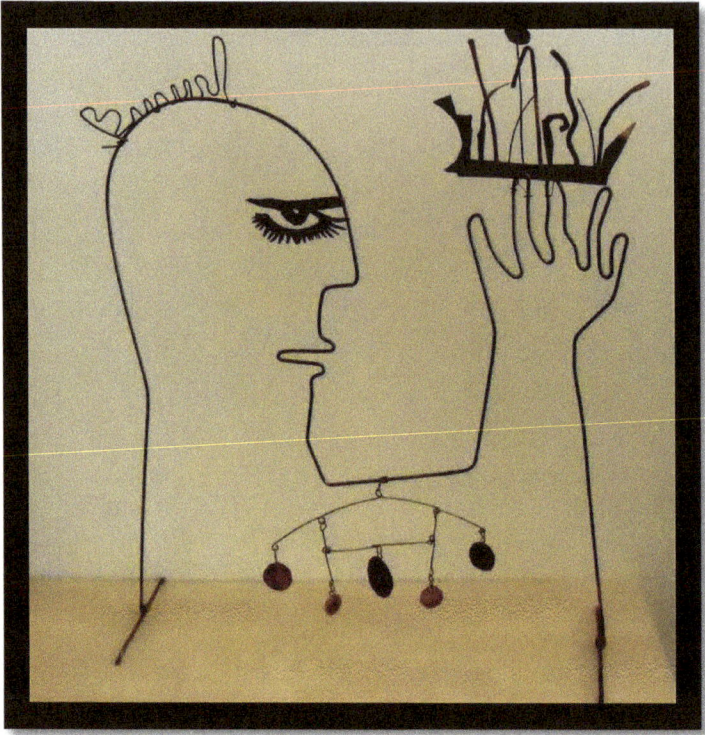

Juggling a sculpture (Juan Luis Buñuel)

Juan Luis' article about Alexander Calder[46]

originally published in the *Jornada de Morelos*

Because the Western democracies did not help the young Spanish Republic, Franco won the Spanish Civil War. Hitler and Mussolini of course, had helped him. And thousands of Spanish people had to leave their homes, spreading out all over the world as political refugees. They went to Mexico, Argentina, France, Peru, Cuba, England and the United States.

Those who found themselves in the non-Spanish-speaking countries had a hard time adjusting. Jobs were difficult to come by. But New York was a home away from home. During the 20's and the 30's, Paris, London and Madrid were the creative home for many American artists. And suddenly, in 1938 and 1939, New York artists opened their arms to their *compadres* (buddies) running from what was to be war-torn Europe.

My father, my mother, and I found ourselves stranded in what they now call the Big Apple. The year, 1940.

We were broke and, to help matters, my brother was born. Of course I have no memories of being broke. It was none of the children's business to know the hardships.

We lived in a kitchenette apartment (the double bed folded into the wall and the kitchen was a pantry that opened up exposing a tiny one-flame gas stove). I slept on a pile of pillows on the floor, my brother in a box.

---

[46] Editor's Note: While many of the stories included in this essay are a recap of earlier stories in the memoir – some fascinating new details are added. This warrants its inclusion.

Later I read letters that showed me what a hard time my parents had. My father, broke and without a job, would try to borrow money from friends. He found out that Dalí was living at the Pierre Hotel, a luxurious establishment in midtown Manhattan. Dalí, along with Federico García Lorca, had been his best friends, and Salvador had co-written my father's first film, UN CHIEN ANDALOU.

They had been very close friends so my father felt free to ask him for a $50 loan to pay the monthly rent. I still have the letter that Dalí wrote back. In so many words, it said that one must not lend money to friends and that he was glad that Franco had won the war. Strange thing to say...his other best friend, Federico García Lorca, had been cowardly shot in the back by a group of Fascists. Murdered.

That was the end of that friendship. But Dalí still kept another card up his sleeve, which I will divulge later on.

Alexander Calder immediately took us into his home. We lived with him for several months until my father was offered a job at the Museum of Modern Art (MOMA).

It was a happy time. Louisa Calder, Sandy's wife (her uncles were Henry and William James), would make delicious bread and every morning we would gather around the large kitchen table, to drink coffee (whenever it was available) and eat the hot buttered (whenever *that* was available) bread. The talk would always center on the Spanish Civil War and the new World War that was looming over the horizon. Being only six years old, I was not very interested in the conversation...but Sandy would absentmindedly make me little animals and mobiles to occupy me. I enjoyed watching him make the objects more than the "things" themselves. So, when he wasn't looking, I would dump them into the garbage. I must have thrown 30 or 40 beautiful little animals away. He didn't seem to mind...nor did he, I think, notice what I was doing. He just kept turning them out.

These were hard times and art wasn't easy to sell. I remember once he and Louisa wanted to go out and they needed one dollar to pay the babysitter. He didn't have one dollar. He offered the young babysitter a beautiful little mobile instead of that dollar bill...she refused and they didn't go out.

Sometimes friends would come over for dinner. They'd all bring bottles of cheap wine...my mother would make *"frites"* (French fried potatoes -excuse me, Freedom Fries) and we ate what was available in the market that day. Once the sun had set, sometimes the sirens would go off (an air raid alert) and everybody -Duchamps, Miró, Calder, other Spanish refugees, and my parents—would rush to the window to see the great spectacle. Watching all of New York's lights going out.

The Calders had a farmhouse and studio not far from the City and at times we loaded up what food we could find...especially the wine...and head out for the weekend on the local train. My mother and father would make big paellas and everyone drank great amounts of wine.

One day, the adults had gone off for a walk in the woods. I stayed behind. Sandy was going to shave.

I was playing in the garden when I spotted a green snake. My father had taught me how to grab a snake from behind, by its neck. I was proud of my catch and rushed into the house to show Sandy my new pet. I banged into the bathroom and there was

Sandy, a huge man, stark naked, his face covered with white lather and an immense straight razor in his right hand. I showed him my snake and he let out a roar, grabbed my beastie, rushed out into the garden and finished it off with a shovel. I can still see him smashing the poor critter. He became my enemy for several months. I guess he thought it was a poisonous snake.

Once we all went out, at Christmas, to José Luis Sert's house in Long Island. José Luis was the Director of the Harvard School of Architecture. They made a paella and someone made a turkey.

My father had bought me a small train. It wasn't electric but had a wind up spring motor. I was happily playing with my new toy when my father, Miró, Calder and Sert stumbled into the living room (they had been drinking red wine since early morning and were feeling good). With little ceremony, they threw me out of the room and spent a good hour playing with my train and laughing loudly. I was furious.

Here Dalí comes back into the picture. He wrote a book denouncing my father as an Atheist and a Communist. This got him some good points with certain political figures, but my father was asked to resign from MOMA.

So we said good-bye to New York friends and moved to California where my father was offered a job dubbing films into Spanish for the Latin American market. The War ended soon and in 1946 we moved to Mexico City where my father could finally make films.

∞ ∞ ∞

I did not see Sandy and Louisa for many years. I studied at Oberlin College in Ohio, wanted to be an English teacher. But instead, after four years of college, I got a job with an American director in Mexico who needed an assistant who could speak both Spanish and English. His name was Orson Welles. Then I worked with a group of American political refugees who had escaped Hollywood during the McCarthy fascist years.

Finally, in 1958, I went back to France to meet my extended family, loved them and Europe, and from then on, spent half of the year there...the other half was divided between New York and Mexico City.

Between films I started twisting wires and pounding metals. I liked being alone...Totally different than film where you work with teams of people.

My first expo was in Mexico. Then I flew to New York and went to see Sandy and Louisa in Roxbury. He welcomed me and helped me get my first show in New York at the Willard Gallery.

Sandy also spent part of his time in New York and then he would fly with no suitcases to Paris where a car would drive him directly from the airport to Saché in the Touraine. He had another house there with clothing and pliers and hammers and a studio...hence no suitcases when traveling. In fact he had another small house, a mill over a river, where he would put up friends.

Our friendship caught on again. I forgave him my dead snake and my little train. I'd go down for weekends, or for a week when I wasn't working on a film.

We would always take down food, to make paellas or Mexican Chicken Molé. Louisa would bring out her accordion and we'd drink and eat and laugh until the wee hours of the morning. Though at times Sandy would go to bed early and we'd continue the fiesta with his daughter Sandra and her husband, Jean Davidson.

At times we met in New York. Once I had another show at the Willard Gallery and Sandy, Miró and other friends would come over for lunch in the back room. Brie cheese, a huge salad and a couple of baguettes...

Once Miró came in and said, "Guess who I saw in Central Park as I was crossing it?" He made the sign with his fingers of the Dalí moustache. "A Rolls Royce pulled up behind me and Dalí jumped out. He called my name, 'Joan' (in Catalan) but I just turned my back and left him standing there."

After Dalí embraced Franco, it was impossible for the old Republican friends to accept him.

At times we'd go to a little restaurant in the Upper East Side. Sandy always fell asleep as the meal neared its end. He seemed fast asleep so, whispering, we decided to get out of there, leaving him to pay the bill.

As we silently stood up and got ready to accomplish our dastardly deed, Sandy's voice rumbled up from the table. "My part of the bill is $6. 75 cents!"

He was on Richard Nixon's blacklist because he generously donated paintings and sculptures to fight against the U.S.'s involvement in Viet Nam. He would give young men a place to stay as they moved north towards Switzerland and Sweden or Norway.

It was an honor to be on that list.

His daughter had built a small swimming pool and whenever the weather was warm he would plunge into the water to take several laps.

Next to his house, which was backed up against a mountain (the inside back wall was made of solid rock), he used the centuries-old wine caves which bit deep into the cliffside to store his wines. The caves were shaped like a three-leafed clover, about ten or 15 meters deep, and an ideal place to stock wine. He had placed hundreds of bottles of wine there, some dating back 20 years....the labels had fallen off most of them. But that didn't stop us. He'd say, "Go into the center cave, deep, and bring back five bottles." That would take care of us for the coming evening.

As he got older, this cliff house of stone by the river became a little too humid for him so he built another, larger place on the rim of the river valley a couple of kilometers from the old house. It was a large airy place with a billiard room in the cellar.

The old house was now used for friends.

One day I decided to sweep up. There were spider webs under the bed. So I poked around and pulled out an early Mondrian. I cleaned it up and when I showed it to him, he said that he had forgotten it years before. I also found a Max Ernst behind the radiator.

Every afternoon, before dinner, we'd shower up and play a game of billiards. He loved billiards. They were like his mobiles...the colored balls would dash around the table.

∞ ∞ ∞

Some times I would take him to the Etablisements Biémont where they would make his huge stabiles. Whenever he got an order for one of his creations, he always checked out where the prevailing winds came from in that region. Some of his stabiles were over 30 meters high, made of thick sheet steel. He would make a small-scale model, maybe three meters high, and test them in a wind tunnel. He would then tell the engineers where and how to point the sculpture. There was always a danger that a freak windstorm could bring the whole structure crashing down. One engineer took me aside once. He said that Sandy's judgment was uncanny. He never failed in his instructions on how to set the big "thing" up.

One Christmas Sandy had bought a huge pork leg. It was really very big and after much discussion, we decided to have it for dinner the next day...roasted over an open fire.

We jammed garlic cloves and bunches of thyme all over that leg, then rubbed salt and pepper all over the outside part. We let it sit all night.

Early next morning, we started a fire, put the creature on a spit and started turning it slowly. We started at 8 that morning. Every one helped with the turning, including Sandy, and by 9 p.m. it was ready. We had a new recipe for a roasted pig's leg.

Ingredients: One pork leg and one tree.... In those 13 hours we did burn up the equivalent in wood of one tree. (Those who worry about forests, this tree had been torn down by a storm.)

It was delicious (The pork leg).

In New York, during the Lincoln Center inauguration, both Alexander Calder and Henry Moore were invited to present their sculptures, which are still there on the great expanse in front of the Center. Moore had a huge round polished marble figure. Sandy's was a razor-sharp stabile. As they walked towards their respective sculptures for the opening ceremonies, Calder leaned over to Henry Moore and whispered in his ear, "Mine's pigeon proof." Both men burst out laughing.

Once there was a big expo of Sandy's "things" at the Guggenheim in New York. The mayor and the rest of the boys were present. Sandy got there a little late, the usual city traffic jams. As he pushed his way through the crowd, he noticed that one of his mobiles had suffered a slight injury and he pulled his trusty pliers from his back pocket. He reached up and started twisting the guilty wire when two security guards grabbed him and threw him out. "You can't touch the sculptures!" they yelled at him. Sandy tried to explain, "But I built them!" The argument was coming to a head as the director of the museum stepped in and saved the situation.

∞ ∞ ∞

Once a French TV crew was interviewing Sandy. The interviewer was an intellectually pretentious man. He kept saying that all the objects in Louisa's kitchen were beautiful works of art. It's true that many of the cooking implements had been made by

Sandy for Louisa's culinary needs: a large fork, a small basket to pluck a soft boiled egg from the boiling water, a broken teacup which he fixed by adding a twisted wire handle.

But this fellow was one boring cretin. At one moment he picked up a common wire coat hanger, looked at it in delight, and went off, in front of the camera, into a long diatribe on Calder's genius. That was it. Sandy let out a rumble, "This fellow's full of horseshit!" We got up and I spirited Sandy into my car and we went off for a ride.... of several hours.

When we got back they were gone.

It was a French farm laborer (the Calder house was surrounded by immense fields of grapevines) who best defined Sandy as a man. He said, "When Monsieur Calder takes his morning walk through the fields or the woodland and you meet up, he's always the first to greet you."

Juan Luis Buñuel

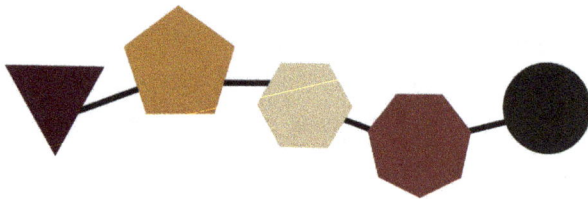

COLLECTIONS

Stones which have a story, which tell me something. I studied Geology in college and the professor taught us how to read stones: their origins ...igneous, sedimentary or metamorphic. I brought back 20 kilos of stones from Patagonia, stones polished by a millions years of hot and cold winds. Stones that were once shark teeth or bones. Semi-precious stones, red and green and blue...and black stones from the beach. A shell-encrusted stone from Sitges. A *pavé* (paving stone) of granite from May '68...

Knives: Great useful objects. Beautiful as to their form and function. I am never without two or three on my person: Swiss knife on my belt, Laguiolle in my tote-bag, small Swiss pen knife on my key chain, hidden knife in my belt buckle and maybe a switchblade in my pocket. Since I can't carry a gun...

I've never stabbed anyone and the very idea fills me with horror. I'd rather shoot someone, or be shot, then stab or be stabbed.

My children's milk teeth. I have several film containers with Juliette's, Diego's and Pablo's teeth.

Paintings: Having many painter friends in Mexico, we indulged in a little ceremony called *"Cambalache"* (bartering, exchanging)...since we can't afford each other's prices...we exchange art work. My little home is a museum.

Guns. Family sickness and obsession. Load them and feel them and master them and shoot them. I hate hunting. Once I went hunting with Charles Fitzgerald in Maine and, holding a shotgun like a pistol, I gunned down a poor dove as it flashed away from me through the dense underbrush. I was so sorry to see the poor dead creature. Of course we ate it that night. As Serge Silberman (my father's French producer) would say, "I went hunting twice in my life, the first time and the last time." Usually he would say that about a restaurant that he didn't like.

French producer Serge Silberman,
with painting by Calder in background.

Paper: I already wrote about that.

Masks from Mexico and Africa: Dreams of the hidden self. Some Mexican masks seem to be made by two different people. The imagination gone riot (trite expression). They hang on my walls. My brother Rafael also collects them. He has ten times as many.

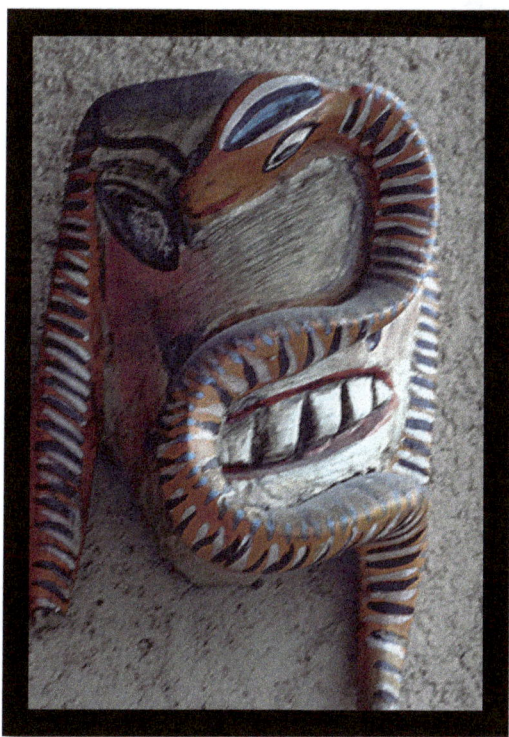

Traditional Mexican mask, face with snake.

Once I went to a painter's house in Cuernavaca and, while we were having lunch on his front lawn, I started to brag about my 30 mask collection. He meekly looked up and stated that he also had a few examples. "Oh, yeah!" I sneered. "How many do you have?" He smiled, "20, 000." The walls, ceilings, rooms and floors of his house (and it was a large house) were covered with masks. Museums from Europe would take a tiny part of his collection for special expositions. I said he was a little *loco* to have so many pieces. He said yes he was...I was a bit jealous.

Traditional Mexican mask, *cuate* (double).

Photos...hundreds of them of friends and events and places and meals...Once I'm gone, these pictures will be meaningless. Probably my children might be interested in them. But right now I enjoy looking back and remembering.

From The Cover

The memoir of Juan Luis Buñuel (b. 1934 in Paris) offers a first-hand look at the life of a vibrant man who has been surrounded by important figures of the twentieth century, including his father Luis Buñuel, Alexander Calder, Joan Miró, and Orson Welles, among many others. A filmmaker, sculptor, painter and raconteur in his own right, Juan Luis' writings reveal a Buñuelian sense of lucid, dark humor and outrage over society's pretensions and inequities.

This memoir, originally written for his children, is here generously offered to the public along with an introduction and a rich selection of illustrations and annotations, assembled by Linda C. Ehrlich.

Juan Luis Buñuel—artist, filmmaker, and bon vivant—tells compelling stories that transport us in waves of exile and artistry from Europe to the U.S. to Mexico and back to Paris.

> I lived and worked in many countries and got to know them intimately. Films are wonderful for that. You go to a foreign country, you get up early like the majority of the population, get to know them, eat with them...and exchange stories. You get a different point of view than that of a tourist. I have enjoyed many good meals, friends, and the strong drinks each country has to offer.

About the Author & Editor

Juan Luis Buñuel, the eldest son of noted filmmaker Luis Buñuel, has made documentaries around the world: in Mexico, the U.S., France, Spain, England, Cambodia, Chile and Venezuela, among other places. His award-winning feature films include *At the Meeting with Joyous Death* (with Gérard Depardieu), *The Lady with Red Boots* (with Catherine Deneuve and Fernando Rey), and *Leonor* (with Liv Ullmann and Michel Piccoli). Juan Luis' imaginative paintings and sculpture have been exhibited in galleries in France, Mexico, the U.S., and Spain.

Linda C. Ehrlich is an innovative writer about world cinema and dance. Her commentary appears on the Criterion DVD of the Spanish film *The Spirit of the Beehive*, and her articles about Spanish cinema have appeared in such journals as *Framework*, *Senses of Cinema*, *Cinema Scope*, and *Cinema Journal*. Ehrlich is the editor of *The Cinema of Víctor Erice: An Open Window* and the author of *Cinematic Reveries: Gestures, Stillness, Water.*

Tributes

This memoir spans continents and straddles important historical events. It makes for an especially illuminating reading that gives us access to both Juan Luis Buñuel's own multi-faceted practice as a filmmaker-artist and the cultures that have come to define our own era.

Linda Dittmar, Emeritus Professor of English,
University of Massachusetts/Boston.
Editor of *From Hanoi to Hollywood; The Vietnam War in American Film*; and author of *Traces: A Memoir of War in Israel/Palestine.*

Here is the book that all of us who know and admire Juan Luis Buñuel have been waiting for— the book that complements the dazzling memoir of his famous father, Spanish filmmaker Luis Buñuel, and that of his delightful and long-suffering French mother. Like a latter-day Yorick, Juan Luis knows how to set the table at a roar. And what stories he has to tell– and with what an array of characters, some of them household names! Here is a book throbbing with life, definitely not to be missed. Hallelujah!

Ian Gibson, Irish-born biographer of Luis Buñuel,
Salvador Dalí, and Federico García Lorca.

www.ingramcontent.com/pod-product-compliance
Lightning Source LLC
Chambersburg PA
CBHW051850090426
42811CB00034B/2279/J